SCOTLAND RESURGENT

SCOTLAND RESURGENT

comments on the cultural
and political revival of Scotland

Paul Henderson Scott

THE SALTIRE SOCIETY

Scotland Resurgent published 2003 by

The Saltire Society
9 Fountain Close,
22 High Street,
Edinburgh EH1 1TF

A catalogue record for this book is available from the British Library.

ISBN 0 85411 083 6

The publisher is very grateful to the Scottish Arts Council for financial assistance in the publication of this book

Cover Design by James Hutcheson

Printed and Bound in Scotland by Bell and Bain Limited

Other Books by Paul Henderson Scott

1707: The Union of Scotland and England Chambers 1979
Walter Scott and Scotland Saltire Society 1994
John Galt Scottish Academic Press 1985
In Bed with an Elephant Saltire Society 1985
The Thinking Nation University of Dundee 1989
Towards Independence: Essays on Scotland Polygon 1991 and 1996
Andrew Fletcher and the Treaty of Union Saltire Society 1994
Scotland in Europe: A Dialogue with a Sceptical Friend Canongate 1992
Defoe in Edinburgh and Other Papers Tuckwell Press 1995
A Mad God's Dream Edinburgh District Council 1997
Still in Bed with an Elephant Saltire Society 1998
The Boasted Advantages Saltire Society 1999
A Twentieth Century Life Argyll Publishing 2002

edited

The Age of MacDiarmid Mainstream 1980 (with A C Davis)
Sir Walter Scott's The Letters of Malachi Malagrowther Blackwoods 1981
Andrew Fletcher's United and Separate Parliaments Saltire Society 1982
A Scottish Postbag Saltire Society 2002 (with George Bruce)
Scotland: A Concise Cultural History Mainstream 1993
Scotland's Ruine: Lockhart of Carnwath's Memoirs of the Union Association for Scottish Literary Studies 1995 (with Daniel Szechi)
Memoirs of the Union Association for Scottish Literary Studies 1995
John Galt's The Member and The Radical Canongate 1996 (with Ian Gordon)
Scotland: An Unwon Cause Canongate 1997
The Saltoun Papers: reflections on Andrew Fletcher Saltire Society 2003

Contents

Introduction

In his book, *The Spirit of Britain*, Roy Strong says that the Union of 1707 "wiped out" the Scottish identity by a "gradual but inevitable anglicisation". Of course, this did not happen, or at least not so completely as he suggests. Strong in fact recognises this by saying later in the same book that Walter Scott wrote in "a country which had lost its political separateness but still retained a cultural identity". Strong's first assumption however, was not unreasonable. Scotland shared a small island with a confident, expansive England. Power, wealth and patronage were concentrated in London, which became for a time the capital of the strongest power in the world. There were periods, particularly at the height of imperial greatness in the 19th century, when it seemed that many Scots were willing to accept assimilation and regard themselves as English.

There were forces on the other side. The Union had suppressed the Scottish Parliament (and in the terms of the Treaty, but not in practice, the English one as well). Almost all of the other institutions of the Scottish state, including the church, the law, local administration, the schools and universities, remained intact. They had much more influence on the lives of the people and on their habits of thought than a distant Parliament which took little interest in Scottish affairs. The Scottish character had been moulded by three centuries of resistance to English pressure, and by the consequent close association with other countries in Europe. The Scottish Reformation, with its emphasis on education, egalitarianism and democracy, was another major influence. All of this was sustained and expressed by a vigorous literature, both written and in song. From Ramsay, Fergusson and Burns to the present many writers and artists of all kinds have resisted the erosion of the Scottish identity.

Because of this conflict of forces, there has been in Scotland an oscillation between Scottish and British attitudes since the 18th century. Scottishness has slowly become dominant in a long process over the last hundred years. Of this, the recovery of the Scottish Parliament, even limited and restricted in power as it still is, has been the most obvious achievement.

This whole complex of questions is one of my main interests and the subject of much of my writing. The present volume is a selection of essays, lectures, and letters on various aspects of the Scottish revival, mostly written in the last ten years. In chapter 5 the papers are arranged in the order in which they were written because they reflect changes in the political and constitutional situation. In the other chapters the sequence depends on the theme. The papers have previously appeared (as I have indicated in each case) in *The Herald, Sunday Herald, The Scotsman, Scotland on Sunday, The Times, Chapman, Cencrastus, Books in Scotland, In Scotland, Scottish Affairs,* and other periodicals as well as in two histories in weekly parts *The Story of Scotland* and *Scotland's Story*. Acknowledgement is due to the editors concerned.

Apart from correction of some minor printing errors, the papers are now republished as they originally appeared. Since they were written for different audiences over several years, the same arguments and questions are sometimes repeated. I have thought it better to risk the irritation which it will cause the reader (for which I apologise) rather than give a false record by substantial cuts or amendment.

P.H.S.
Edinburgh
March 2003

A Personal Declaration

1.1

Life After the Foreign Office

'Foreign Service', Spring 1992

I joined what was then called the Senior Branch of the Foreign Office, through the post-war examinations in April 1950. I retired in November 1980 and returned to live in my native Edinburgh.

Since that time I have been writing books, essays and reviews about Scottish history, literature and politics. I am a member of many, and chairman of several, organisations devoted to these matters. For the last three years I have been a member of the National Executive Committee of the Scottish National party. I am the party spokesman for education and the arts and am prospective candidate for the parliamentary constituency of Eastwood. The title of my latest book, a collection of essays and articles, is, with deliberate intent, *Towards Independence* (Polygon, 1991).

The object of the SNP is, of course, to restore independence to Scotland as a member of the European Community. You could therefore say, I suppose, that I have spent about 40 years of my life working for the British state (for I was in the Army and Control Commission before the Foreign Service) and the last 11 doing my best to dismantle it. A journalist recently made that point to me; but, as far as I can remember, no one else has. Perhaps this is because the people of Scotland are accustomed to the SNP and its objectives are a familiar part of political life. For some years the party has been oscillating with the Conservatives for second place in the opinion polls, but it is likely to surge ahead at the next election. About 80% of the Scottish people are in favour of constitutional change, divided about equally between those who want full independence and those who want a parliament limited to domestic affairs.

I do not think there is any inconsistency between my two careers. As long as Scotland remains in its present association with

England, the only way you can become a diplomat, if that happens to interest you, is in the British Service. We trust that the parting of the two countries will be achieved by democratic process and amicable arrangement, unlike the bribery and intimidation which brought us together in 1707. The demand for Scottish independence has nothing to do with hostility towards England, even if the English sometimes exasperate us. One of the benefits of independence is that it should lead to a more equitable and friendly relationship between the two countries.

I have been in favour of Scottish independence since my schooldays and have never made a secret of it. To their credit, the FCO accepted this without comment; although it is possible, I suppose, that it may have been discretely held against me. Not that I was alone within the Office in this opinion. In the 1970s, when it seemed that Scotland was about to achieve a measure of self-government, many of my Scottish colleagues used to talk about the agreeable possibility of transferring to a Foreign Office in Edinburgh. I hope that they are now doing it again.

It might be thought that diplomatic experience is likely to encourage a respect for the constitutional status quo. In fact, I think the opposite is true, at least as far as the Scots are concerned. The principle of self-determination is embodied in many international instruments and is generally accepted as axiomatic. Why should it not apply to Scotland which is one of the oldest nations in Europe? I was the Assistant Head of the United Nations Department at a time when the main activity was 'decolonisation', the conversion of colonies into independent countries. If that was good enough for them, why would it not also be good for Scotland which is so much better prepared in experience, education, industry and infrastucture?

In the course of my diplomatic work I met many people from countries which had recently become independent. Almost always, you could sense the satisfaction, confidence, optimism and self respect that comes with freedom and responsibility. That is what I want to see in Scotland as well.

1.2

Edinburgh in 1980 and 1995

'The Scottish Review', No. 4, October 1995

This is an essay in two parts. I wrote the first part shortly after I left the Diplomatic Service and returned to Edinburgh in 1980. It had been commissioned for a collection of essays which Norman Wilson, the Scottish publisher, was planning. Wilson did not live to complete the project, and the book never appeared. The second part, written in 1995, is effectively a postscript taking into account what has happened to Edinburgh, and Scotland, in the intervening period.

Part 1: 1980

Stevenson says in *Weir of Hermiston*: "Archie went the usual round of other Edinburgh boys, the high school and the college." So did I. And it was when the High School was still in Hamilton's noble Grecian building overlooking Holyrood, with an inescapable view bounded by Arthur's Seat and the Castle Hill. It was a view that made the history of Scotland almost palpable and visible. You could not grow up with it without feeling that you were part of a demanding tradition and that you had an obligation to do what you could to preserve and enlarge it. The move of the school to a nondescript new building, lost in the anonymous suburbs, is one of those acts of wanton self-destruction recently not uncommon in Edinburgh. It is some compensation that the old school has now been made ready as the seat of a revived Scottish Parliament.

If I had a good Edinburgh start to life, I soon went wrong. The war caught up with me and I went off to the Army. I became so involved in Berlin that I took the Foreign Office examination. Before I knew where I was, I was committed to the nomadic life of the diplomat. That did not stop Edinburgh remaining at the centre of my life. Wherever I went, I took the essential Edinburgh books, *The Heart of Midlothian*, *Weir of Hermiston*, *Magnus Merriman*, Cockburn's *Memorials*, Lockhart's *Scott* and *Peter's Letters*, Fergusson and Garioch, Mossner's *Hume*. Most of the pictures on my walls were Edinburgh scenes. I came back to Edinburgh whenever I could. Part of my mind was always in Edinburgh. Of course, this is a common enough phenomenon, like Stevenson writing *Weir of Hermtston* in Samoa and saying in his dedication:

> I saw rain falling and the rainbow drawn
> On Lammermuir. Hearkening I heard again
> In my precipitous city beaten bells
> Winnow the keen sea wind.

I am writing this on a wet and windy Sunday in the precipice of Drumsheugh Gardens, with the snell wind from the Forth battering against the windows. Stevenson's memory was as accurate as his language was precise. For my part, I am back in Edinburgh and here I propose to stay.

I identify with Edinburgh to the extent that I can hardly bear the place praised in my presence without embarrassment. Whenever I had to tell anyone that I came from Edinburgh and meant to go back to live there, I felt that I was boasting shamelessly. I feel any damage to the fabric of Edinburgh as a personal injury. When the University, to their eternal shame, were contemplating the ravaging of George Square and Bristo Street, they sent a circular to graduates asking for financial help. It was like being invited to dig one's own grave. I wrote back to say that I would gladly contribute to a fund to stop them. They went ahead, of course, and tried to appease the outraged ghosts by giving names like David Hume and William Robertson to the structures erected on the ruins.

Mention of Hume reminds me of another set of vandals, an English insurance company, who destroyed the house in South St. David Street where Hume lived ("Never mind, lassie, many a better man has been made a sanct of afore"), and where Walter Scott came when he had to sell 39 Castle Street. There was no excuse for this. The building was both elegant and soundly built of good stone before they turned it into a synthetic structure which might be anywhere. No wonder we need the Cockburn Association. Without constant vigilance, commercialism would soon bring everything to the indiscriminate and tawdry mess to which they have already reduced the north side of Princes Street.

Edinburgh would not command the affection, admiration and love that she does if this process of destruction had gone too far. In my more pessimistic moments I sometimes feel that we are close to that sorry end. We cannot survive many blows like the loss of George Square or the imposition of the detestable St. James Centre.

Fortunately, the basic topographical structure of Edinburgh is tough and endurable. It lies between a coast line and a range of hills which are accessible and still relatively unspoilt. Other hills, like miniature mountains — for Arthur's Seat has every feature that a mountain should have — lie close to its heart. There are unexpected angles of vision that bring glimpses of distant sea and hill to every part of the town. The Waverley Novels, wrote Alexander Welsh, "originate from the city of Edinburgh, and could not have been written by a citizen of any other land but Scotland. To the present day, from the window of a library or from the confusion of city traffic in Edinburgh, one can be shocked by the sudden prospect of sublime nature crowding in upon civilisation."

The New Town, and its extension westwards to the precipices overlooking the Dean, are also reasonably enduring and largely intact. These "draughty parallelograms", as Stevenson called them, are so confident and assured that they impose something of their own character on everyone that lives among them. They are the Enlightenment made visible, rationality incarnate. "This is the town of Hume," said Edwin Muir. "Everything in it breathes spaciousness, order and good sense . . . It shows that little over a hundred years ago Edinburgh possessed a boldness of foresight and a standard of achievement which at that time were remarkable." The New Town, like the view from the High School, is a challenge, an encouragement to effort and a reproach to back-sliding. It is an environment which flatters human dignity and radiates an idea of permanence; but you have to live up to it.

So in spite of the blemishes (and, of course, the more you are devoted to Edinburgh, the more you resent them) both the stone and the essential character of the city are more durable than most things in this evanescent and volatile age. Sydney Smith who helped to found the *Edinburgh Review* wrote this description of the town nearly 200 years ago:

> I like this place extremely and cannot help thinking that for a literary man, by which term I mean a man who is fond of letters, it is the most eligible situation in the island. It unites good libraries liberally managed; learned men without any other system than that of pursuing truth; very good general society; large healthy virgins, with mild pleasing countenances and white swelling breasts; shores washed by the sea; the romantic grandeur of ancient, and the beautiful regularity of modern buildings; and boundless floods of oxygen.

That still conveys the look and feel of Edinburgh. The libraries are indeed liberally managed and one of the great assets of Edinburgh. You can still find plenty of only slightly polluted oxygen on the slopes of the Pentland or the shores of the Forth. I am not sure about the virgins, but scholarly and intelligent society is still much as it was. When Amyat made his celebrated remark at about the same time as Smith, "Here I stand at what is called The Cross of Edinburgh, and can, in a few minutes, take fifty men of genius and learning by the hand", he went on to talk about this accessibility:

> In London, in Paris and other large cities of Europe, though they contain many literary men, the access to them is difficult; and, even after that is obtained, the conversation is, for some time, shy and constrained. In Edinburgh, the access of men of parts is not only easy, but their conversation and the communication of their knowledge are at once imparted to intelligent strangers with the utmost liberality. The philosophers of Scotland have no nostrums. They tell what they know, and deliver their sentiments without disguise or reserve.

That was at a time when, as Walter Scott said, there were giants in the land. Perhaps our men of wit and learning are less gigantic than they were then, but it is still easy to find them and to talk to them.

The size and compactness of Edinburgh is one of the reasons for this accessibility. Scotland is about the ideal size among countries, large enough for diversity and small enough to be comprehended by the individual. So Edinburgh is large enough to sustain all the essentials of civilisation: theatres, bookshops, libraries, societies and organisations of all kinds. It is small enough for the individual to feel part of it and to be thoroughly at home. The centre is still a real town where people live and meet one another, not an empty shell which is dead when the shops and offices close. Everything is within walking distance. It is rare to go anywhere without meeting by chance someone you know. You can keep your friendships in repair without agonising effort. Edinburgh is still small enough to have the country, and genuinely wild and open country at that, within easy reach. There is still a sharp division between town and country, in some directions at least, not an endless urban sprawl. We are fortunate in our natural boundaries, the Pentlands and the Forth, because nobody can build on them.

Also people in Edinburgh are accessible because social pretentiousness and exclusivity do not come easily to us. We have some people who try, but there are not many who do it with any conviction or success. I think that people tempted in this direction have an uneasy feeling that they are more likely in the sceptical air of Edinburgh to excite ridicule than admiration. Our poetry is full of examples, such as this from Robert Garioch:

> The function was held in the aipen air
> a peety, that; the keelies of the toun,
> a toozie lot, gat word of the affair.
>
> We cudnae stop it: they jist gaither roun
> to mak sarcastic cracks and grin and stare.
> I wish I hadnae worn my M.A. goun.

Perhaps, as John Grierson has suggested, the flitting of the king to London in 1603 has something to do with it. Since then we have had no resident monarch, no royal court, and no hangers on. This has had deplorable political effects because it led to our loss of independence; it was disastrous for the patronage of the arts and ruinous for the Scots language; but perhaps its social effects were beneficial. We enjoy, Grierson said, "the happy absence of an arrogant and ignorant gentry gone south".

Also, and this is a point which is embarrassing and difficult, but I have to try to be honest. I have to admit that I find the people of Edinburgh overwhelmingly helpful and kind. To say anything like this is to run the risk of being accused of sentimentality, nowadays the most damning of accusations. And, yes, I have heard that there is violent crime and mindless vandalism in Edinburgh as in other places. The truth is whenever I have come back to Edinburgh the thing which astonishes me most is the sheer kindness of people. John Leyden once referred to the "true hearts and sound heads of Edinburgh". I would say the same. What about the sound heads? Perhaps they too are partly a consequence of 1603. J. G. Lockhart suggested that the best of Edinburgh talk, "which might be transferred without alteration to a professor's notebook or the pages of a critical review", was "the talk of a society to which lawyers and lecturers had given the tone". In the absence of Grierson's "ignorant gentry", conversation in Edinburgh has long aspired not to fashionable chit-chat but to serious intellectual qualities. To use Saunders Fairford's words, it aims at solidity not the waggish and scatter-brained. It is also vigorously argumentative, and all the better as a training for the mind in consequence. Walter Scott called it the "Edinburgh *pruritus disputandi*", and Benjamin Franklin said that he had noticed that disputatiousness was the habit of men of all sorts that had been bred in Edinburgh.

I have always felt that closely argued conversation with your opponent seizing at once on any chink in your logic is one of the traditional sports in Edinburgh. It has its disadvantages, of course. It can easily descend into pedantry or become the excuse for the endless postponement of any decision or any action — one of the reasons why our politics often seems curiously impotent. Like all pleasures, it is subject to the damages of excess, but it is a very real and very Edinburgh pleasure for all that. Once in the lamented L'Aperitif, for long the best restaurant in Edinburgh and one of the best anywhere (see Eric Linklater's *Edinburgh*), a group of us talked over dinner, playing little attention to a rather silent couple at the next table. When it was time to leave, the man, who was a professor from America, said that he felt that he had to thank us for the pleasure which our conversation had given them. He said that he had never heard anything like it, but it was only the usual sort of Edinburgh talk. In some circles and in some places it is thought to be inappropriate, ill-bred or unsuitable to talk about philosophy, politics, or religion. I remember hearing someone in Sussex say in shocked tones: "He talked about religion and the vicar was there, too!" Edinburgh has no such inhibitions. Metaphysics has always been the proper stuff of conversation.

Possibly again because of the importance of the law in Edinburgh life, there is a certain ponderousness or formality about it. "There is kind of a decency to be observit". The words are those of Stevenson's Hermiston and he, like his creator, was an Edinburgh lawyer. It is the social equivalent of the architecture of the New Town. In neither case should you be deceived by the formality of the facade.

Dr Jekyll and Mr Hyde is often said to be quintessentially Edinburgh, although it pretends to be set in London. By this theory, Deacon Brodie, respectable citizen by day and criminal by night, is supposed to be representative of the split in the Edinburgh soul. In fact, Brodie seems to have been amiable in his respectability and harmless in his crimes.

Edinburgh avoids extremes. Those who are not used to it may be put off by the apparent reserve of its society — "East windy, west endy", as they say. They may think it hypocritical when they discover the conviviality beneath the surface. We are not really trying to deceive anybody, but we like our lives and pleasures to have some shape and control about them. Sometimes I wonder if part of the pleasure of living in Edinburgh is merely that it is rather old-fashioned. We are a little isolated in our remote northern periphery and less subject to some of the pressures that make life harsh and disagreeable. Other places, no doubt, used to be more formal, more dignified and more amiable than they are now. Edinburgh resists change. That is why, in talking about Edinburgh, it is quite natural to quote Boswell, Fergusson, Scott, Lockhart, Cockburn or Stevenson. It is recognisably still the same place.

That does not mean that Edinburgh is dull, complacent and uneventful. On the contrary I find that it is almost too crowded with activity. I have to resist all sorts of temptations if I am to keep the time I need for writing and reading.

Certainly, the hectic pressure of the Edinburgh Festival relaxes, but it is only a change of degree. When the official Festival was started, immediately after the War in an atmosphere of exhaustion, shortage and rationing, it seemed improbable that anything so ambitious could succeed. The Festival not only went from strength to strength, it generated the Fringe, spontaneous, uncontrolled, multifarious and diverse. There is nothing like it for sheer scale, energy and range anywhere in the world. Now it is true that most of these events came from outside; but they would not have come to Edinburgh if the atmosphere had not been congenial, and most of the audiences and many of the participants are Edinburgh born and bred.

The Scottish Renaissance of the 1930s was centred on Edinburgh, when the conversation in the Abbotsford and Milne's Bar was enlivened by men like Hugh MacDiarmid, Sydney Goodsir Smith, Sam MacLean, Norman MacCaig, Robert Garioch and Hector MacIver. This is a chapter of the literary history of Edinburgh which has still to be written, and it has already taken off on a new wave. The town, as always, is full of literati. The Traverse Theatre is an exciting place. There are scores of societies, like the admirable Saltire. Almost every evening it seems a group of people is meeting somewhere to promote such things and plan the survival of Scotland. The town is a hive of activity.

What about the weather? Often that is the question when I

have told people that Edinburgh is where I am determined to live.

Scott was fond of saying that there was nothing wrong with Scotland except the climate; but I notice that when he complains about it in his *Journal* or his letters, it is always because the day was too hot: "Almost overcome by the heat in walking home, and rendered useless for the day". Stevenson, poor man, was sensitive to the cold: "The weather is raw and boisterous in winter, shifty and ungenial in summer, and a downright meteorological purgatory in the spring. The delicate die early." On this matter, I am more with Scott than Stevenson. The climate suits me precisely because it is seldom too hot. You cannot do much to avoid the discomfort of heat; Edinburgh has its defences against the cold and wet:

> Auld Reikie! thou'rt the canty hole,
> A bield for mony caldrife soul,
> Wha snugly at thine ingle loll,
> Baith warm and couth;
> While round they gar the bicker roll
> To wet their mouth.

In short, I agree with Bernard Levin, who explained the whole matter with admirable brevity when he wrote in *The Times*:

> . . . one of the most glorious cities on earth, and Scottish to boot. The openness and warmth: the grave beauty of the architecture: the indefinable genius loci, which pours its spirit into the air so that I walk about, even in the invariable rain, feeling as though I am listening to Figaro from morning till night: these are true qualities of Edinburgh, for which I love it . . .

Edinburgh suits me. I am constantly delighted by the changing views under the changing sky. Walking in Edinburgh is a positive pleasure. I am at home with the people and in the libraries and clubs. I like the judicious blend of scepticism and warmth, formality and irreverence, egalitarianism and style. I like the feel of history and the sense that we still might make Edinburgh again the real capital of a real country.

Part 2: 1995

Reading the foregoing is a little like hearing a voice from the past. Would it be so full of the first flush of enthusiasm of the returning exile that it could not survive the critical eye of experience? In fact, I would not wish to retract a word of it.

I am a little surprised to see that my confidence that Scotland would soon recover independence was undimmed in the immediate aftermath of the Referendum of 1979. I evidently did not foresee the wasted years that were to follow. To me, the case for Scottish independence is so strong that I have never doubted that it would before long prevail. My confidence in this has been reinforced by experience abroad. When you see the quality of life in other small European countries, all less rich in natural resources but with their own government, you inevitably speculate about the frustrated potential of Scotland.

The question is, of course, inescapable in Edinburgh. It was for hundreds of years the capital of a country, in Walter Scott's words, "once proud and independent". It has never ceased to be a partial capital, the seat of a national Kirk, law and education, all with their integrity invaded but still surviving. Many of the symbols of nationhood also remain, the Crown, Castle, Palace and Heralds, even if only as historical relics. We have even created new, and functioning, national institutions from the Scottish Office to the Portrait Gallery. When Edinburgh was invaded by political journalists for the European Summit in December 1992, several of them remarked that Edinburgh was unmistakably a European capital.

But we, the residents, or most of us, are not deceived. We know that Edinburgh, as Owen Dudley Edwards once said, is a past and future capital, but at present only a shadow of one. The Scottish Office is not controlled by Scottish votes, but by the majority in England; it exists to impose policies on us for which we have not voted and which we do not like. It has more of the nature and function of a colonial headquarters than of a democratic administration. In a rare outburst of honesty, a recent Secretary of State described himself as the Governor-General.

This semi-colonial status is a humiliation and a curb on our pride and self-esteem and it also has substantial disadvantages. A real capital, which has a government and a parliament, draws to it, not only government departments and embassies, but head offices of all kinds. It means a great concentration of the most influential and highly paid jobs. A city which ceases to be a real capital, on the other hand, gradually loses the head offices and all the activities that go with them. This has been the fate of Edinburgh since 1603, when we lost the king and court, and even more since 1707, when we lost the parliament as well.

It is a process which still goes on. In spite of many assurances we recently lost the head office of Distillers, as one example among hundreds. On a lesser scale, the shops on Princes Street in my youth were locally owned. Now, with the conspicuous exception of Jenners, they are branches of companies with their head offices south of the Border and that is where their profits go and the taxes based on them are paid. To add insult to injury, government spokesmen then use these distorted statistics to argue that they spend more in Scotland than we pay in tax.

The whole of Scotland would benefit immeasurably from the stimulus of independence (and even from the half-way house of devolution), but the effects would be most obvious and immediate in the capital. It is one of the paradoxes that the people of Edinburgh have been slow to realise this, and that their support for the SNP is below the Scottish average. Perhaps it is because it is so agreeable to live in Edinburgh, even as it is, that its people are lulled into complacency.

For the same reason, Edinburgh has been outclassed by Glasgow in energy and determination to improve. In the past, Glasgow was one of the great industrial cities of the world, building ships and locomotives for the Empire. That has gone, but Glasgow has not been content to sink into post-industrial decay. It has put formidable vitality and zeal into finding a new role. In the process, it has acquired many of the institutions which you would expect to find in the capital: the national orchestra, opera and ballet, and the television studios. To general astonishment and incredulity in Edinburgh, it has seized the prizes of the Years of European Culture and of Architecture and Design. It is proposed as the site for a new National Gallery. All of this has at last persuaded Edinburgh that it cannot simply rest on its laurels. The transformation of the old Empire into the Festival Theatre is a sign of the new spirit.

I am optimistic about the future. I am sure that we are moving closer to the day when Edinburgh will recover its proper role as a real capital with a parliament and a government, visibly involved as a full partner in the affairs of Europe and the rest of the world.

Literature and the Survival of Scotland

2. 1

Scotch Myths

'The Bulletin of Scottish Politics', No. 2
Spring 1981

The *Scotch Myths* exhibition, assembled by Barbara and Murray Grigor for the St. Andrew's Festival in February (and now touring Scotland) is an astounding monument to misdirected energy. It is astounding in the effort and research which must have gone into the collection of over 1,000 old postcards, whisky advertisements, shortbread tins and the like, and in mounting them with flair and imagination worthy of less lamentable material. It is misdirected because it is firing at the wrong target. The whole conception is based on too limited a view of the real nature of the myths which have undermined our self-confidence and bedevilled our political development.

The Grigors' view of the myth is the Scotland of Harry Lauder, the comic or sentimental post-card of *Punch* in its less sophisticated days. It is obsessed with parsimony, porridge, whisky and what goes under the kilt. Unmitigated vulgarity is tempered only by maudlin sentimentality. Allen Wright summed it up in *The Scotsman*:

> The material which the Grigors have assembled is enough to make even an inanimate object weep—the whole panoply of postcards, labels and posters proclaiming that Scotland is a wilderness of heather and thistles, and that its inhabitants are daft.

Most of this stuff is happily old and largely forgotten with its heyday in the early part of this century. Some of it was produced in Scotland itself by Scots, to their shame, jumping on a profitable bandwagon, but a flood of it came from publishers south of the border and beyond. Lingering traces of it are still around of course. It created an idea of Scotland which still haunts us. Any one who takes his view of Scotland from this sort of thing is bound to regard us with a mixture of pity and contempt.

Where did it all start? On the evidence of a television interview and of the exhibition itself, I gather that Murray Grigor blames Macpherson's Ossian, Mendelssohn and Walter Scott. A model of Fingal's Cave (in tartan!) is the centrepiece of the exhibition, a piano (which gushes with water) plays the Hebrides Overture continuously, against a background of slides of Ossian; busts of Scott and Mendelssohn look on benignly. No doubt Macpherson, Mendelssohn and Scott, all in their various ways, brought the Highlands to the attention of Europe, and encouraged (deliberately or not) a romantic view of them; but there is nothing in common between the spirit of any of these and the comic postcards. As Scott said in the *General Preface* to the Waverley Novels, his object was to place the Scots, and—he emphasises—both Highlander and Lowlander, in a "more favourable light than they had been placed hitherto". He succeeded triumphantly, as the enthusiasm of the whole literate world demonstrates.

The origins of the comic postcards are to be found much further back in a literary form—the less favourable light—against which Scott was consciously reacting. This was the long tradition of the abuse of the "beggarly Scots" which was a commonplace of English polemical writing, encouraged by the 300 years war, careerists in London from 1603 onwards, the Jacobite Rising and the agitation against Bute. The *North Briton* of Wilkes and Charles Churchill is a sustained example. This whole tradition is an early example of hate propaganda or psychological warfare. (As such, it might be worth a scholarly investigation, which, as far as I know, no one has yet attempted). Anyone who reads any of this stuff will very soon find precisely the same old jokes and gibes which were the endlessly repeated themes of the comic postcards. Both rely more on the power of repetition than on originality and invention. This sort of animosity is not yet dead. A. N. Wilson in his recent book on Scott says, "Even now a modern Frenchman or Russian is likely to come out with unself-consciously anti-semitic feelings rather in the way that an Englishman might make no bones about disliking the Scots or the French". He indulges in it himself.

Murray Grigor has done a useful service in exposing the full horror of a particular *genre*, but he clearly has quite a false idea both of its origin and of its significance. He might even start a new misapprehension by implying that this is how the Scots see themselves and that this is the important myth about Scotland. In fact, we are not misled by the comic postcards, whatever may happen elsewhere, because they obviously have so little to do with the reality that surrounds us. If this were the only myth, it would be humiliating, infuriating and deplorable enough, but its practical consequences inside Scotland would be limited. Unfortunately, there is another and quite different myth which is much more powerful and subtle and which has direct and serious political consequences.

In crude and blunt terms, this is the view that Scotland before 1707 was backward, bloody and barbarous, that it was saved by the Union, which is seen as an enlightened act of statesmanship, and that thereafter economic progress and civilisation flowed benignly northwards from England. The thesis is seldom expressed as bluntly as this, because that would provoke thought and discussion that would reveal its unreality. It is more damaging as an unspoken assumption which undermines Scottish self-confidence and sustains the unionist argument.

Certainly in the past there was violence and bloodshed enough in Scotland, but probably less than in most places. In the massacre of Glencoe, which horrified Scottish opinion then and since, 36 people were killed. That is moderation compared to, say, Edward I's sack of Berwick, to say nothing of Hiroshima. The Scottish legal system was always remarkable for its lenience and never hanged petty malefactors with the indiscriminate zeal of the English. Nor did it have anything approaching the barbarity of the English penalty for treason. The Scottish Parliament has been maligned as unrepresentative and ineffective, but the much vaunted English one was no more representative and had to wait for that, long after the

Union, for the Reform Acts of the 19th Century. The Scottish Parliament, after all, made the first attempt in the world to bring education to the whole population. As James Mackinnon said of it:

> It has been contended, not without reason, that the old Scottish Parliament has anticipated many of those reforms, which it has been the endeavours of modern liberalism to secure for the people. It is certain, at all events, that the Scottish Statutebook contains many Acts, tending to secure the liberty as well as to foster the well-being of the subject, which even yet may stand as models of legislative wisdom ... In their benevolent care of the poor, both from starvation and the litigious oppression of the rich, in the protection of the subject from arbitrary imprisonment, in the recognition of the right of all prisoners to be defended by counsel, in the establishment of an excellent system of popular education, in the humane restriction of the death penalty, the old Scottish Parliament had anticipated legislation which came to the people of England more than a century after the Union.
>
> (*The Union of England and Scotland*, 1907)

The 18th Century was a period of rapid economic and intellectual development in Scotland. This followed the Union and *post hoc* has often been confused with *propter hoc*. In fact, during the whole of the century, the policy of the Government in London was to leave Scotland to sink or swim by its own devices, apart from the military intervention at and after Culloden. When James Stuart Mackenzie took over the Scottish Office in London in 1761, he was astonished to find no papers and no sign that any business was being carried on. Certainly, the Scottish economy was stimulated by access to the colonial trade, especially in the brief period between the Union and American independence, but the internal economic growth was self-generated and self-sustained. The triumphs of the Scottish Enlightenment, as Richard Pares has remarked in *The Historian's Business and Other Essays* (1961), owed something to French and Dutch influence but little to England. The English universities were moribund, "steeped", as Edward Gibbon said, "in port and prejudice". It was only after the Government in London started to intervene in Scottish affairs from about the beginning of the 19th Century that the achievement of this great age started to falter and lose pace.

The process by which Scotland began to accept a false and denigratory view of its own history is one of the great mysteries, although George Davie's *The Democratic Intellect* made an important contribution to our understanding of it. It was a process carried out by the schools and universities. They turned their backs on Scottish history and literature, and replaced their earlier obsession with ancient Rome by an Anglo-centric view of the world. They did their best to suppress Gaelic and Scots and made generations inarticulate and insecure in consequence. We all know about the process (of which, by the way, an interesting example is described in Joy Hendry's recent pamphlet, *Literature and Language: the Way Forward*). It is less easy to understand why it happened. I suppose that the influence of England, at the acme of its Victorian wealth, self-confidence, and power, was simply irresistible. It is, or should be, different now.

After so much brain-washing, it is not surprising that the myth which it created should be powerful, all the more so because it is largely unconscious. Its power was demonstrated by the substantial minority who voted 'No' in the Referendum. Myths do not matter too much if they are benign, but this one is destructive, corrosive of self-confidence and a realistic approach to our own affairs. We cannot hope for a constructive attitude to the problems of Scotland until the myth is seen for what it is, and that can only come from an unprejudiced look at our own history. As *The Scotsnan* said on 8th February 1979:

> In every country except Scotland, it is taken for granted that national history and literature should be well taught in the schools.

That is where we have to begin.

2. 2

Obstacles and Diversity

Paper for the 50th International PEN Congress, Lugano May 1987

The border between Scotland and England is one of the oldest in Europe. It has remained in the same position for many centuries and it is very close to the line of Hadrian's Wall, the northern extremity of the Roman Empire. It was the front line of the longest war in European history, as Scotland for more than 300 years defended her independence against repeated English attempts to overthrow it. This struggle was the background to the Border Ballads, a rich body of poetry which is remarkahle for the force and economy of its language. Paradoxically, therefore, a bitter and bloody struggle helped to bring about a great literary creation.

There is a paradox also in the peaceful relationship which has existed across this border since James VI of Scotland became by dynastic accident also King of England in 1603. In her long independent history, Scotland was cut off from England but she developed a close relationship with the rest of Europe, including especially the interchange of scholars and writers and the free flow of ideas. This helped to stimulate a distinctive literary and cultural tradition in Scotland which has made a particular contribution to our common civilisation. This is of value both for its own sake and as part of the enriching diversity of human expression.

This is where the other paradox arises. The former Canadian Prime Minister, Pierre Trudeau, expressed it well when he said that sharing a continent with America was like sharing a bed with an elephant (a phrase which I have borrowed for the title of an essay on Scotland's experiences of similar elephantine pressure). Modern technology enables large countries, without any malicious intention to exercise a peaceful but suffocating pressure on their smaller neighbours, especially when they share a common language. The pressure is exercised through the sheer weight of numbers, and their consequent financial strength, by means of the press, publishing, radio, television, and the cinema. It works for conformity with the big battalions in language, attitudes, tastes and ideas; it tends to smother and suppress the distinctive character of the smaller community. Modern communications have enormous benefits, but if we are not careful they can also lead to a dull and sterile uniformity. The paradox is that in some senses modern peaceful pressures can be more destructive than the border wars of the past.

We therefore need to find ways to do two opposite things simultaneously. We have to demolish obstacles to the free circulation of ideas, but we must also defend diversity against the dangers of an imposed uniformity.

2. 3

The Power of Books

The first PEN Lecture at the Edinburgh Book Festival August 1999

There is a remark by Andrew Fletcher of Saltoun which is very often quoted, but usually in isolation from its context. It occurs in a pamphlet written in December 1703 shortly after the Scottish Parliament had made a firm assertion of Scottish independence in the Act of Security. The title is descriptive: *An Account of a Conversation Concerning a Right Regulation of Governments for the Common Good of Mankind*. This conversation, real or imaginary, is set in London. Apart from Fletcher himself, the participants are another Scot, the Earl of Cromarty, and two members of the English House of Commons, Sir Edward Somers and Sir Christopher Musgrave. The two Scots were political opponents. Cromarty was one of the very few Scots at the time who were genuinely in favour of an incorporating Union with England; Fletcher was the chief architect of the Act of Security, which was tantamount to a declaration of Scottish independence. The main subject of the conversation was the constitutional future of Scotland and much of it is still remarkably topical; but the remark I have in mind is a more general one and one which is perhaps surprising from a man who was so deeply concerned with the survival and the powers of the Scottish Parliament.

The conversation is at first about the wealth and comforts of London, which Cromarty says is the greatest city in the world. It then turns to the pleasures of the town, and that, says Musgrave, spoils all. The corruption of manners "has infected the whole nation and must at length bring both the city and nation to ruin . . . Even the poorer sort of both sexes are daily tempted to all manner of lewdness by infamous ballads sung in every corner of the streets.

At this point in the conversation Fletcher makes his celebrated remark:

> I knew a very wise man so much of Sir Christopher's sentiments, that he believed if a man were permitted to make all the ballads, he need not care who should make the laws of a nation.

And he continues:

> And we find that most of the ancient legislators thought they could not well reform the manners of any city without the help of a lyric, and sometimes of a dramatic, poet. But in this city the dramatic poet no less than the ballad-makers has been almost wholly employed to corrupt the people, in which they have had most unspeakable and deporable success.

Usually when the first of these passages is quoted it is to suggest that ballads have a desirable effect. It is clear from the context that both Fletcher and Musgrave thought that they could be a pernicious as well as beneficial. The general idea has persisted. Shelley in the 19th century said that poets are the unacknowledged legislators of the world. Recently in a discussion on television Jim Sillars remarked that poets and novelists often had more influence on ideas and values than generations of politicians.

This is the proposition which I should like to discuss with some adjustment in vocabulary to take account in changes in the usage of words and in social conditions. Fletcher was writing before cheap books, public libraries, mass circulation newspapers, even, in England if not in Scotland, general literacy. Literary influence on the people at large therefore came from its oral forms, songs sung in the streets, plays in the theatre or, although he did not mention it, sermons in the churches. Now, when we are all subject to the written word as much as the spoken, we should broaden the term, "ballads" to include all forms of literature.

Also, the word, "manners" has changed in meaning since the 18th century. Then it embraced the whole of behaviour, reflecting character, morals, values and assumptions about society. When

Fletcher talks about the manners of a nation, he means the peculiarities which constitute what is now called a national character.

The pen is said to be mightier than the sword. Is it also mightier than the parliaments in determining our ideas about ourselves? Since it is the country and literature with which I am most familiar, I shall draw most of my examples from Scotland. What influence has our literature had in the past on our ideas and attitudes and can we draw any conclusions about Scotland in the New Era which begins with the restoration of the Scottish Parliament?

If we want a definition of national character, I do not think we can do better than turn to David Hume. In his *Enquiry Concerning Human Understanding* he said: "Mankind are so much the same, in all times and places, that history informs us of nothing new or strange in this particular". He meant, of course, that there was a basic similarity in the appetites, needs, emotions and instincts of people everywhere and at all periods; but that did not mean that he supposed that there was not also considerable diversity. Indeed he devoted one of his essays to the subject of national characters. Men of sense, he said, "allow that each nation has a peculiar set of manners, and that some particular qualities are more frequently to be met with among one people than among their neighbours". At the same time he warned us that there were always exceptions, and time brings change. Hume divided the causes which made national characters into the physical, by which he meant such factors as the climate and geology, and the moral, such as the nature of government and relations with other countries. The physical causes hardly change from century to century, but the moral are in constant movement. It is to be expected, therefore, that some of the national characteristics will remain fairly constant, but that others will change with historical circumstances, including the movement of people from and into Scotland.

From the evidence of Scottish literature are there attributes which persist for centuries? I think that the most obvious is a strong spirit of egalitarianism, a sceptical irreverence towards anyone who claims superiority and fellow feeling for the unfortunate, including animals. The Declaration of Arbroath of 1320 is a document of state, but it is also an impressive work of literature. It tells the King, who is no less than the national hero, Robert Bruce, that he will be sacked if he fails to carry out the will of the people. This is the spirit which runs through Scottish literature from Henryson in the 15th century to Burns in the 18th and to MacDiarmid, Maclean, Garioch and MacCaig in the 20th. I do not know of another literature which is so constantly egalitarian and from so early a time. When Gregory Smith considered the character and influence of Scottish Literature in a book of that title in 1919 he concluded that one of its prominent and continuous features was a "combination of opposites ',which he called the "Caledonian Antisyzygy". The French historian of philosophy, Charles de Remusat, remarked on the same thing in the *Revue des Deux Mondes* in 1856:

> Pride and respect, violence and restraint, intelligence and simplicity, practical sagacity and religious exaltation, these are some of the contrasts which occur all the time among the people of a country of which one can say that no other is so poetically reasonable . . . This nation is among the most enlightened in the world. Politics, religion and literature have made Scotland incomparable.

Religion, as de Remusat says, is another of the factors which make a national character, and it is related to literature. For centuries the Authorised Version of the Bible was by far the most widely read book in Scotland and, apart from anything else, it is a great work of literature. Sermons, hymns, and psalms are a form of literature as well. Before the Reformation, Catholicism helped to involve Scotland closely with the rest of Europe. It was a period of outstanding achievement in poetry, philosophy and music. The Reformation in Scotland was a revolutionary change. It established a Presbyterian Church, egalitarian in its structure and principles, and with strong convictions about the importance of education. In Walter Scott's *Rob Roy* he has Frank Osbaldistone say about a

Scottish church service:

> The Scotch, it is well known, are more remarkable for the exercise of their intellectual powers, than for the keeness of their feelings; they are, therefore, more moved by logic than by rhetoric, and more attracted by acute and argumentative reasoning on doctrinal points, than influenced by enthusiastic appeals to the heart and the passions.

This attitude, and the availability of a wide, general education encouraged habits of metaphysical and moral speculation. The Scottish Enlightenment of the 18th century is a product of this and of the long traditions of Scottish philosophy and close cultural interchange with the rest of Europe.

So too is the remarkable fertility of Scotland in innovative ideas. Religion and literature together helped to create a certain national character. The reformed Kirk tended to disapprove of the arts and the other pleasures of life as frivolous distractions from serious things, although one must always remember the contradictions of the antisyzygy. Many years ago I wrote an essay for *Blackwood's Magazine* [1] in which I suggested that some aspects of the Scottish character, which were the consequence of these influences, bore a close resemblance to certain qualities which the ancient Romans admired: *gravitas*, a sense of the importance of the matter in hand, *industria*, hard work, *frugalitas*, simple tastes, *severitas*, being stern with oneself.

Now that secularism and modern consumerism has made inroads in Scotland as elsewhere, *frugalitas* and *severitas* are not as prominent as thy once were. Still, elements of the old attitudes survive. In an article in the *Herald* on 18th May 1999, Lindsay Paterson argued that the "passion for ideas", encouraged by Calvinism, was still evident in Scotland:

> Writers as diverse as Hugh MacDiarmid, Nan Shepherd, Lewis Grassic Gibbon, Fionn MacColla, William McIlvanney, Alasdair Gray, Robin Jenkins, Liz Lochhead and James Kelman have represented characters in their novels and plays with an interest in philosophical debate. The cumulative effect from this literary tradition is that there is something about the national identity that is indeed passionately intellectual.

There was, of course, a distinct possibility that this national identity might have been eroded or destroyed by the consequences of the Parliamentary Union with England in 1707. In the course of the 18th century there many signs of a tendency to make the best of something which could not be changed and to adopt English ways, English ideas and English speech. After the defeat of the Jacobite Rising of 1745, which had the repeal of the union as one of its objectives, it became dangerous to admit any tendency to resist assimilation. Even robust spirits like David Hume, who made his feelings plain in his private letters, was very discrete in his published works. He might write an essay about the virtues of small states, but he avoided any suggestion that this applied to Scotland. The fact that, in spite of all of this, the national character survived is usually attributed to the survival after the Union of the Scottish Church and the systems of law and education, all of which for the next two centuries or more affected the lives of the people and their ideas and attitudes far more than the distant Parliament. All of these institutions were involved with books or at least with words.

It was the writers, and especially at first the poets, Allan Ramsay, Robert Fergusson and, above all, Robert Burns, who led the defence of the Scottish identity. They all wrote poems against the Union. They wrote in Scots, partly because it was the language which most effectively expressed what they wanted to say, and partly as a defiance of Anglicization. They made a conscious effort to re-establish links with the Scottish literary tradition, Ramsay by publishing his two volume anthology of early Scottish poetry, *The Evergreen*, Burns by his great patriotic endeavour to rescue Scottish songs from oblivion. Scott, a little later, did the same by collecting the Border ballads.

In his autobiographical letter to Dr John Moore, Burns describes the effect on him of a particular part of the Scottish literary tradition, Blin Hary's *Wallace* or the version of the 15th century poem which was widely read in 18th century Scotland:

> the story of Wallace poured a Scottish prejudice in my veins which will boil along there till the flood-gates of life shut in eternal rest.

This is as clear a declaration as one could wish of the effect which poetry can have on ideas and attitudes. His enthusiastic response to everything Scottish is apparent throughout his life from his letters and poetry. In spite of his egalitarianism, he even approved of the Stewart kings because they had been kings of an independent Scotland. He wrote on a window of an inn in Stirling:

> Here Stewarts once in glory reign'd
> And laws for Scotland's weal ordain'd
> The injured Stewart line is gone,
> A race outlandish fills their throne:
> An idiot race, to honour lost—
> Who knows them best despise them most.

Burns was not the last Scot to be both Jacobite and Jacobin. Towards the end of his life when he was threatened with a government investigation, which could have led to transportation or worse, he felt obliged to write one or two letters and one or two poems to profess conformity. It is contemptible that modern unionists are prepared to point to them to claim that Burns was one of themselves.

The work of these poets in the rescue of the Scottish identity was consolidated by Walter Scott by his poetry and even more by his novels. Again the best passages of the novels are the dialogues in Scots. In *Paul's Letters to his Kinsfolk*, Scott's son-in-law and biographer, J. G. Lockhart, discusses the effect of Scott s work on Scotland itself. The generation of Hume had "employed only the national intellect, and not the national modes of feeling". Since they dealt with intellectual abstraction and not with Scotland, the country and its history and character were liable to be forgotten. It had been left to Scott to restore "the richer and warmer spirit of literature in Scotland". In Scott's own lifetime, Lord Meadowbank expressed the gratitude of the people of Scotland and many others have done so since. Alexander Gray, for instance, said: "What Scotland owes to Burns and Scott is beyond all computation". That Scotland has survived as something more than a geographical expression is due to the determination of the Scottish people as a whole; but the impulse, definition and sense of direction has been given by the writers, the makers of the ballads.

Some people have gone further and suggested that Scott not merely restored the Scottish identity, but that he invented it. An exhibition now open in the Scottish National Portrait Gallery, *O Caledonia* has the sub-title: "Sir Walter Scott and the Creation of Scotland". Scott was an international best-seller for more than a century, and he is still popular in many countries, if not at present so well established at home as he once was. This has meant that people all over the world, who might otherwise scarcely have heard of Scotland, have formed an image of the country from his work. In that sense he created an idea of Scotland, but he was dealing with a reality which had existed for centuries before.

Duncan Macmillan in commenting on the same exhibition made a similar but a more far-reaching point:

> He (Scott) invented cultural identity, or at least popularised the notion that those communities searching for political autonomy as nations, are actually cultural constructs, a peculiar psychological package of feelings rooted in myth and memory. These ideas have had an impact far beyond Scotland.

Of course, Scott had no such conscious purpose; but it is probably true that in making the world aware of the national identity, or peculiar package rooted in myth and memory, of Scotland, that he made other people realise that their country too could claim something similar.

In his book, *Scotland and Nationalism*, Christopher Harvie refers to Fletcher s remark about ballads and laws and says that it "was to be prophetic in describing the course of Scottish nationalism over the course of the next 250 years". I think that he means by this that the loss of the Scottish legislature in 1707 meant that an even greater responsibility, for the evolution and expression of the national identity, fell on Scottish writers. They have responded to the challenge. But I think that everywhere writers have an essential role, because they establish and express the "myths and memories". A character in Alasdair Gray's *Lanark* says that "if a city hasn't been used by an artist not even the inhabitants live there imaginatively". In the same way, I doubt if a people can be aware of a national character if it has not been expressed in literature.

In this respect, the most influential writer in Scotland in the 20th century has been Hugh MacDiarmid. When he died in 1978 David Murison, the editor of the *Scottish National Dictionary*, said that he would make an unlikely comparison and that was with John Knox. This was because after MacDiarmid, as after Knox, Scotland would never be the same again. As he admitted himself, MacDiarmid was not afraid of self-contradiction; but in one thing he was entirely consistent in all his poetry and polemics, his insistent demand for the political and cultural independence of Scotland as part of the modern world. He was not alone of course, but his was the most powerful voice in changing the whole climate of opinion in Scotland.

In the latest issue of the *Edinburgh Review* (No 100 of May 1999) a number of writers reply to the question: "what do you expect from the Scottish Parliament?" Their replies echo Andrew Fletcher. Janice Galloway says: "Writers don't follow politicians, rather the reverse." Duncan McLean says the same thing and adds: "After all, hasn't Scottish writing been one of the major causes in bringing the Scottish Parliament into existence? . . . It was the writers (not alone among the artists, but possibly leading from the front) who articulated a sense of Scottish identity, of Scottish values, of Scottish concerns".

So the idea of Andrew Fletcher, or of his wise friend, is still very much alive and at least some Scottish writers are confident that they are unacknowledged legislators. But if that has been so in the past and in the present, how confident can we be that Scottish writers, or writers of any kind, will still have an influence in Scotland in the new era? Perhaps new era is too grandiose a term for the changes which can be introduced by a half-way Parliament with very limited powers and which has to work under very severe financial restraints imposed from the outside. But, if only in expectation, it has already transformed Scotland by its mere existence. There is a new hope and a new confidence in the air and a new conviction that Scotland really does exist after all. In 1935, in his book, *Scottish Journey*, Edwin Muir said that Scotland is "now falling to pieces for there is no visible and effective power to hold it together" and that "Edinburgh is a handsome, empty capital of the past". We now have a Parliament to hold Scotland together and Edinburgh already has the feel of a real capital once again. The writers now have to compete with parliamentary legislators, but they are legislators on our door-step who will have to respond to the demands and expectations of the writers and the people at large. A process has begun which will have an irresistible momentum of its own.

Not only Scotland is changing. So is the rest of the world and it is changing very fast. We now live in a global economy. At the beginning of the 20th century Scottish industry was a major economic force and it was mostly owned and controlled by Scots in Scotland. Now, at the end of that century, such industry as remains is almost entirely owned and controlled from outside. Factories are opened, or more often closed, by decisions taken in New York, Tokyo or London. It is an age too of global, instant, electronic communication, global fashion and global ideas. In the developed world at least, we all wear much the same clothes, live in much the same buildings and eat much the same food. There is hardly a high street in the world that does not have a MacDonald's, of which only the name is Scottish. We are more than ever a multicultural nation. Travel to the ends of the earth is commonplace. We no longer take our holidays in Rothesay or North Berwick, or even in Spain or Italy, but in America or Thailand. International organisations play a much larger role in our lives and the European Union is steadily harmonising social and economic legislation in the member states.

Andrew Marr in the *Observer* of 9th May 1999 asked: "Is Scotland regaining her Parliament at just the historical moment when real political choice is dying off, killed by a global market?" Is it perhaps far more than political choice that is being killed? Can the "peculiar set of manners" and the "particular qualities", which David Hume recognised survive in a world where the pressures and influences, or many of them at least, are not local or national, but as global as the market? The influence of Robert Burns or of Walter Scott is unlikely to be great in an age when few people read either or read very much at all. We may perhaps hear a song or two of Burns round about Burns Night, but the normal listening of most people is trans-Atlantic or mid-Atlantic pop. Television, the internet and computer games leave little time for books of any kind. Are we then entering a new era where national character and national literature are of no account and where particular qualities are being replaced by a global uniformity?

I do not know if such a world is imaginable or desirable, but I think that it is unlikely. I think that it is more probable that while some things become more uniform, other national or local differences will become more pronounced. I say this because there are many signs that external pressures towards conformity usually produce a compensating tendency towards the opposite. We have many examples of this in our own experience in Scotland. It was so, for instance, with the 18th century poets. The Gaelic and Scots languages have gradually retreated before English, the language of the all-powerful Government, for about 300 years. The external pressure only became intense with the introduction of talking films and broadcasting. Before that most people in Scotland, as elsewhere, hardly ever heard any other voices but those immediately around them. Now English and American voices were in their ears every day of the week. What happened? At first, standard English gained ground, but then there was a conscious revival of both Gaelic and Scots which are now resisting more strongly than ever before.

A similar response to a similar situation is happening all over the world. Some years ago, at a Congress of International PEN, George Steiner predicted that English, the "killer language", as he called it, would before long displace all the other languages of the world. I do not suppose that the other major languages will surrender all that easily; but many others, which are used much less extensively, are, like Gaelic and Scots, fighting back. In June 1996 in Barcelona 220 people from about 90 countries and all five continents met to sign the Universal Declaration of Linguistic Rights in defence of languages under threat. This is based on the principle that all languages are of equal value and should have equal rights. UNESCO are working towards an intergovernmental agreement at the UN on similar lines. The revival of interest in the langages is likely to be accompanied, as in Scotland, with a revival of their literatures and therefore an enhancement of their national characters.

Resistance to conformity is not confined to language. All over the world, the empires and multi-national states have dissolved into their component parts. More than 50 former colonies of the British Empire have become independent states and more recently and abrubtly the same thing has happened to the Soviet Union. In Scotland, since we are patient and long-suffering, progress has been slower; but we have at last taken a decisive step forward.

In Scotland in the 18th century Fletcher, Hume, Ferguson and Millar all argued that small states were the most conducive to human happiness and civilisation. They were more responsive to the wishes of their citizens, less liable to become oppressive, and more productive of a variety of ideas in the arts and sciences. In 1826, in the *Letters of Malachi Malagrowther*, Walter Scott made a passionate case for diversity and against uniformity. "National diversity between different countries", he said, "is but an instance of that general variety which nature seems to have adopted through all her works".

It seems to me that the dissolution of the empires and the large states suggests that there is a large measure of world wide agreement with these ideas. Most people prefer self-government to external control and prefer to follow their own inclinations than accept conformity imposed from the outside.

The modern world has revealed another advantage of the small states. They are more adaptable and responsive to the conditions of the global market. The small independent states of north west Europe are among the most prosperous in the world. At the same time, of course, we all have the advantages of the vast market of the European Union, within which there is no barrier to the free movement of goods and people. Within it also, there is general agreement that, whatever else may be harmonised, cultural diversity is one of the great virtues of Europe and that it must be preserved. We can conclude, I think, that not only have Scottish writers had a decisive influence on how we think and act in Scotland,— but that many of their ideas have spread well beyond our borders.

The recovery of the Scottish Parliament and of increasing control over our own affairs should remove the psychological damage of the Union. I mean by this the so-called Scottish cringe, a sense of inferiority which can amount to self-hatred. This is the result, I think, of dependence on decisions taken elsewhere and of the impression, conveyed by our educational system and London control of the media, that everything of importance happens somewhere else. Scottish writers have a vital role in the recovery of cultural self confidence.

But will books themselves survive? Will they be displaced by all the rapidly expanding wizardry of electronics? If that were to happen it would only be another means of conveying the same material. The basic tool is the word, conveyed at first by speech, then by writing, then by printing, now by electronics. They all still require the human mind to put the right words in the right order. Even if we were to banish books entirely from our houses and replace them by television and computer screens, there would still be writers behind them, using words to convey ideas, emotions and experiences.

Even so, I am confident that the book will survive. It is more adaptable, more diverse and wide-ranging in time, subject and space, more convenient, more attractive in appearance, touch and even smell, more user friendly that any electronic screen. Many people seem to agree. In spite of the spread of the internet and all that, we now have more, larger, better and busier bookshops than ever before. Long may it continue.

Reference

1. In *Blackwood's Magazine* of November, 1976. Reprinted in *Towards Independence* (Polygon, Edinburgh, 1991 and 1996).

2. 4

Burns and Scotland

'The Herald' Essay, 6th January 1996, a shortened version of a paper for the International Bicentenary Burns Conference at Strathclyde University, 11th to13th January 1996

I have been reading Burns for almost as long as I have been reading anything; but in the last few months I have systematically read through everything of his which survives, the poems, letters, Commonplace Book and travel diaries. I am left with a strong impression of a man of warm humanity, lucid intelligence and firm nationalist convictions. This last quality is so obvious that it is surprising how little is said about it in the vast literature about him. It seems that we are still suffering from a hangover of nineteenth century attitudes. Then the Monarchy, the Empire and the Union were all regarded as above criticism and any awkward evidence against them was simply ignored. That is why we have had to wait for more than a century for new editions of Walter Scott's *Malachi Letters* and Lockhart of Carnwath's *Memoirs* and why this aspect of Burns has been forgotten or even denied. It is time that we had a new look at one of the strongest feelings which inspired him, his love of Scotland and his detestation of the Union.

Burns himself tells us how he thought it began. In his famous autobiographical letter to Dr John Moore on 2nd August 1787 he said: "the story of Wallace poured a Scottish prejudice in my veins which will boil along there till the flood-gates of life shut in eternal rest." Thomas Carlyle said that it was not a prejudice but a "deep and generous" patriotism, for "certainly in no heart did the love of country ever burn with warmer glow than in that of Burns."

If Burns placed Wallace first, no doubt because of his humbler origin, uncompromising patriotism and dreadful end, he also held

Bruce in high regard. He refers to both of them in a letter to Robert Muir on 26th August 1787, where he describes the first day of his tour to the Highlands:

> This morning I Knelt at the tomb of Sir John the Graham, the gallant friend of the immortal Wallace; and two hours ago I said a fervent prayer for Old Caledonia over the hole in a blue whinstone, where Robert de Bruce fixed his royal standard on the banks of Bannockburn.

Burns's diaries of his Border and Highland tours consist mostly of very brief notes, but his entry about this event is passionate. He imagines his "heroic countrymen" approaching "the oppressive, insulting, blood-thirsty foe" and "gloriously triumphant, exulting in their heroic royal leader and rescued liberty and independence."

These thoughts on the field of Bannockburn immediately suggest the words of "Scots Wha Hae", although the song was not written until sixteen years later on about 30th August 1793. He described the circumstances in a letter to George Thomson and added after the words of the song: "So may God ever defend the the cause of Truth and Liberty, as he did that day! Amen!" There is a further postscript to the letter: "the accidental recollection of that glorious struggle for Freedom, associated with the glowing ideas of some other struggles of the same nature, *not quite so ancient*, roused my rhyming mania."

What were these other struggles? Burns may have been thinking generally of French revolutionary ideas, but there was another event much nearer home and of a precise co-incidence of date. On the same 30th August the trial of Thomas Muir of Huntershill for sedition began in Edinburgh. Muir, who advocated parliamentary reform and Scottish independence, was sentenced to transportation. In "Scots Wha Hae" therefore, Burns was drawing a parallel between Bruce's struggle for the independence of Scotland and the situation in his own time. Murray Pittock has pointed out that the song also uses Jacobite language. "For Scotland's King and Law" is a Jacobite phrase, and "chains and slaverie" could refer to the Jacobite prisoners who had been transported as slaves to the colonies. Pittock says that "the idea of a heroic, traditional Scotland as having to wage perpetual war against English might and gold in order to secure its very very existence was one central to Jacobite images of native heroism."

It may seem paradoxical that a man of egalitarian spirit like Burns should have looked back nostalgically, not only to Bruce, but to the entire line of the Scottish monarchy. In his "Address to Edinburgh", for instance:

> Edina! Scotia's darling seat!
> All hail thy palaces and tow' rs,
> Where once, beneath a Monarch's feet,
> Sat legislation's sov'reign pow'rs.

That last line is quite specific. His regret for the loss of the Scottish monarchy is regret for the loss of sovereignty and legislative power. His bitter sense of loss, and his Jacobitism, is even more apparent in the lines 'written on the Window of an Inn in Stirling'. (See page 32 above).

These feelings for the "injured Stewart line", more, I think because they were Scottish than because they were royal, were no doubt an element in Burns's Jacobitism; but there were others which were probably even more compelling. George Rosie has recently drawn attention to a passage in the writings of Hugh Miller where he suggests that Burns was in a state of intellectual confusion in professing both Jacobitism and Jacobinism at the same time. In fact, this combination of ideas was not unusual and was certainly not confined to Burns. There were solid reasons for it. Jacobitism in Scotland was largely a patriotic, nationalist attempt to overthrow the Union. Also, as Murray Pittock has argued, Jacobite and Jacobin shared the the view that the Hanoverians had caused "something rotten in the state of Scotland" and that there was a need to defend traditional values against an oppressor for whom money was all that mattered.

In supporting Jacobitism, Burns knew exactly what he was doing. He did not imagine that a Stewart could be restored to the throne. It was an expression of his detestation of the Union and of the arrogance and corruption of wealth. Walter Scott, who had Jacobite leanings himself, wrote of Burns that "a youth of his warm imagination and ardent patriotism", brought up at that time could "hardly escape" Jacobitism. Burns wrote or adapted about 30 Jacobite songs and they include some of his best and most passionate.

Andrew Noble has suggested that Burns's analysis of the Scottish situation is as valid now as it was in his time. In Noble's words, Burns was concerned with "the corrupting politics and psychology generated by the Union: the degeneration of parliament and other British civic and fiscal institutions, causing increasing disparity between rich and poor." All of these things are at least as obvious now as they were in the eighteenth century.

There are other ways in which the ideas of Burns are still apposite to our present situation. He wrote in a letter to Mrs Dunlop on 10th April 1790: "Alas! have I often said to myself, what are all the boasted advantages which my country reaps from the Union, that can counterbalance the annihilation of her Independence, and even her very name?" That is precisely how many of us still feel. The same is true of;

> We're bought and sold for English gold—
> Such a parcel of rogues in a nation.

In his autobiographical letter to John Moore, Burns said that that it was after coming across Fergusson' s Scotch Poems that he "strung my wildly-sounding, rustic lyre with emulating vigour." Both in verse and prose he paid many tributes to Ramsay and Fergusson as his models and inspiration, from the reference to them both in the Preface to the Kilmarnock edition to the inscription which he placed on Fergusson's grave: "My elder brother in misfortune / By far my elder brother in the muse." Like Burns, Ramsay and Fergusson wrote in Scots, and like him again, both were strongly nationalist in feeling and wrote poems against the Union. Does this suggest that writing poetry in Scots was in itself a nationalist act of defiance against the prevailing pressures of Anglicisation?

Burns told James Johnson on 16th September 1792 that he had an "enthusiastic attachment to the Poetry and Music of old Caledonia". This was an enthusiasm which he often expressed in his letters and Commonplace Book. He was determined to preserve the melodies of Scottish songs by writing new words where the old ones had been lost, were inadequate or where only the refrain survived. It was a patriotic labour of love, for which he refused to take any payment, similar in spirit to Walter Scott's collection of the Border Ballads. Burns began to contribute songs to Johnson's *Scots Musical Museum* in November 1787 and to Thomson's *Select Collection of Scottish Airs* in September 1792. He contributed 213 songs to Johnson and 114 to Thomson. With the important exception of "Tam o Shanter", this meant that for the last nine years of his life Burns's writing of poetry was almost entirely devoted to songs.

Alexander Scott has suggested that there were two reasons for the decline in Burns's satirical writing after the publication of the Kilmarnock edition in 1786 ,"rootlessness and respectability". Burns was rootless because he had left the community which had given him the substance for his attacks on religious orthodoxy and aristocratic privilege, and respectable because he had become an officer in the Excise. That last point is probably the main reason, and in fact the dates neatly coincide. Burns began to collaborate seriously with the *Scots Musical Museum* in November 1787 and in January 1783 he wrote to Robert Graham of Fintry to solicit his patronage for an appointment in the Excise. He began work as an Excise Officer in September 1789, and was therefore a civil servant of a government that was in a state of panic over its fear of revolutionary ideas from France. Muir and the others who were sentenced to transportation in 1793 were no more revolutionary in their ideas thanBurns himself and he had even attempted to send guns to France to support the Revolution.

Burns clearly understood his vulnerability. He wrote to Mrs Dunlop on 6th December 1792 about an episode in the theatre in Dumfries when "God save the King" had been hissed and the French revolutionarysong song, "Ça ira" repeatedly called for:

> For me, I am a *Placeman*, you know, a very humble one indeed, Heaven knows, but still so much so as to gag me from joining in the cry. — What my private sentiments are, you will find out without an interpreter.

His caution was not sufficient to prevent a denunciation of him as a person disaffected to Government, and the Board of Excise ordered an enquiry. He sent two abject and frantic letters to his patron, Robert Graham. Even dismissal from the service, without any more serious penalty, would, he wrote on 31st December 1792, turn his wife and family adrift "without the necessary support of a miserable existence." In the second letter of 5th January 1793 he went through the humiliation of obligatory conformity: "As to Reform Principles, I look upon the British Constitution, as settled at the Revolution, to be the most glorious Constitution on earth, or that perhaps the wit of man can frame." (The Revolution in this case is, of course, that of 1688-89, in which Scotland was still nominally independent with her own Parliament) Graham knew Burns well enough to understand how seriously to take these loyal protestations, but they were sufficient to satisfy the inquisition. It was, no doubt, as part of the same insurance policy that Burns joined the Dumfries Volunteers on 31 January 1793 and wrote their anthem, "Does Haughty Gaul Invasion Threat?",with the lines:

> Be Britain still to Britain true,
> Amang ourselves united!

There have been people who have seized on these prudent insincerities to try to represent Burns as a pillar of the establishment and the Union. These were the grounds for Hugh MacDiarmid's complaints about the Burns Clubs which he thought had done precisely that. MacDiarmid ended his celebrated essay on the subject with a call for us to follow the lead of Burns at long last. "We can, if we will . . . We can still affirm the fearless radical spirit of the true Scotland." I suggest that this is the appropriate objective for the Bicentennial year.

2.5

Burns the Radical

Review of Liam McIlvanney's 'Burns the Radical: Poetry and Politics in Late eighteenth-century Scotland'. 'The Sunday Herald' 20th October 2002

This is said to be the first book-length study of Burns's politics, which is surprising since his passionate radicalism and nationalism are evident on almost every page of his poems and letters. McIlvanney says that his purpose is to show that Burns was not a "simple, uneducated rustic" (does anyone suppose that?) but a man whose view of politics "was shaped by a critical engagement with a variety of political discourses", and who wrote rich and complex political verse. The subject has been enlarged, as McIlvanney acknowledges, by the discovery by Patrick Scott Hogg of previously unknown poems, now published in the *Canongate Burns.*

The book is an innovative and fascinating account of the political influences to which Burns responded. The first, and this may come as a surprise, is the Presbyterian kirk. "It remains unfortunate", McIlvanney says, "that Burns's run-ins with the kirk have obscured the extent to which his own political philosophy is grounded in his religious inheritance". The kirk was egalitarian in spirit and democratic in structure long before the state and it believed firmly in the right of resistance to unjust authority. Burns did not have to wait for the French Revolution to be persuaded of the virtues of equality, liberty and fraternity. His satires on the kirk were themselves products of his Presbyterian instincts. So too was his support for the New Light ministers who put personal interpretation of the scriptures above the acceptance of dogma.

These ministers with whom Burns associated were mostly graduates of Glasgow University where they had come under the influence of the Scottish Enlightenment thought of Hutcheson, Millar and the Adam Smith of the *Moral Sentiments*. As McIlvanney says, "Burns's poems are saturated in the idiom of Enlightenment moral philosophy, and palpably influenced by the concept of sympathy expounded by Adam Smith".

The "Real Whigs", a loose grouping of political thinkers in various parts of the British Isles, also held the Presbyterian belief in the right of resistance. Burns was familiar with their ideas from his own reading in the circulating library of which he was a member and even from the schoolbook to which his teacher, John Murdoch, introduced him, the *Collection of Prose and Verse*, edited by Arthur Masson of Aberdeen.

In all of McIlvanney's lucid analysis of the political influences on Burns there is one conspicuous omission, and it is one to which Burns himself attached importance. He said in his autobiographical letter to John Moore: "The story of Wallace poured a Scottish prejudice in my veins which will boil along there till the flood-gates of life shut in eternal rest". And indeed it is very clear from the frequent invocation of Wallace, Bruce and the Scottish struggle for independence in his poems and letters that Burns was an ardent Scottish patriot.

McIlvanney is curiously reticent about this aspect of Burns's ideas. He says very cautiously that a reference in "The Author's Earnest Cry and Prayer" faces us with the "intriguing possibility" that Burns might be calling for the restoration of the Scottish Parliament. Elsewhere he says that Burns is "very much part of a politicised cultural nationalism which developed in response to the 1707 Union". That is all. There is no mention of any of the passages where Burns makes his hatred of the Union specific, such as in "Such a parcel of rogues" or in the letter to Mrs Dunlop about "the boasted advantages" claimed for the Union.

McIlvanney also has an unusual response to the crisis which faced Burns in 1792, four years before his death. He had been denounced as "a person disaffected to Government". This was a serious threat. It was at the height of official panic over the French

Revolution. In the following year Muir and Palmer were sentenced to transportation, and Burns knew that he was vulnerable to similar treatment. He wrote a frantic letter to his patron, Graham of Fintry, on 31st December 1792 and a further letter on 5th January in response to the charges against him. In this he said that he looked upon "the British Constitution, as settled at the Revolution (he meant that of 1688-9) to be the most glorious Constitution on earth". But at about the same time he wrote to Mrs Dunlop to say: "What my private sentiments are, you will find out without an interpreter." He joined the Dumfries Volunteers and wrote a song for them, "Does haughty Gaul invasion threat?", in which are the lines: "Be Britain still to Britain true, / Amang oursels united."

In explanation of this apparent volte face, McIlvanney argues ingeniously that there were escape clauses in both the letter to Graham and the song which show that Burns had not completely abandoned his principles. It seems to me obvious enough that Burns was simply doing what was needed to save himself from prosecution. In the circumstances of the time who could blame him? The book has a final chapter about the Ulster Scots poets who were among Burns's most enthusiastic admirers and have been too much neglected. McIlvanney tells us that they were bitterly disillusioned by the song for the Dumfries Volunteers. In Ulster they probably did not know the gravity and urgency of the risk to which Burns was exposed.

This book is an important contribution to the understanding and appreciation of the work of Robert Burns. It is scholarly, lucid, full of fresh ideas and a pleasure to read.

2.6

The 18th Century Vernacular Revival

'Scottish Studies Review', No 3:1, 2001

An amended version of a paper for the Conference 'Brothers in the Muse', Strathclyde University, January 2000

At the the Bicentenary Burns Conference in 1996 I gave a paper on the nationalism of Robert Burns, his strong feeling for Scottish history, particularly of the Wars of Independence, his detestation of the Union, and his love of Scottish poetry, music and song and of the Scots tongue.[1] In the present paper I should like to consider the attititudes of his predecessors, Allan Ramsay and Robert Fergusson.

There exists a short manuscript biography of Allan Ramsay of which two copies have survived. They are in the handwriting of his son, the portrait painter of the same name, and are almost certainly by him. It describes his father's early reading in these words:

> Before he left Leadhills he had no opportunity of reading any books but such as were then in the hands of the country people all over Scotland. Amongst those were the History in verse of King Robert the Bruce, the exploits of Sir William Wallace; and the poems of Sir David Lindsay, a favourite of King James the fifth, which coming at an early period to one not distracted by a variety of studies, made a deep impression upon his mind, and gave a cast to all his after sentiments, particularly with regard to the dignity and independency of Scotland, in the history and antiquities of which he became very knowing.

The biography then refers to Ramsay's long poem, *The Vision*, which was included in his anthology, *The Evergreen*, of 1724. It purports to have been written originally in Latin about 1300 and translated into Scots in 1524. The subject is the suffering inflicted on Scotland by the invasions of Edward I. It is signed "A. R. Scot", which, as the biography points out, are Ramsay's initials with his nationality. It continues:

> His notions about the independency of Scotland had made him, for some time, consider the Union of the two Crowns as a hardship; an opinion which he held in common with many worthy men, and sincere friends of their country, in those days; and there is a poem of his in print called *The Tale of the three bonnets*, in which the manner of bringing about that Treaty is handled with a great deal of satirical humour. But his good sense and observation getting, at length, the better of his early prejudices, this Poem never obtained a place in any of his two volumes, and is now difficult to be met with. [2]

In this passage the younger Allan Ramsay, if he was indeed the author, is evidently trying to play down and explain away the nationalist views of his father. He also suggests that his father's objections were to the Union of the Crowns, not to that of the Parliaments, although he does confusingly also refer to "that Treaty". The son was, of course, a highly successful portrait painter in London with the royal family and other members of the establishment among his clients. He therefore had good reason to avoid any hint of political unreliability. Pressures of this kind are a subject to which I shall return.

There is an obvious similarity between what the the biography says about the early influences on Ramsay and what Burns says about himself in his autobiographical letter to Dr John Moore about the story of Wallace.[3]

Ramsay expressed his nationalist feelings and his opposition to the Union in more poems than those mentioned in the short biography and more explicitly. One has the title: *On the B(ritish) P(arliament's) design of Taking the Bounty off Victual exported. Decem 1724.* It begins:

> Poor slav'd tho' covenanted Land
> anes Independent brave dominion
> how like ane Idiot dost thou stand
> Sair Payd and forc'd to kiss the wand
> and bend thy Craig beneath the U— . [4]

His first published poem, *To the Memory of the famous/ Archibald Pitcairn M.D. / By / A Member of the/ EASY Club / In / Edinburgh*, is even stronger in its language. (This by the way is the poem of which no copy could be found in time for inclusion in the Scottish Text Society edition. Dr Fred Freeman in 1979 discovered a copy in the Edinburgh Room of the Edinburgh Public Library) It says of Pitcairn:

> For like a Noble Scot of Antient Race,
> He spurned at our Slavery and Disgrace,
> Poor Slaves to England, Wretched, O ye Gods

In heaven Pitcairn meets Bruce, Wallace, Douglas, Graham and Belhaven. Bruce asks him:

> O Gods. Is the Great Soul of Scotland fled;
> Or does She dream on some dark drowsy Bed
> Will She not rise to gain Her Old Renown,
> And show She wears an Independent Crown. [5]

Alexander Kinghorn in his biographical note in the Scottish Text Society edition says of the Easy Club: Ramsay in his late twenties "entered into association with a number of young men of strong nationalist political leanings and, on 12th May 1712, helped to form a group calling itself the 'Easy Club' ". Kinghorn quotes Lord Woodhouslee, the joint editor of an edition published in 1800:

> The political principles of Ramsay were those of an old Scotsman, proud of his country, delighted to call in mind its ancient honour, while it held the rank of a distinct Kingdom, and attached to the succession of its ancient princes... The chief friends of the poet were probably men, whose sentiments on those subjects agreed with his own, and the Easy Club, of which he was an original member, consisted of youths who were anti-unionists. [6]

All the contemporary evidence is that the Union was vastly unpopular in Scotland. There were demonstrations in the streets and a flood of petitions against it from all over Scotland. Sir John

Clerk was a prominent figure on the government side, but he said in his *History of the Union* that not even 1% of the people were in favour.[7] Ramsay was 23 or 24 in 1707 and it is not in the least surprising that he shared the views of the great majority of his contemporaries. What is more surprising is that even the Easy Club, at least at first, welcomed certain English literary influences, as we can see from their minute book.[8] The members each chose a *nom de plume* for himself. Ramsay's was Isaac Bickerstaff, a name used by both the *Tatler* and Jonathan Swift. On 8th August 1712 the Club resolved that an issue of the *Spectator* should be read at every meeting and that the said Bickerstaff would provide the first volume. It sounds as if the chief object of the Club was to imitate London literary society.

The Club soon abruptly changed course. By November 1713 it had evidently lost its initial appeal and a meeting, with Ramsay in the chair, discussed the reason for this. One of the members (who significantly had chosen from the beginning the name of George Buchanan) offered an explanation. "Representing what Scotland has suffered, what we in a More inglorious manner are like to suffer by the Perfidy, pride and hatred of England and how great an affront was put upon the Scots Nation by Condemning our own Country and choosing English men for our Patrons", he proposed and it was resolved, that the members would choose Scottish, in place of English, patrons, "to pay a dutiful Respect to the heroes and authors of their own nation". Ramsay chose Gavin Douglas.

On 9th February 1715, the year in which Mar raised the standard in Braemar on 6th September, the Club approved an address to the King. This appealed for the dissolution of the Union and its replacement by a federation of the two Parliaments "as a safeguard against the eternal discord engendered by the Union". It added: "if this Union be not speedily dissolv'd Scotland will be Ruin'd".

In spite of this strong language, it is evident from the earlier history of the Club that even so soon after the traumatic shock of the Union to national pride and even in a club of enthusisatic nationalists, there were pressures in opposing directions. They were distressed and outraged by the Union, but they had to survive and make their way in a society where all advancement was by patronage. Control of that patronage was in the hands of the London establishment and of a small aristocratic circle in Scotland who collaborated with them. They were, by and large, those who had voted for the Union, "having gotten, it was thought, a rug of the compensations", (to use the words of *Wandering Willie's Tale*), that is to say a share of the bribes and were doing well out of it. In the 18th century, if you wanted to find employment in the Church, the law, the universities, the army or other government service, you were well advised to keep your feelings about the Union to your self.

Robert Fergusson shared the pride of Ramsay and Burns in the "ancient honour" of Scotland and the glories of the independent past. Like Burns, he was inspired by the history of Wallace. He wrote two acts of a tragedy about him, which unfortunately have not survived. A contemporary called him "a rank Jacobite". [9] The following lines are from his poem *Auld Reekie*:

To Holy-rood-house let me stray,
And gie to musing a' the day;
Lamenting what auld Scotland knew
Bein Days for ever frae her view:
O HAMILTON, for shame, the Muse
Would pay to thee her couthy Vows,
Gin ye would tent the humble Strain
And gie 's our Dignity again:
For O, waes me the Thistle springs
In DOMICILE of ancient Kings,
Without A Patriot to regrete
Our PALACE, and our ancient STATE. [10]

Fergusson also shared with the other poets their detestation of the Union. He said in his poem, *The Ghaists*:

Black be the day that e'er to England's ground
Scotland was eikit by the Union's bond. [11]

There were other conflicting pressures, apart from patronage. Most Scots for most of the century were opposed to the Union, but the majority of them were also presbyterian. On the other hand, resistance to the Union had become associated with Jacobitism. The Jacobites had opposed the Union in the Scottish Parliament and had made the Risings of the '15 and '45 crusades against it. But Jacobitism was also associated in the minds of many people with Episcopalianism or Catholicism and with arbitrary royal power. What was a Presbyterian Scot, opposed to these things but also to the Union, to do? It became still more difficult because, after the Risings, Jacobitism could be treated as treasonable and subject to the most severe penalties of the law. By association, opposition to the Union could be interpreted as a symptom of Jacobite leanings. To make matters still worse, the failure of the Risings, and the ruthless and brutal suppression after the '45, proved that resistance was hopeless and that the Union, whether you liked it or not, was there to stay for the foreseeable future.

In all these circumstances there were two possible responses. The first was to decide that since resistance was hopeless, the best course was to swallow your pride and dislike of the Union and try to make the best of a bad job. That meant accepting the fact that England was now dominant politically and that London, in James Boswell's phrase, "was now the metropolis of the whole island". [12] So you had to conform. That involved the abandonment of your own history, language, and ways of thinking and behaving and doing your best to ape those of the English. This, you might say, was the policy of the literati of the Enlightenment.

At the same time, the attitude of the literati was by no means homogeneously pro-Union and pro-England. Their Scottish feelings repeatedly showed through in spite of their prudent pose of Unionist conformity. In his private letters Hume was frank about his opinion of those he called "the Barbarians who inhabit the Banks of the Thames". [13] In his published writings he was more discreet, but even so he argued in his essays that "a small commonwealth is the happiest government in the world". Like Andrew Fletcher, whom he admired, he took the city states of ancient Greece as a model of the advantages of diversity. [14] Adam Ferguson in his *Essay on the History of Civil Society* said that the advantages of society may frequently be obtained "where nations remain independent, and are of small extent". [15] John Millar said that small states are usually successful in establishing a free constitution, but that large and expansive nations are more likely to terminate in despotism. [16] Adam Smith said that the colonies of ancient Greece were successful because they were allowed to control their own affairs, but that those of Rome were stifled by centralised control. [17]

It seems to me that remarks like these suggest that these men of the Enlightenment regretted Scotland's loss of independence, even if they felt that rational self-interest now required acceptance of the *fait accompli.* In the turmoil of conflicting pressures and emotions caused by the Union, it is not surprising that people veered in more than one direction. Boswell, who has told us more than anyone else about his emotions and ideas, is a case in point. He longed to share in the power, wealth and fashion of London, but throughout his life he repeatedly expressed his detestation of what he called the "cursed Union" that had reduced Scotland to a province. [18]

The alternative course to Unionist conformity was to struggle to preserve from the wreck as much as you could of Scottishness and to resist culturally, even if political resistance was impossible. That meant a determination to preserve and build on the history, language, literature, sense of values and social habits of the independent Scotland before the Union. That was the policy of Ramsay, Fergusson and Burns. The opposition between acceptance of assimilation and resistance to it has continued to the present. It is essentially the distinction between unionism and nationalism. In the 18th century the unionists tried to write and speak like the English; the nationalist poets wrote in Scots or Gaelic (although the Gaelic poets are outside the scope of the present paper) as an act of political and cultural defiance.

Ramsay, Fergusson and Burns all wrote verse in English as well as Scots or in a mixture of the two. As David Daiches remarked, Burns often wrote in "English sprinkled with Scots" [19], although I should prefer to say, enriched with Scots. Apart from one letter by Burns, all their prose which survives is in English. This habit of using both Scots and English, and of mixing them, has long been, and still is, common in Scottish writing and speech. I do not think that it should be considered as a defect or weakness. It arises naturally because the two languages share a common origin and remain in many ways so close and because English was mainly the language of school and church. Ramsay regarded this bilingualism as an advantage. He said in the Preface to his *Poems* (1721) that the Scots were masters of English "by being taught it in our schools, and daily reading of it; which being added to our native Words of eminent Significancy, makes our Tongue by far the completest." [20] Just over a hundred years later John Galt made the same point. In the Introduction to his short story, *The Seamstress*: he referred to "the fortunate circumstance of the Scotch possessing the whole range of the English language, as well as their own, by which they enjoy an uncommonly rich vocabulary."

R. D. S. Jack has argued that the use by the poets of English as well as Scots proves that that the revival of literary Scots was not an expression of a "defensive spirit of linguistic nationalism". [21] On the contrary, I do not think that there can be any doubt that this is exactly what it was, an act of resistance to anglicisation. That seem to me to be clear from the nationalist declarations of the poets themselves, the determination with which they insisted on using Scots in spite of all the pressures against it and the contrast with those who took pains to eliminate Scotticisms from their speech and writing.

Ramsay's *Evergreen* (1724), a collection of medieval Scottish poetry, and his *Tea-Table Miscellany* of traditional Scots songs and ballads were, like his use of Scots, a patriotic undertaking to establish continuity with the independent Scotland of the past. It is significant that an earlier such anthology, James Watson's *A Choice Collection*, was first published in 1706, precisely at the time when the Union was under debate. John Oliver, one of the editors of the Scottish Text Society's edition of Ramsay, and an accomplished versifier himself in Scots, says in an essay, after a reference to Andrew Fletcher's celebrated remark about ballads and laws:

> And now when the Union, which Fletcher had opposed so bitterly, was an accomplished fact, and Scotland had lost the power of making her laws, Watson and Ramsay gave her back her ballads . . . No influence was stronger in the preservation of national characteristics, national sympathies, and national pride. [22]

Burns's tireless collection of songs and fiddle tunes and later Walter Scott's work on the Border ballads were undertaken in the same spirit

Some surprising remarks about Fergusson and Burns have been made recently in two important and influential books. The first was Lindsay Paterson's *The Autonomy of Modern Scotland* (1994). He says:

> The poets Robert Burns and Robert Fergusson, for instance, resented that the Union had not in fact created one realm; and they expressed their resentment in Scottish nationalist terms . . . Thus Robert Burns or Robert Fergusson wanted a more complete Union in order to remove any political obstacles to Scots' following their own special ways of living and feeling. [23]

The other book was T.M.Devine's *The Scottish Nation: 1700-2000* (1999) which has the following passage:

> Robert Fergusson and Robert Burns, major Scottish poets of the later eighteenth century, waxed eloquent on the theme of Britain. Fergusson referred to 'Thrice happy Britons . . . the sons that hem Britannia round from sudden invasion', while Burns, in the "Ode for General Washington's Birthday", spoke of "the freeborn Briton's soul of fire". [24]

I have mentioned my paper of 1996 on the attitude of Burns to Scotland and the Union. I shall not repeat it, except to say that I do not think that anyone can read through his letters and poems without being convinced that enthusiasm for Scottish independence and detestation of the Union were among his strongest feelings. It is true that towards the end of his life, when he was threatened with a Government investigation, he wrote one or two letters and one or two poems to defend himself against the very real risk of deportation, like Thomas Muir, or worse. At the same time, he wrote to Mrs Dunlop: "What my true sentiments are, you will find out without an Interpreter." [25]

Burns's *Ode for General Washington's Birthday* [26] has the opposite significance from the one which Devine attributes to it. It is true that the poem speaks of "the freeborn Briton's soul of fire", but this refers to bards at the time of King Alfred and it goes on to say that they: No more thy England own'. Now:

> England in thunders calls—'The Tyrants cause is mine.'
> That hour accurst, how did the fiends rejoice,
> And Hell thro' all her confines raise th' exulting voice
> That hour which saw the generous English name
> Linkt with such damned deeds of everlasting shame.

Then, as Burns himself said in a letter to Mrs Dunlop on 25th June 1794, [27] with which he enclosed a copy of the poem: "After having mentioned the degeneracy of other kingdoms I come to Scotland thus:

> Thee, Caledonia, thy wild heaths among,
> Famed for the martial deed, the heaven-taught song,
> To thee, I turn with swimming eyes.—
> Where is that soul of freedom fled?
> Immingled with the mighty dead.
> Beneath that hallowed turf where WALLACE lies.

In the same letter Burns said: "The subject is LIBERTY; you know, my honoured friend, how dear the theme is to me". So far from celebrating the idea of Britain, as Devine would have us believe, he is condemning it as the friend of tyrants and celebrating Scotland as the home of freedom. He links Wallace and the Scottish struggle in the Wars of Independence with the same struggle in America and by implication, (as Thomas Crawford has pointed out) [28] with the aspirations of the French Revolution and the Friends of the People in Scotland.

As we have seen, Fergusson's attitude to the Union was very similar. The lines which Devine quotes come from a polite poem in English which Fergusson wrote in appreciation of a sail in a whaler from Dunbar to Fife. His real feelings are, I think, those which I have quoted from *The Ghaists*.

I do not think that there is any doubt that Fergusson and Burns, and Ramsay too for that matter, did not want a more complete Union, as Lindsay Paterson suggests, but no Union at all. I fail to see how it can be suggested that a more complete Union would help Scots to follow "their own special ways of living and feeling". Paterson does not tell us how he arrived at his conclusion. The only possible source that I can think of is a phrase in a letter which Burns sent to an Edinburgh newspaper on 9th February 1789 to protest against a tax which discriminated against Scottish distillers. He says in it that Scotland, after many ages of struggle for independence, had at last agreed to a Union with her more powerful neighbour, "which should ever after make them one People". [29]

In that context, it was perfectly natural to argue that the Union, whether you like it or not, should accord equal treatment in the matter of tax.

The influence on Ramsay, Fergusson and Burns of our early history, of our independence and the struggle to defend it are, of course, by no means all that these three poets had in common. They all wrote in Scots, shared the same feelings for the language and for Scotland, hated the Union, and used the same themes and verse forms. It is perfectly appropriate that they have always been regarded as a coherent school, the poets of the vernacular revival.

It seems to me that the nationalism of these three poets involves two elements which are interrelated. The first is a strong belief in what we now call the right of self-determination, a conviction that the history and the distinctive character of the Scots gives them a right and a need to run their own affairs, of which they were deprived by the Union and which they should recover. The second is a deep affection for the poetry, languages, music, traditions and habits of thought and behaviour of Scotland. It was once described by Maurice Lindsay in relation to his own feelings as a love affair, "the fervour, the obsession with Scottishness for its own sake, the strongly emotional response to whatever carried even the faintest Scottish overtone." [30] In the work of these poets, these feelings extend even to Scottish food, drink and dress.

In an essay where she discusses Fergusson, Janet Adam Smith asks if there is something narrow about such feelings as these, but she concludes that Fergusson's "concern is really at a deeper level". He sees all of these things "as standing for Scotland's separate identity; nationality is for him not just a matter of institutions or of 'high culture', but of all the elements that make up the texture of life". Later in the same essay she says that "Burns's pride and independence as a man, his pride in his country's struggle for independence, led him to value freedom everywhere. Scots must be inspired by their past to a concern for the freedom of others". [31]

This reference to "pride in his country's struggle for independence" is reminiscent of a remark by the English historian, J. A. Froude: "No nation in Europe can look with more just pride on their past than the Scots, and no young Scot ought to grow up in ignorance of what that past has been". [32] For so small a country, Scotland has made a remarkable contribution in the arts and sciences to world civilisation; but Janet Adam Smith and J. A. Froude evidently agree with Ramsay, Fergusson and Burns that the greatest source of pride must be the long and heroic struggle for independence against very heavy odds. All nations and all nationalisms depend on their view of the past. The circumstances of our past have disposed us to value freedom, social justice and equality, the qualities which find powerful expression in the poetry of Robert Burns. Perhaps that is why he has been adopted as a spokesman for the nation to an extent which is not equalled, I think, in any other country or by any other poet.

Nationalism is a word which is easily misunderstood because it is used in two very different, or even entirely opposite, senses. It is often used pejoratively to mean aggressive chauvinism, a desire to dominate, expel or destroy other people, justified by an assumption of superiority. On the other hand, the word is also to mean opposition and resistance to these deplorable atttitudes. In this sense it is a liberalising and constructive force, and it is in this sense that the word is used in Scotland and in many other small European countries.

I think that the remarks by Janet Adam Smith, which I have quoted, amount to a good definition of Scottish nationalism as it was expressed by these 18th century poets and as it has remained. It is a belief in the value of the Scottish approach to life and a conviction that it can only be adequately expressed and developed through self-government, towards which the present constitutional arrangements are a decisive step. It is not aggresive, exclusive or ethnic, but democratic, egalitarian and compassionate, open to ideas from other countries and sympathetic to similar struggles everywhere. As Janet Adam Smith concludes, "concern for Scottishness becomes a moral concern".

References

1. Published in *Love and liberty: Robert Burns - A Bicentenary Celebration.* Edited by Kenneth Simpson. (East Linton, 1997) pp. 266-273 and in Paul Henderson Scott, *Still in Bed with an Elephant* (Edinburgh, 1998).

2. Scottish Text Society edition of the Works of Allan Ramsay. Edited by Alexander Kinghorn and Alexander Law. (6 Vols. Edinburgh, 1954-74) Vol. IV (1970) pp.1, 58, 73-4.

3. *The Letters of Robert Burns*, Edited by J. De Lancey Ferguson (2 vols. Oxford, 1931) Vol.1 pp. 1067.

4. As 2 above. Vol.111 pp.181-2.

5. *The Biblioteck*, Vol. 9, No. 5. (1979) pp 455-157.
6. As 2 above, Vol.IV pp.10, 13, 55 and Vol V. pp. 27-8.
7. Sir John Clerk of Penicuik, *History of the Union of Scotland and England*, translated from the Latin and edited by Douglas Duncan (Scottish History Society, Edinburgh, 1993) p. 118.
8. As 2 above. Vol. V (1972) pp. 27-8.
9. Scottish Text Society edition of the Works of Robert Fergusson. Edited by Matthew P. McDiarmid. (2 Vols, Edinburgh, 1954, 1956) Biographical introduction, Vol. I p. 19.
10. As 9. above. Vol. II p. 117.
11. As 9. above, Vol.11 p. 143.
12. James Boswell, *Boswell, Laird of Auchinleck*, Edited by J.R.Reed and F.A. Pottle (New York, 1979) p. 66.
13. David Hume, *Letters*. Edited by J.Y.T.Greig. (London, 1932) Vol I, p. 436.
14. David Hume, *Selected Essays*. Edited by Stephen Copley and Andrew Edgar. (Oxford, 1993) pp. 311, 64.
15. Adam Ferguson, *An Essay on the History of Civil Society* (1767). Edited by Duncan Forbes. (Edinburgh, 1966) p. 59.
16. John Millar, *Origin of the Distinction of Ranks* (Chapter 5) in *The Scottish Enlightenment: An Anthology*. Edited by Alexander Broadie. (Edinburgh, 1997) p. 542.
17. Adam Smith, *The Wealth of Nations*, Everyman's Library edition (London, 1971). Book IV, Chapter 7. Vol. II pp. 64, 65.
18. James Boswell, *Grand Tour in Germany and Switzerland*, Edited by F.A.Pottle (London, 1953) pp.126, 218. *The Applause of the Jury*, Edited by I.S.Lustig (London, 1981) pp. 83, 84.
19. David Daiches, *Robert Burns* (London, 1952) p.32.

20. As 2. above. Vol.1 p.xix

21. R.D.S.Jack, "Which Vernacular Revival? Burns and the Makars" in *Studies in Scottish Literature*, Vol. XXX. Edited by G. Ross Roy. (Columbia, South Carolina, 1988). p. 17.

22. John W. Oliver, "The Eighteenth Century Revival" in *Edinburgh Essays on Scottish Literature.* Edited by H.J.C.Grierson (Edinburgh, 1933) pp. 91-2.

23. Lindsay Paterson, *The Autonomy of Modern Scotland* (1994) pp. 41-2.

24. T.M.Devine, *The Scottish Nation: 1700-2000* (1999) pp. 28-9.

25. As 3. above. Vol. II. p. 137.

26. Robert Burns, *Poems and Songs* Edited by James Kinsley. (Oxford Standard Authors, 1969) pp.580-581.

27. As 3. above. Vol. II. p. 246.

28. Thomas Crawford, *Burns: A Study of the Poems and Songs* (Edinburgh, 1994).

29. As 3. above. Vol. p.305.

30. Maurice Lindsay, *By Yon Bonnie Banks.* (London, 1961). p. 220.

31. Janet Adam Smith, "Some Eighteenth Century Ideas of Scotland" in *Scotland in the Age of Improvement.* Edited by N.T.Phillipson and Rosalind Mitchison. (Edinburgh, 1970). pp. 118, 121, 122.

32. J. A. Froude, Quoted by Gordon Donaldson in his Inaugural Lecture in the University of Edinburgh, 1964.

2.7

Boswell and the national question

Paper for the ALS Boswell bicentenary conference, Edinburgh, 19-21st May 1995. Reprinted in 'Boswell in Scotland and Beyond', edited by Thomas Crawford, Glasgow, 1997.

At the beginning of his *Life of Samuel Johnson* Boswell says that Johnson "will be seen in this work more completely than any man who has ever lived." [1] I am not sure if that is true of Johnson but it is certainly true of Boswell himself from the record preserved, to use his own word, in his journals and letters. Although he realised the risks of a frank journal (31st July 1779), there seems little doubt that he did his best to follow the advice which Johnson twice gave him to write down everything that he could remember fully and minutely. [2] So we have a vast body of evidence of the way in which Boswell acted and thought and about the society that surrounded him. This evidence has to be treated with some caution because Boswell recorded his feelings at the time and he was, as he said, changeful. Any one extract in isolation might be misleading, because you can often find another which says the opposite. You have to look at the overall effect. The picture is all the more honest and complete for that very reason. It has all the uncertainties and contradictions which are part of the normal human experience.

The aspect that I propose to consider is a theme that runs throughout the journals, the tensions between the opposing influences of Scotland and England, their religions, languages, social conventions and intellectual attitudes and the ways in which they had been affected by the new relationship established by the parliamentary Union of 1707. Boswell was living at the time when the Scots were coming to terms with the Union. He was only five when Culloden destroyed any hope of escape from it in the forseeable future. The Scottish economy was beginning to recover from its immediate damaging conseqences. By the 1760s the people had largely decided to make the best of it. There is a letter of April 1760 in which Adam Smith explains why all classes of people had been utterly opposed to the Union, but that the "views of their Posterity were now very Different". [3] A few years later Boswell himself at Avignon on 26th December 1765 records a conversation in which he agreed that the greatest part of the people in Scotland were by then reconciled to the Union because, as he said, they had "lost all principle and spirit of patriotism". Boswell remained constantly opposed to the Union throughout his life, in spite of his love for London and English society.

A decisive moment in Boswell's life was when he ran off to London when he was 19. It was an act of rebellion against his father with whom Boswell's relations were always difficult, like those of Hermiston and his son in Stevenson's novel. The father, Lord Auchinleck, was a Whig and Prebyterian, of blunt and direct Scots speech and committed to solid and steady devotion to duty. Boswell reacted against all of these things. His long suffering father treated him generously and financed him for another visit to London, law studies in Utrecht and a long Grand Tour. But for Boswell, Edinburgh was indelibly associated with his father's disapproving eye and tongue. London meant freedom and self indulgence, and, after he met Samuel Johnson in May 1763, an alternative father figure.

For the rest of his life, or at least until he went to live there permanently, Boswell was besotted with London. Nearly every year he went there for some months in the spring, and his journals are vibrant with the excitement of it. When he arrived there on 17th March 1778, for instance:

> I was struck with agreeable wonder and admiration by contemplating the immensity of the metropolis and the multitude of objects; above all by the number and variety of people; and all melancholy was as clearly dissipated as if it had never existed in my mind.

Johnson, you remember, said that "when a man is tired of London he is tired of life; for there is in London all that life can afford", but he also said that he had never known a man "with such a gust" for London as Boswell. [4]

His longing for London bred an impatience with Edinburgh. His journals are full of such phrases as: "my aversion to the narrow ill-bred sphere was very strong" (18th Nov 1792); "a comfortable sense of superiority over any Edinburgh society" (8th Nov 1792); "I passed as dull a day as if I had been in Edinburgh (2nd Dec 1792). Occasionally, but not very often, he says the opposite. On 12th January 1786 he "sat some time in the room behind Creech's shop, and had an impression of Edinburgh being a very good place" and on the 19th he "judged it unreasonable to be dissatisfied in Edinburgh".

Throughout the journals he constantly expresses his dislike for certain Scottish institutions and characteristics. He was no friend of Presbyterianism. On 20th April 1765 in Rome he prayed to "drive away melancholy and keep clouds of Prebyterian sundays from rendering mind gloomy". In Woodford on 8th April 1781 he played whist with some Scottish friends on a Sunday. No wild indulgence you might think, but they hugged themselves that they "were out of the reach of Presbyterian prejudices". On 12th November 1780 he "regretted that we had not the decency of the Church of England established in this country". None of this is surprising, of course. Quite apart from the revolt against his father, Boswell was fond of ritual and display and of many things of which the Kirk disapproved, the theatre, card playing and sexual freedom.

Boswell was not at ease with the general tone of Scottish social behaviour. The journals are full of complaints about "Scotch tones and rough and roaring freedom of manners" (2nd June 1763); "familiarity and inquisitiveness" (3rd Sept 1769); "sarcastical temper" (17th Sept 1769); "uncouth Scots manners" (16th February 1766); "rude Scots sarcastical vivacity" (31st July 1764)) and so on. On the other hand, he had a "fondness of English manners" (20th February 1788.) He praises London for "the freedom from remark and petty censure, with which life may be passed there". [5] I think all of this is consistent with Boswell's social and political attitudes. Not to put too fine a point on it it, he was a bit of a snob, priding himself on his ancient baronial family. Like Johnson, he was a strong upholder of what he called "the subordination of rank, by which all the elegance of life is produced". (8th Sept 1792) In a pamphlet which he published in November 1772 he complained: "For some years past there has been in Scotland an abominable spirit of levelling". [6] Evidently Boswell was not treated in Scotland with the deference to which he felt entitled but his vanity was cosseted by the the greater reserve and formality of London.

Then there is the complex question of language. In his early years at least Boswell was an enthusiast for the Scots language. When he was in Utrecht in 1764 he began to compile a dictionary of it and he wrote in his journal on 24th February:

> The Scottish language is being lost ever day, and in a short time will become quite unintelligible . . . To me, who have the true patriotic soul of an old Scotsman, that would seem a pity.

In October 1769 he showed a specimen of the dictionary to Johnson who encouraged him to complete it. "Make a large book, a folio". *Boswell*: "But of what use will it be, Sir?" *Johnson*: "Never mind the use; do it. Unfortunately, that seems to be the last that was heard of the idea. In 1773 Boswell told Johnson that Allan Ramsay's *Gentle Shepherd* in Scots was "the best pastoral that had ever been written". [7]

It may seem strange (although in fact it is by no means unusual) that the enthusiast for Scots should also take pains to speak like an Englishman. He took lessons from Mr Dove of the Drury Lane Theatre and from Sheridan who, although Irish, gave classes on pronunciation in Edinburgh. To some extent Boswell wanted the best of both worlds. In the *Life of Johnson* he speaks with approval of getting rid of what he calls the "coarse part" of the Scottish accent, but retaining enough "as to mark his country; which, if any Scotchman should affect to forget, I should heartily despise him". [8] Even so, increasingly as he grew older Boswell expressed his displeasure or disgust at the sound of a Scots voice. Twice he gives examples by imitating the sound in his spelling of the sort of thing which he dislikes. One concerns no less than Hugh Blair who was an arbiter of literary taste at the time and, as the first occupant of the Chair of Rhetoric and Belles Lettres in Edinburgh, was the first professor of English Literature at any university. On 20th July 1784 Boswell says in a letter from Edinburgh to Temple: "The coarse vulgarity all around me is . . . shocking . . . Dr Blair accosted me with a vile tone, '*Hoo did you leave Sawmuel?*' " But Boswell does have the grace to add, "What *right* have I to be so nicely delicate?" In a letter from London to his wife in Auchinleck on 28th January 1789 he says that his former law clerk from Edinburgh has turned up "and quite sunk my spirits by renewing former coarse, vulgar sensations, the Parliament *Hoose* etc, etc." On 26th September 1793 he says in his journal that it had hurt him a good deal that "his daughters were at no pains to acquire the English pronunciation and tone, and were fond of associating with Scotch people who could do them no credit".

Of course Boswell was not alone in his anxiety to acquire an English accent. Tom Crawford has described the anglomania which gripped a generation of Edinburgh literati about 1755 to 1760. [9] The Select Society, which had the cultivation of English as one of its purposes, was founded in 1754 and Sheridan came to Edinburgh to give his lectures in 1761. Boswell was involved in both. This is also the time, as I have mentioned, when many Scots were beginning to accept the Union in a spirit of if you can't beat them, join them.

The decline in status of Scots, the language in which some of the finest poetry in mediaeval Europe had been written, was a consequence of the Unions first of the crowns and then of the Parliaments. When James VI flitted to London in 1603, royal patronage and the right to make all state appointments went with him. James's successors were all brought up in England, spoke English and were surrounded by English courtiers and ministers. Anyone in Scotland with political or social ambition had to go to London and make himself acceptable in the dialect of the Court.

The wide circulation in Scotland of the James VI Bible made English seem the appropriate language for serious discourse. After 1707 London became even more completely the source of power and prestige. First the aristocrats and then the snobbish and ambitious made English speech the badge of social acceptability and Boswell was both snobbish and ambitious. The rejection of Scots had many unfortunate conseqences. It undermined the confidence of the people in their own language and impaired self expression. It is also a short step from the rejection of the language to contempt for those who speak it and the rejection of the country itself. Boswell shows many signs of this complex, although he never entirely lost his Scottish patriotism.

One example of this complex is Boswell's failure to realise that in Edinburgh he was living in the great age of innovative thought which we now call the Scottish Enlightenment. He was on intimate terms with David Hume, Adam Smith, William Robertson, Lord Kames and many others, but still thought that he had to go to London for intellectual conversation. His journals are full of such remarks as "London has made my taste too high" to enjoy conversation in Edinburgh, (11th February 1780) or "London and Dr Johnson have made me unhappy in ordinary company". (26th February 1780) Boswell accepted Johnson's view that there more learning and science within ten miles of where they sat in London than in all the rest of the kingdom. He says the they both loved London "for the high and varied intellectual pleasure which it furnishes". [10]

There are many contemporary tributes to the quality and accessibility of intellectual society in Edinbugh at the time, but one from Boswell's friend William Temple is as good as any:

> Indeed I should prefer Edinburgh to London: it is less expensive, the men of letters are all known to one another, their character is honourable, and their conversation the instruction and delight of the best company. In England our literati are generally pedants, ill-bred and not fit to live in society: they are therefore with reason avoided by men of the world and of common sense. [11]

The energy which Boswell spent in collecting material for his *Life of Johnson* might have been more usefully employed in Edinburgh. His failure to respond to an approach from his neighbour at Auchinleck, Robert Burns, is one of the saddest missed opportunities in literary history.

Johnson told Boswell (and it was no doubt meant as a compliment) that he was the "most unscottified" of his countrymen, almost the only one "who did not at every other sentence bring in some other Scotsman". [12] Even so, and in spite of Boswell's rejection of Scots speech and Scots manners, he freqently makes his Scottish feelings very apparent. In the *Life* he more than once mentions the Scots who assisted Johnson with his Dictionary. When Johnson writes to Reynolds to recommend Cruikshanks to succeed Hunter as Professor of Anatomy in the Royal Academy, Boswell adds a footnote to remark that they were both Scots. [13] He adds corrective comments to many of Johnson more extreme sallies against Scotland and the Scots. Towards the end of the book, he offers a general apology: "Had he in his early life been in Scotland, and seen the worthy, sensible, and independent gentlmen, who lived rationally and hospitably at home, he never could have entertained such unfavourable and unjust notions of his fellow-subjects". [14] Boswell is even more outspoken in his *Journal of a Tour to the Hebrides* where he says that he treats the English as children when they indulge in "an outrageous contempt of Scotland" and adds, "thus I have, at some moments, found myself obliged to treat even Dr Johnson". [15]

Boswell's Scottish patriotism was most evident in his detestation of the Union of 1707. On 5th October 1764, just before his 24th birthday, Boswell on his Grand Tour visited a library in Leipzig with some scholars of the place. He describes his reaction when he came across the text of the Declaration of Arbroath in a copy of Anderson's *Diplomata Scotiae*:

> My old spirit got up, and I read them some choice passages of the Barons' letter to the Pope. They were struck with the noble sentiments of liberty of the old Scots, and they expressed their regret at the

> shameful Union. I felt true patriot sorrow. O infamous rascals, who sold the honour of your country to a nation against which our ancestors supported themselves with so much glory. But I say no more . . . only Alas, poor Scotland.

On 3rd December 1764 Boswell had his great interview, as he called it, with Rousseau at his house at Motiers. Boswell referred to "our cursed Union" and agreed with Rousseau that it had "undone" Scotland. He undertook to provide Rousseau for a life of Fletcher of Saltoun with information about the making of the Union, "but with the warmth of an ancient Scot." When Johnson was in Edinburgh at the beginning of the Hebridean tour, Boswell took him to Parliament Hall and the Advocates' Library. He says that he "began to indulge *old Scottish* sentiments, and to express a warm regret, that, by our Union with *England*, we were no more; our independent Kingdom was lost". When the Keeper of the Records remarked that "half our nation was bribed by English money", Johnson replied: "Sir, that is no defence: that makes you worse". [16] On this subject of the Union, Boswell's views were unchanging. Towards the end of his life, when he had at last moved to London, he notes on 15th February 1790 that "he attacked the Union and said that the nation was gone".

Consistently with this, as is not unusual in Scotland, Boswell also sympathised with struggles for national liberation elsewhere, as in his support for Corsican independence. When he published his *Account of Corsica* in 1768, Boswell used as the epigraph on his title page the great sentence in the original Latin from the Declaration of Arhroath: "For we do not fight for glory, riches or honours, but for liberty alone, which no man surrenders but with life itself". Johnson said to him in a letter of 23rd March 1763, "I wish you would empty your head of Corsica, which I think has filled it rather too long", but Boswell's response was to call on him to feel for "an oppressed nation struggling to be free". [17] They had a similar disagreement over America. Johnson said that the Americans were "a race of convicts, and ought to be thankful for anything we allow them short of hanging". Boswell tells us he had a "clear and settled opinion, that the people of America were well-warranted to resist" taxation without their consent. [18]

In November 1785 Boswell at last sought admission to the English Bar so that he could move to London, which he did in January 1786. He had been agonising over it for years. His journals record both his rational self-analysis and the movements of his instincts and prejudices. When he was on one of his visits to London on 30th March 1772 a solicitor, George Urquhart, urged him to come to the English Bar. "I argued against it", Boswell said, "but was pleased to hear him, because I really do often wish to do it . . . My only objection is that I have a kind of idea of Scottish patriotism that makes me think it a duty to spend my money in my own country". He thought (against all probability) that he might be able to spend as much time at Auchinleck if he practised at the English Bar instead of the Court of Session. He might be able to make more money in England, but then he reflects that he would be "leaving a certainty of tolerable business for an uncertainty".

In the same entry, Boswell said that Auchinleck was his great object. It was one of the finest country houses of a moderate size in Scotland with a magnificent estate. He told Johnson in 1777 that he could ride for ten miles from his front door on his own land and that 600 people were dependent on him. [19] There were other good reasons for staying in Scotland. It was no disadvantage for an advocate to be the son of a judge and his career was well established. In England he would have to try to start again. His wife and children were opposed to the move. His swithering was agonising. "My fancy roved on England and the English Bar", he wrote on 24th July 1781, "yet I had faint hopes of happiness even in the metropolis, which I dreaded would pall on me; and I thought it would be very wrong to desert Scotland. In short I did not know what to do".

Boswell thought that he had made up his mind on 6th July 1734 when he wrote in his journal that after years of wavering the resolution to move to London came upon him with wonderful power; but he continued to be pulled in both directions. On 28th November 1785 he wrote that "the idea of making my children *aliens* from Scotland was dismal"; but on 3rd July 1739 he told Temple in a letter, "But were my daughters to be *Edinburgh-mannered girls*, I could have no satisfaction in their company". His admirable, patient and sensible wife, Margaret Montgomerie, was always unhappy in London. On 23rd March 1787 Boswell noted that "she seemed to have no comfort in view but being at home at Auchinleck" and on 18th November in the same year:

> I was very uneasy, for my wife complained of the expense of London, of the injury it did her health and that of of both my sons, and of the obscurity in which my daughters must be. I was sensible of all this. But my aversion to the narrow, ill-bred sphere was very strong.

Boswell evidently felt driven by an irresistible compulsion to leave Edinburgh even when it was clear to him as he wrote on 16th September 1793, that in solid reason he was wrong. No doubt his difficult relationship with his father had something to do with it, but if that had been the only reason it would have disappeared in August 1762 when Lord Auchinleck died but Boswell did make the move until nearly four years later. I think that at least part of the explanation is to be found in the melancholy, or as we should now say depression, which plagued Boswell for his whole life. He refers to it frequently in his letters and journals, but I give only two examples. From Rome he wrote to John Johnson on 11th May 1765, "Were it not for melancholy, I am one of the most fortunate young men alive", and then goes on to worry about not being able to live up to his father's expectations when he returns to Edinburgh: "he expects me to be a solid, steady man, who shall apply to business with perservering assiduity . . . there is hardly any probabilty that I shall ever be such a man". I think that Boswell felt like that because he knew that he had to try to escape from his melancholy by his pursuit of great men, his wenching and drinking. The other example is from his journal on 28th February 1786, two years after he had moved to London: "I felt a reluctance to *descend*, as I felt it, to the narrow situation of Scotland, in which I had suffered so sadly from melancholy, fancying myself excluded from any chance of figuring in the great circle of Britain".

I think that when Boswell was working in Edinburgh he was living an illusion, of which he was at least partly conscious, that he could escape from melancholy by leaving Edinburgh for London. Johnson, another victim of melancholy, understood this very well. On 3rd July 1778 he wrote to Boswell: "I wish you would a little correct or restrain your imgination, and imagine that happiness, such as life admits, may be had at other places as well as London". [20]

It is a pity that Boswell did not take Johnson's advice, because the last nine years of his life which he spent in London were the most miserable of all. He failed to get work at the English Bar; he was humiliated by attaching himself for a time to a bullying patron; he was tormented by thoughts of the harm he had inflicted on his family by dragging them to London. He had burned his boats. He could not bear the thought of admitting failure by returning to Edinburgh and had in any case now lost any chance that he had of appointment as a Scottish judge. On 15th December 1787 he "observed that the high admiration for London went off". He was working on his *Life of Johnson*, but "felt himself degraded from the consequence of an ancient Baron to the state of a humble attendant on an author". He wrote to his wife, who was in Auchinleck, on 3rd November 1788: "Oh that I had never come to settle in London. Miserable I must be wherever I am. Such is my doom". On 26th September 1793, he says that his old friend, Temple, found him "more wretched than he could have imagined".

As an escape from melancholy, the move to London had only made things worse, but throughout the journals there runs also a rational explanation of Boswell's desire to seek his fortune there. It is one which is consistent with his perception that the Union had destroyed Scotland. He said in a letter to a London newspaper on 6th April 1779: "since the union of the two kingdoms, which deprived us of all national dignity and all the advantages of a vice-court and of a parliament in our own district, London is now the metropolis of the whole island". London was now the centre to which all power and wealth gravitated and the place where all important appointments were made and exercised. This is why

Scotland had become what Boswell calls "a narrow sphere". The ambitious had to be in London and Boswell was ambitious. He makes the point frequently as, for example, on 23rd March 1783:

> I am clearly persuaded that a man of my family, talents and connexions may reasonably endeavour to be employed in a more elevated sphere than in Scotland, now that it is in reality only a province.

Boswell was constantly torn between his Scottish patriotism and his ambition, between his devotion to the Scots language and his preference for the smoother tones of the metropolis; his admiration for the wealth and power and social tone of London and his feeling that it was wrong to desert Scotland. These tensions were all consequences of the Union. They are still the cause of a malaise which torments us, but they have never been discussed at such length or so frankly as by Boswell. That is why his journals are still so topical.

References

References to extracts from Boswell's Journals and to letters printed in the 'reading' editions are indicated by the dates of the entry from which the appropriate volume and page can be readily traced.

References to *Life* are to the Everyman's Library edition of Boswell's *Life of Samuel Johnson* (2 vols; 1906 and freqently reprinted).

1. *Life* Vol. I p.8.
2. *Life* Vol. I pp 457 and 554.
3. Adam Smith, *Correspondence*, edited by E.C.Mossner and I.C. Ross. (Glasgow Edition; Oxford, 1977) p. 68.
4. *Life* Vol.11 p. 130.
5. *Life* Vol. II p. 269.

6. James Boswell, *Reflections on the late Alarming Bankruptcies* (1772) quoted in *Boswell for the Defence* (1960) p. 148.
7. *Life* Vol. I pp. 368 and 459.
8. *Life* Vol I p. 239.
9. Tom Crawford, "Boswell and the Tensions of Enlightenment" p. 183 in *The Science of Man in the Scottish Enlightenment*, edited by Peter Jones (Edinburgh, 1989).
10. *Life* Vol. II p. 7.
11. Quoted by Tom Crawford in "Enlightenment, Metaphysics and Religion in the Boswell-Temple Correspondence" p.55 in *Studies in Scottish Literature* V01 XXV.
12. *Life* Vol I p.473.
13. *Life* Vol II pp. 468-9.
14. *Life* Vol II p. 434.
15. James Boswell, *Journal of a Tour to the Hebrides* (Oxford Standard Authors, 1934) p. 172.
16. Ibid pp. 184-5.
17. *Life* Vol I p.349.
18. *Life* Vol I p. 526.
19. *Life* Vol II p. 131.
20. *Life* Vol II p. 258.

2. 8

The Legacy of Waverley

'The Story of Scotland' (1988) part 35, pp.961 to 963

"At this moment, his position, take it all for all, was, I am inclined to believe, what no other man ever won for himself by the pen alone". With these words, J. C. Lockhart, Walter Scott's son-in-law and biographer, begins a chapter of his *Life*. He is speaking of 1816 when Scott had published only five of his twenty-seven novels and long before he had openly acknowledged any of them. But Lockhart was not exaggerating. Through his long narrative poems and his novels Scott achieved an international reputation and influence which few, if any, other writers have matched in their own life-time. His books were vastly popular and universally admired throughout Europe and North America. Goethe said that he was "a great genius who does not have an equal" and Byron called him "certainly the most wonderful writer of the day". In Scotland he became a sort of uncrowned king so that it was natural that he should dominate the reception of that other monarch, George IV.

The influence of Scott changed the course of literary history in virtually every country of Europe. In Russia Pushkin remarked that his influence could be felt in every branch of literature. In Germany he was so popular that it was said that he might almost be a German writer and that his effect on German literature was incalculable. In France he was acclaimed and imitated by Hugo and Balzac. The greatest of Italian novelists, Manzoni, said that if it had not been for Walter Scott it would never have occurred to him to write a novel. Many other writers in many other countries might have said the same. From Hungary to Quebec the first novels to be written were imitations of Scott.

Scott's influence was not confined to literature. He created a fashion for the middle ages with profound effects on music, painting, architecture and taste generally. At least 70 operas and many plays have been based on his poems and novels. The number of paintings of scenes from his work runs into thousands. He profoundly affected attitudes to the writing of history. Thomas Carlyle in an essay published in 1838 said that Scott was the first to teach "writers of history and others" that the past was "filled by living men, not with protocols, state-papers, controversies and abstractions of men... History will henceforth have to take thought of it". And history has. Scott gave a great impulse to the development of archaeology and ethnology and to the collection, publication and study of original documents as the basis of history.

How are we to account for the extraordinary impact of Scott's Waverley novels? Partly it was because they gave their first readers a new kind of pleasure which they had not found in books before. They were, said Byron, "a new literature in themselves". In a famous passage in his *Memorials of his Time* Henry Cockburn described the "instant and universal impression" made by the publication of Waverley in 1814: "The unexpected newness of the thing, the profusion of original characters, the Scotch language, Scotch scenery, Scotch men and women, the simplicity of the writing, and the graphic force of the descriptions all struck us with an electric shock of delight".

You might suppose that the Scottishness of the best of the Waverley novels would have been attractive only to the Scots themselves. In fact, and it is another reason for Scott's phenomenal success, the novels were published precisely at a time when there was an insatiable curiosity all over Europe for everything Scottish. This was an appetite which had been stimulated fifty years earlier by the publication by James Macpherson of what he claimed to be translations from the work of an ancient Gaelic epic poet, Ossian. Even if they were largely fraudulent, they admirably met the fashionable taste of the time for the noble savage. All over Europe, Ossian was hailed as a new Homer. He became the favourite reading of Napoleon. The romantic movement in Europe, which dominated taste for the best part of a century, responded enthusiastically to the work of three Scots, Macpherson, Scott and Byron.

Ironically enough, none of these men was predominantly romantic in the nineteenth century sense of the term. Scott, in particular, was strongly influenced by the rational and sceptical attitudes of Enlightenment Edinburgh. As a recent biographer, Edgar Johnson, says: "Certainly Scott, like almost all of us, had a romantic strain, but the fundemental nature of his mind and feeling was realistic, rationalistic and stoic". One of the consequences of the novels appearing in an age of romantic enthusiasm was that generations of readers and critics failed to understand the implications of the novels as a comment on the nature of the historical process. David Daiches hardly exaggerated when he said in 1975 that it was only recently "that we have really understood what Scott's novels are about".

Scott' s enormous popularity and critical esteem lasted for about 100 years. In about the 1920s or 1930s he became unfashionable and was widely assumed to be unreadable. There had been an inevitable change in interests and attitudes. Generations of school children had been put off him for life by being forced to read one of his less successful novels before they were ready for it. The curious fact is that schools seem to have preferred novels like *Kenilworth* or *Ivanhoe*, set in England in the distant past, and not the best, like *Waverley*, *The Antiquary*, *Guy Mannering*, *Old Mortality*, *Rob Roy*, *The Heart of Midlothian* or *Redgauntlet* which are set in Scotland and much closer to Scott's own time. Critical opinion began to discover new strengths and interests in Scott, particularly in that group of novels, from about the 1950s, but the popular view has not yet caught up with the critics.

Impressions of the effect which Scott has had on Scotland itself have also changed with the years. No one doubts that he was a powerful force who made a great impact on Scottish life and on attitudes to Scotland. The argument has been whether the effect has been good or bad. In his own life-time, and for long afterwards, he was invariably regarded as a great benefactor, symbolised by the monument on Princes Street. In 1827 at the dinner in the Assembly Rooms in Edinburgh at which Scott for the first time publicly acknowledged that he had written the novels, Lord Meadowbank said: "We owe to him, as a people, a large and heavy debt of gratitude". And he explained why: "He it is who has conferred a new reputation on our national character, and bestowed on Scotland an imperishable name".

It was certainly part of Scott's intention to do all he could to defend the identity of Scotland and to enhance its reputation. Lockhart says of him: "The love of his country became indeed a passion;... he would have bled and died to preserve even the airiest surviving nothing of her antique pretensions for Scotland". In the Introduction to his first substantial work, *The Minstrelsy of the Scottish Border*, Scott said that he offered it us a contribution to the history of his native country, "once proud and independent". Towards the end of his life, in the General Preface to the Waverly novels, he said that his object was to present the Scots "in a more favourable light than they had been placed hitherto, and tend to procure sympathy for their virtues and indulgence for their foibles".

In recent years, for reasons which are obscure, quite a different view of the effect of Scott's novels seems to have become widely accepted. According to this, he encouraged a romantic and false image of the Scottish past which had little relation to reality. This is said to have the effect of persuading us to accept the Union and gradual assimilation with England. The theory is that the poems and novels stimulated the tourist trade (it certainly did that) but to a Scotland so romanticised and distorted that the Scots themselves were living in a fog of complacency which impaired any attempt to face up to the real problems and assisted a decline into provincial mediocrity.

Such a view of Scott is often held by people who have read hardly a word that he wrote. If they read more, they would probably come to quite a different conclusion. So far from creating a romanticised view of history, Scott is notably realistic in his account of political, economic and social conditions. Walter Bagehot, for instance, speaks of his "plain sagacity, digested accuracy and theoretical completeness". He continues, "you might cut paragraphs, even from his lighter writings, which would be thought acute in the *Wealth of Nations*". So far from encouraging assimilation and the disappearance of the Scottish identity, his whole purpose is to resist precisely these things. He made this very specific in his *Letters of Malachi Malagrowther*. This has been called the first manifesto of modern Scottish nationalism because it is a passionate call for the assertion of the Scottisn identity and for resistance to English attempts to assume control of Scottish affairs.

Scott grew up in the Edinburgh of the Scottish Enlightenment and accepted many of its ideas and attitudes. As Lockhart pointed out, there were however important ways in which Scott differed from men like Hume, Smith and Ferguson. They employed, Lockhart said, "only the national intellect, and not the national modes of feeling". Along with national feelings, they disregarded Scottish history and tradition. Scott restored these things. He was, Lockhart said, "the great genius to whom whatever is Scottish in thought, in feeling, or in recollection, owes so large a share of its prolonged, or reanimated, or enobled existence".

Of course, Scott was not alone. The poets and the song writers embodied and transmitted a large part of the Scottish tradition. Scott yielded to no one in his appreciation of Robert Burns. Other novelists, particularly James Hogg and John Galt, also celebrated and recorded Scottish manners, speech and ideas. Even so, it needed a man with Scott's ability to command an audience as wide as the literate world to win international awareness and respect for Scotland at a time when cultural identity might have followed political independence into limbo. Scott himself was afraid that Scotland was about to disappear into the mists of forgotten things. He resisted and in the long run was more successful than he supposed.

2.9

Was Walter Scott a Tory?

Paper for 'Scottish Dimension' Conference
Ruskin College, Oxford 24-5th March 1995

'The Herald' Essay, 4th July 1948

To the question, "Was Walter Scott a Tory?", the simple answer is "yes"; but it is an answer which requires several qualifications.

Scott himself gave a straightforward answer. For example, he said in a letter to Anna Seward on 13th January 1807:

> I was not only very early disposed to what have been called Tory principles by the opinions of those whom I respected & was bound to respect, but the favours I received, the intimacy in which I lived with many of Lord Mellville's family, his nephew & son in particular, was founded as much upon attachment to their measures in 1792-3 as to gratitude for favours received at a time when they were truly valuable.

This is a slightly muddled sentence, but it is clear that Scott frankly attached at least as much weight to the favours which he had received as to agreement with opinions and policies. The first sense in which Scott was a Tory was as an active participant and beneficiary of the system of patronage on which the political power of the party depended. In Scott's day, (and not only then) the Tory party was a device to dispense favours and jobs in exchange for political support or acquiescence.

This was so much part of the accepted order that Scott evidently participated in it without question or shame. He was indebted to the system for his own appointments as Clerk of the Court of Session and Sheriff of Selkirk, and he used it to further the career of his two sons. He was generous of his time and energy in using the system on behalf of innumerable friends and acquaintances. As

Graham McMaster says in his book, *Scott and Society*, "At one time or another he seems to have tried to find jobs for half of the unemployable gentry of the borders."[1] His correspondence is full of letters of recommendation of this kind. When he wrote to Lord Melville on 15th January 1825 on behalf of his son-in-law, J. G. Lockhart, he is quite explicit about the nature of patronage: "Make him your own, my dear Lord, by your countenance and patronage as your father made me his many years ago."[2]

Scott was also active, although usually discretely, as a propagandist for the Tory cause. He helped to launch the *Quarterly* as a Tory riposte to the Whig *Edinburgh Review*, and when Lockhart became editor of the *Quarterly* Scott was profuse with political advice. In 1819 he wrote three newspaper articles, afterwards published as a pamphlet, *The Visionary*, to attack parliamentary reform and ideas of equality and democracy. He played a part in the wheeling and dealing to arrange elections among the handful of men entitled to vote. Even towards the end of his life he appeared on a public platform in Jedburgh to call for resistance to parliamentary reform.

Scott then was an active Tory who was not ashamed to admit that he had sold himself to Melville and his party; but there was much more to his Toryism than self-interest. He was a Tory also by instinct and philosophy, if they can be distinguished because one is very often a rationalisation of the other.

In a letter to George Ellis on 9th October 1801 Scott said that "a tincture of Jacobitism, which tho' rather an Instinct than a principle adopted from reason, forms a frequent feature in the character of the animal calld a thorough bred Scotsman." Scott offers an explanation of his own instinctive Jacobitism in the Memoir of his early years which Lockhart used as the first chapter of his Life. He speaks of "a very strong prejudice in favour of the Stuart family, which I had originally imbibed from the songs and tales of the Jacobites. This latter political propensity was deeply confirmed by the stories told in my hearing of the cruelties exercised in the executions in Carlisle, and in the Highlands after the battle of

Culloden. One or two of my own distant relations had fallen on that occasion, and I remember of detesting the name of Cumberland with more than infant hatred." Jacobitism and Toryism are historically connected. In Scotland the Tory party began in Jacobite resistance to the Revolution settlement of 1688-9 and then to the Union of 1707.

Scott's Jacobitism did not mean that he was in favour of anything so wildly unrealistic as a new attempt to restore the Stuarts. He told Marianne Clephane in a letter of 13th July 1813 that if he had been alive in 1745 he would have fought for Charles "even to the bottom of the gallows; but I am not the least afraid nowadays of making my feelings walk hand in hand with my judgement. Though the former are Jacobitical the latter inclined for the public weal to the present succession." In fact, Scott's Jacobitism was more conservative than revolutionary in the sense that it aimed, not at constitutional or dynastic change, but at the preservation of what Scott saw as the traditional virtues of the Scottish past. He is explicit about this in a famous passage in the last chapter of *Waverley* where he says of the Jacobites that they, "averse to intermingle with the English, or adopt their customs, long continued to pride themselves upon maintaining ancient Scottish manners and customs." He then adds:

> This race has now almost entirely vanished from the land, and with it, doubtless, much absurd political prejudice; but also many living examples of singular and disinterested attachment to the principles of loyalty which they received from their fathers, and of old Scottish faith, hospitality, worth, and honour.

In this, as in all passages where Scott speaks about the erosion of Scottish characteristics, there is an unmistakeable tone of regret. One of Scott s strongest impulses was the desire to resist assimilation and preserve the distinctive character of Scotland.

Jacobitism also implies respect for the principle of inherited right and privilege. Scott's attitude to the aristocracy, noticed by all of his contemporary biographers, is consistent with this. James Hogg in his *Familiar Anecdotes of Sir Walter Scott* said:

> The only foible I ever could discover in in the character of Sir Walter was a too strong leaning to the old aristocracy of the country. His devotion for titled rank was prodigious and in such an illustrious character altogether out of place. It amounted almost to adoration. [3]

Lockhart attaches even more significance to it: "The whole system of conceptions and aspirations, of which his early life was the exponent, resolves itself into a romantic idealisation of Scottish aristocracy". He also offers an explanation:

> His imagination had been constantly exercised in recalling and embellishing whatever features of the past it was possible to connect with any pleasing ideas, and a historical name was a charm that literally stirred his blood. But not so a mere title. [4]

Scott's first biographer, George Allan (who published a Life in 1834) noted an essential contradiction in Scott's attitude to class:

> There was an extraordinary inconsistency in his character. In his habits, his demeanour and desires, he was decidedly aristocratic. On the other hand, if we examine his prose writings, it will be found that a spirit of what is termed 'Liberalism' predominates throughout. It will be found that almost his best, that is to say, his most virtuous and amiable specimens of human character, are taken from the lower classes. Scott's heart was evidently with the great mass of society. [5]

This is a perfectly fair point. We have only to think of such characters as Jeanie Deans and Edie Ochiltree. In his historical writing as well as in the novels, Scott constantly shows that he was under no illusion that the so-called nobles could be relied upon to act with nobility. In his *Tales of a Grandfather*, for instance, he is scathing about the Scottish politicians, most of whom were aristocrats, who accepted the Union of 1707:

> When they united with the degradation of their country the prospect of obtaining personal wealth and private emoluments, we cannot acquit them of the charge of having sold their own honour and that of Scotland.[6]

Scott's characters from "the great mass of society" were convincing because he mixed easily and made friends with people of all classes and kinds. One of his workers at Abbotsford said, "Sir Walter speaks to every man as if they were blood-relations."[7] One of his closest friends was Tom Purdie, a reformed poacher. He told Lockhart that although he had conversed with many eminent and cultivated minds, he had heard "higher sentiments from the lips of poor *uneducated* men and women" than he had "ever met with out of the pages of the Bible." [8]

But, a contradiction within a contradiction, even if Scott was egalitarian in practice, he was entirely opposed to equality as a political principle and to democracy as an expression of it. Here he was at one with the Tory party of his day. His three political essays, published as *The Visionary* in 1819, were written at a time when he was in a bad state of political panic at what he thought were signs of incipient revolution. They were attacks on the ideas of equality, parliamentary reform and universal suffrage, which, he said in his Preface, were worthy only of "scorn and derision." This was because, "the bulk and mass of the population are rendered incapable of the due exercise of an elective franchise, by their want of education and violence of passions, as well as by their dependent situation, which must place their votes at the command of those who pay them daily wages to buy daily bread." [9]

Scott saw property, by which he meant the ownership of land, as involving responsibilities as well as privilege. The introductory chapters of his *Life of Napoleon* gave him an opportunity to express his political ideas for, to his mind, the excesses of the French Revolution were a convincing proof that he was right. He said that the reason why it was only in La Vendée that a stand was made against the Revolution was that "there alone the nobles and the cultivators of the soil held towards each other their natural and proper relations of patron and client, faithful dependants, and generous and affectionate superiors." [10] This was the kind of relationship which he sought to establish with his own dependants at Abbotsford, and it was in the same spirit in which he helped to organise volunteer forces against the threat of invasion from France or of rebellion by discontented weavers.

Scott's instinctive wish for continuity and political and social stability was strengthened by his awareness of the human suffering involved in the suppression of the Highlands after the '45 and by the events in France in his own lifetime. He was influenced also by the ideas of the Scottish Enlightenment which surrounded him as he grew up, and in particular, I think, by those of Adam Ferguson, the father of one of his close friends. Scott often echoes the thought and even the language of Ferguson's *Essay on the History of Civil Society*. Both believed that the inequality of ranks was necessary for the progress of civilisation, and that society, an essential part of human happiness, was a complex organism with which it was dangerous to tamper recklessly. Consistently with these views, they were both disturbed by industrialisation because it tended to degrade the worker and destroy the 'natural' relationship between patron and client. Scott said in a letter to John Morritt on 19th May 1820:

> The unhappy dislocation which has taken place betwixt the Employer and those under his employment has been attended with very fatal consequences. Much of this is owning to the steam engine. . . . The manufactures are transferd to great towns where a man may assemble 500 workmen one week and dismiss the next without having any farther connection with them than to receive a weeks work for a weeks wages nor any further solicitude about their future fate than if they were so many old shuttles. A superintendence of the workers considerd as moral and rational beings is thus a matter totally unconnected with the Employer's usual thoughts & cares.

Scott's Toryism was benevolent and patriarchal with a social conscience.

George Allan, who wrote the *Life* which I have already mentioned, was evidently no Tory. He said of Scott that he "had thrown himself, with the blind vehemence of youth, into the ranks of the British tories, the most narrow minded politicians of the age. Dogged adherence to what was established, be it right or wrong;

deep, bitter and enduring hatred of every opponent, was what they required." [11] Scott did not meet either of these "requirements".

He was cautious about change, but not invariably opposed to it. Abbotsford was full of mediaeval relics, but it was also one of the first houses to be lit by gas. In his *Life of Napoleon* Scott suggested that a major cause of the French Revolution had been the suppression of criticism of the government and the consequent failure to "make such alterations as the lapse of time and change of manners may render necessary." [12] He advocated a balance between reckless experiment and necessary improvement and change: "If there were no Whigs, our constitution would fall to pieces for want of repair; if there were no Tories, it would be broken in the course of a succession of rash and venturous experiments." [13]

As might be deduced from that last remark, Scott did not believe either in hating his political opponents. In his letter to Anna Seward in which he declared his Toryism, he went on to say: "I am candid enough to esteem the principles and cherish the friendship of many whose political opinions are different from my own, because I know they are adopted by those who hold them from an internal conviction of their rectitude." He always preferred conciliation to confrontation and conflict. Another of his contradictions is in his attitudes to violence and war. He would have been a soldier if his lameness had not prevented it and his imagination was stirred by the courage and panache of battle. At the same time, he had a clear conviction of the futility and waste of war and he was always in favour of peace and stability.

When it came to the defence of the Scottish interest Scott's instinct was to close ranks and to urge all parties to work together. He said in his *Journal* on 20th January 1826, "So the Tories and Whigs may go be damned together, as names that have distracted old Scotland, and torn asunder the most kindly feelings since the first day they were invented." He would like to have seen an all-embracing party devoted to the national interest of Scotland. "Why should not old Scotland have a party among her own children?", he said in a letter to Henry Francis Scott on 10th January 1831. There is the same thought in the second of his *Letters of Malachi Malagrowther*:

> The Scottish members of Parliament should therefore lose no time — not an instant — in uniting together in their national character of the Representatives of Scotland . . . do not let us, like our ancestors at Falkirk fall to jealousies among ourselves, when heart, and voice, and hand, should be united against the foreign *enemy*. [14]

The Letters of Malachi Malagrowther were three essays which Scott sent to the *Edinburgh Weekly Journal* in February and March 1826 and which were afterwards published as a pamphlet. Their immediate purpose was to oppose a Government proposal to abolish the right of the banks to issue one pound notes, then the main form of currency in Scotland, and in this they succeeded. Scott seized the chance to protest about a much wider matter which had long disturbed him, English interference in Scottish affairs in the previous fifteen or twenty years. Before that time, and in spite of the Union, Scotland had been left "under the guardianship of her own institutions, to win her silent way to national wealth and consequence." Now the Government seemed to be determined to change everything in Scotland to an English model, uniformity for the sake of uniformity, whether it was to the benefit of Scotland or not. "There has been in England a gradual and progressive system of assuming the management of affairs entirely and exclusively proper to Scotland, as if we totally unworthy of having the management of our own concerns." [15] The *Letters* are the fullest and strongest expression of his deepest feelings and convictions. He wrote to James Ballantyne on 26/7th February 1826: "I will sleep quieter in my grave for having so fair an opportunity of speaking my mind".

The English, he said in the first *Letter*, had a wise policy of resisting "all hasty and experimental innovations" when England was in question. Scotland, however, they were treating as "a sort of experimental farm" by imposing their system on a country, which has been hitherto flourishing and contented under its own. He would like Scotland to resist with "just so much ill-nature . . . as may keep her good-nature from being abused", but not to resort to violence on the Irish model. Rather than that, "we had better remain in union with England, even at the risk of becoming a subordinate species of Northumberland." [16]

This last passage has been misquoted out of context by unionist propagandists to suggest that Scott wanted Scotland to remain in the Union in a similar status to Northumberland. On the contrary, the whole pamphlet is a passionate plea for the autonomy of Scotland, for respect for Scottish traditions and for cultural diversity. "For God's sake, let us remain as nature made us, Englishmen, Irishmen and Scotchmen, with something like the impress of our several countries on each." [17] Scott's Tory friends in London were gravely displeased. Scott had shown that he was indeed ready to put the interests of Scotland before those of the party.

Hugh MacDiarmid has remarked that Scott's arguments lead "naturally to the separatist position". [18] He is right. In *The Letters of Malachi Malagrowther* Scott wrote the first manifesto of modern Scottish nationalism.

So to return to the question with which we started. Scott was a Tory , but one of his time and place. With his distrust of reckless innovation he was very different from a modern conservative. He was a Tory of a Scottish and Jacobite kind which hardly now exists. His class instincts and ideas were moderated, and even displaced, by his essential decency, social conscience and Scottish patriotism.

References

Quotations from Scott's letters are from *The Letters of Sir Walter Scott*, edited by Sir H. J. C. Grierson. (12 Vols. London, 1932-37) and are indicated in the text of this paper by the date and name of the recipient. References to J. G. Lockhart's *Life* are to the edition of 1900 (London, 5 Vols). Those to Scott's *Life of Napoleon Buonaparte* are to the edition of 1827 (Edinburgh).

1. Graham McMaster, *Scott and Society* (Cambridge, 1981) p. 30.
2. Lockhart, Vol. I p. 14.
3. James Hogg, *Familiar Anecdotes of Sir Walter Scott* (1834). Edited by Douglas S. Mack (Edinburgh, 1972) p. 95.
4. Lockhart, Vol. V p.439 and Vol. IV pp. 329-30.
5. George Allan, *Life of Sir Walter Scott* (Edinburgh, 1334) pp. 314-5.
6. Sir Walter Scott, *Tales of a Grandfather* (1828). Edition of 1839 (Edinburgh) p. 751.
7. Lockhart, Vol. IV p. 147.
8. Lockhart, Vol. IV pp. 294-5.
9. Sir Walter Scott, *The Visionary* (1819). Edited by Peter Carside (Cardiff, 1934) pp. 12-13.
10. Sir Walter Scott, *Life of Napoleon* Vol. I p. 31.
11. Allan, p. 159.
12. *Napoleon* Vol. I p. 68.
13. Ibid Vol. I p. 278.
14. Sir Walter Scott, *The Letters of Malachi Malagrowther* (1826). Edited by P.H.Scott. (Edinburgh, 1931) p. 72.
15. Ibid. pp. 4,10,136.
16. Ibid. pp.8,9,10,17.
17. Ibid. p. 143.
18. Hugh MacDiarmid, *Lucky Poet* (London, 1943) p. 203.

2.10

Walter Scott's 'Journal': an essential book

'The Scotsman' 12th December, 1998

It is very good news that Walter Scott's *Journal* now takes its proper place in the admirable series of Canongate Classics. This is something which I have long advocated because I think that it is such an enthralling and important book that it should be permanently in print in an easily available edition. I should like to explain why. Scottish literature is very rich in the frank and informal writing that you find in the best diaries and letters, such as Boswell's many volumes of *Journals*, Cockburn's *Memorials*, Elizabeth Grant's *Memoirs*, Naomi Mitchison's *Diaries* and the letters of Hume, Burns, Byron, Stevenson, MacDiarmid and, of course Scott himself. This is very distinguished company, but Scott's *Journal* is of very special value for a number of reasons.

First of all, there is the extraordinary reversal of fortune, a modern Greek tragedy in prose. When Scott wrote his first entry in the *Journal* on 20th November 1825, he was at the pinacle of a life of achievement. Probably nobody before or since had won so much influence, popularity and wealth by his pen alone. He had enlivened the historical imagination of Europe and North America and made them aware of Scotland as never before. In Scotland itself, he was almost an uncrowned king, the natural leader of every good cause. He had built a great house on the banks of the Tweed and was surrounded by devoted friends and family. Now he could relax in the civilised ease which he had certainly earned, and, since he had the time, he would begin a journal. In that long first entry you can feel the atmosphere of agreeable and unhurried leisure. But in a few weeks all had collapsed abruptly around him. He was faced with financial ruin from which he could recover only by constant work; his wife died; he fell ill and was often in pain and so he remained for the rest of his life.

So the *Journal* became a record of response to disaster. In his honest account of it, Scott gradually gives us a living self-portrait. In his novels he had created scores of memorable characters; but, as John Buchan says, "the greatest figure he ever drew is in the *Journal* and it is the man, Walter Scott". In reading the *Journal*, you feel that you meet him and that is a pleasure. You can understand why Byron described him in a letter to Stendhal in these words: "of all men he is the most *open*, the most *honourable*, the most *amiable* . . . I say that Walter Scott is as nearly a thorough good man as man can be, because I know it by experience to be the case." Much more recently, Bernard Levin wrote in a review of W. E. K. Anderson's excellent edition of the *Journal* when it first appeared in 1972: "I have rarely enjoyed making any new acquaintance as much as I have enjoyed meeting Sir Walter Scott in his own words".

It is a reponse to disaster, but that does not mean that it is gloomy. Scott's good nature keeps breaking through and the book is highly entertaining. When Moore grows lyrical over the beauty of a sunset in Venice, Byron replies: "Ah come, damn me, Tom, don't be poetical". (9/2/26) Scott says of Jane Austen: "The Big Bow-wow strain I can do myself like any now going, but the exquisite touch which renders ordinary commonplace things or characters interesting for the truth of the desciptions and sentiments is denied to me". (14/3/26) Scott again: "The conversation is seldom excellent among official people. So many topics are what Otaheitans call Taboo".(24/10/26)

There is another important aspect of the *Journal*. Scott was familiar with people of all kinds in Scotland and, through his legal work and his travels, with every aspect of life in the country. He was steeped in the history, legend and literature, had read virtually everything and had a formidable memory. When he was asked to write a history of Scotland, he commented, "This would be very easy work. I have the whole stuff in my head". (16/4/29) Nor is it true, as is often supposed, that he had a romantic or distorted view of that history; his ideas were clear and well informed. His chapter on the Union in *Tales of a Grandfather*, although a book written for children, is the fullest and frankest account of that affair written by anyone in the whole of the 19th century. He had a grasp also of economics. Walter Bagehot remarks on "the digested accuracy and theoretical completeness" of passages about economic points in the novels, "which would be thought acute in the *Wealth of Nations*". For these reasons, the whole *Journal* is an informed digest of Scottish attitudes and conditions, much of which applies not only to Scott's own times but also down to the present.

In the 19th century the Empire, and therefore the Union by reason of which Scotland was involved in it, were regarded generally as above criticism. The view seems to have emerged that Scott was an uncritical enthusiast for the Union, if only because that was then the usual expectation. Nothing can be further from the truth, as can be clearly seen from his *Letters of Malachi Malagrowther*, the fullest and most explicit statement of his views on the matter, or indeed from the *Journal* where the strength of his feelings about the effects of the Union on Scotland are obvious. Thomas Crawford in his book about Scott says that there is a strain of melancholy in his poetry, "to the point where it becomes mourning for Scotland's vanished independence". Precisely the same strain runs through the *Journal*. Some examples: "I set about Malachi Malagrowther's Letter on the late disposition to change everything in Scotland to an English model . . . They do treat us very provokingly". (18/2/26) "I should rejoice to see the old red lion ramp a little, and the thistle again claim its *Nemo me impune*". (24/2/26) "Surely we ought to close one volume at least of Scottish history at a point which leaves the kingdom triumphant and happy; and, alas. where do her annals present us with such an era excepting after Bannockburn?" (28/12/27) "Thus London licks the butter off our bread by opening a better market for ambition. Were it not for the difference of the religion and laws, poor Scotland could hardly keep a man that is worth having; and yet men will not see this". (24/3/29)

Scott was far too realistic to suppose that escape from the Union was a political possibility in his own time when so small a part of the population had the vote. If he could have foreseen future events,

2. 11

The Life of Sir Walter Scott
by John Sutherland (1995)

'The Scotsman', 25th December 1995

This is a book of great strength but it also has some veritable howlers about Scottish institutions and history. We are told, for instance, that all the professors at Edinburgh University were members of the Speculative Society and that law lords are "enobled". Sutherland says that in 1707 Scotland "lost its traditional right to a Scottish monarch". When Scott's son joined the army, he is said to have become an English soldier, serving in England's colonial possessions. Sutherland implies too that Mary Queen of Scots was a subject of the English Elizabeth. He is generally dismissive and derogatory of things Scottish. When Shortreed is quoted by Lockhart in good Scots, Sutherland thinks it mysterious that he should "lapse" into Lallans. He thinks it "quaint" that Scots songs and ballads were sung in aristocratic families. Presbyterianism is "pinched" and Allan Ramsay's *Gentle Shepherd* is "kitch".

Scottish national feelings were a passion for Walter Scott and much of his best writing is in his dialogues in Scots. You might, therefore, suppose that an indifference or hostility to these things would incapacitate anyone from writing a useful book about him. In fact, this is a book which clearly has been deeply and comprehensively researched and is, I think, an important addition to the extensive literature about Scott's life and work.

If Scott had to stand trial, not as a writer but as a man, this would be an extended speech for the prosecution. All the evidence for his actions and motives are examined and generally the least charitable interpretation is suggested. Most of the accepted ideas about Scott's life and character derive from Lockhart who was, after all, writing a biography of his father-in-law. Sutherland accuses him of "stomach-turning" pomposity and frequent invention to show Scott in a favourable light. He dismisses many of Lockhart's best anecdotes on the grounds of "chronological contradiction". Scott is accused of bigoted Toryism, indulgence in the "bulging coffers of Tory patronage" (some things don't change), reverence for social rank, obsession with money, and, even if it is contradictory, carelessness over his business transactions.

Possibly, Sutherland errs as far in one direction as Lockhart does in another. At one point, Sutherland refers to Scott's "usual unobtrusive kindness". There are many examples of this in the accounts of his contemporaries. He used the resources of patronage for others as well as himself. He had, as Hogg said, an exaggerated respect for ancient families; but he had the common touch as well. His devotion to Scotland was stronger than his party ties. Sutherland does mention the *Malachi* letters where this appears most clearly, but he represents them as concerned only with the matter of the bank notes. In fact, they were a passionate protest against English interference in Scottish affairs and the first declaration of modern Scottish nationalism.

Scott emerges from Sutherland's cross examination, not as the unblemished saint of Lockhart's account, but as more human, credible and courageous. Sutherland's treatment of the evidence is sceptical, but also imaginatively creative. He gives a very convincing picture of many episodes in Scott's life, particularly of the early days at Sandy Knowe and of the last months when he continued to write through a succession of strokes. Sutherland's unflinching approach applies also to the other members of Scott's family who added in various ways to the difficulties. Scott's massive output, which Sutherland calls "one of the wonders of literature", becomes even more remarkable.

This book is part of a series intended to rebut the modern heresy that only the text matters. Its aim is "to re-establish the notion that books are written by people who lived in particular times and places", and, of course, Scott is a perfect example. Sutherland constantly relates the atmosphere, events and characters of Scott's writing to his own experience. He makes illuminating comments about almost all of Scott's work and finds merits even in the *Life of Napoleon* and the later novels which are usually ignored. Sutherland may have set out to debunk, but he ends by celebrating Scott's towering genius. His book will do more to consolidate Scott's reputation than to damage it.

2.12

"The Last Purely Scotch Age"

Contributed to Volume 3 of 'The History of Scottish Literature' (Aberdeen, 1998)

The late 1830s mark one of the most obvious and drastic turning points in the literary history of Scotland. Before lay a long period of high achievement: Ramsay, Fergusson and Burns, the Gaelic poets of the 18th century, the philosophers and historians of the Enlightenment, Scott, Galt and Hogg. Afterwards there was a loss of cohesion and self-confidence, a decline which lasted about 50 years. In George Davie's famous and precise phrase, it was a time of "failure of intellectual nerve". [1] Historians of Scottish literature all take a similar view of the period. Kurt Wittig, for instance: "The less said about the two generations after Scott the better . . . The tradition seemed really to have come to an end, and not with a bang, but a whimper".[2] In Roderick Watson's recent history there is a chronological table of important publications. It is conspicuously thin from 1830 to 1880. [3] William Power says of the 1830s that "Scots literature fell at once from a national to a provincial level".[4] David Craig makes fun of this suggestion that the change was abrupt ("overnight?"), but himself gives an even more final significance to the year 1830 in which he ends the period of his *Scottish Literature and the Scottish People: 1630-1830*. With a sublime indifference to what was going on around him as he wrote, he says that his period "includes the last flowering of the vernacular poetry and the rise and hey-day of the native novel". He takes an even more terminal view of what happened to Scotland as a whole at that time, "the point at which Scotland was all but emptied of native talents during the early Industrial Revolution and the increase of emigration". [5]

William Power had good reason for using language which implied that the change was sudden and abrupt. The great figures of the previous age all died within a few years of one another, Scott in 1832, Hogg in 1835 and Galt in 1839. Of the writers who survived them, many left Scotland. Lockhart emigrated to London to edit the *Quarterly* in 1825 and Carlyle also finally moved there in 1834. Nor were they by any means alone in yielding to the pull of what Lockhart called the "immense magnet" of "triumphant and eclipsing England" [6], or more specifically London. Walter Scott remarked in his *Journal* on 24th March 1829: "Thus London licks the butter off our bread, by opening a better market for ambition. Were it not for the difference of the religion and laws, poor Scotland could hardly keep a man that is worth having". The most accomplished and prolific novelist between Galt and Stevenson, Margaret Oliphant, became in J. H. Millar's words, "thoroughly acclimatised in England". [7] James Thomson of *The City of Dreadful Night*, the most interesting poet of the same period, also lived in, and wrote of, London, even if he was not so happily acclimatised. By death or emigration, therefore, Scotland was emptied of major writers in the ten years or so before the Disruption of 1843, which was itself a turning point with far-reaching consequences.

Scotland's loss was England's gain as John Gross recognised in his book, *The Rise and Fall of the Man of Letters*:

> . . . It would be hard to exaggerate the part played by Scotsmen in the development of the English periodical press. They helped to create not only the great quarterlies and monthlies, as is well known, but the weeklies as well; the first editors of the *Spectator*, the *Economist* and the *Saturday Review*, for example, were all Scotsmen. And right through the nineteenth century critics and essayists made their way south across the border. Lockhart, Masson, Andrew Lang, William Archer are a few random instances, the list could easily be extended — and it would become positively daunting if one were allowed to include the second generation of the diaspora: men like Ruskin, who still spoke with traces of a Scots accent, or Macaulay, whose features in repose struck Carlyle as those of 'an honest good sort of fellow, made out of oatmeal'. [8]

Recently, William Donaldson has challenged the "prevailing view" that "the nineteenth century after the death of Scott was a period of decine and failure". He does this by examining articles, stories and novels published in the Scottish newspapers. His conclusion is that the later nineteenth century so far from being a period of failure of writing, especially in Scots, was one of "resurgence, renewal and growth almost without precedent". [9] This is an exciting theory which may make us all change many of our old ideas and assumptions, although we can only test it when more of the texts become generally available. But even if Donaldson is right, I do not think that his discoveries fundamentally challenge the view that there was a marked change for the worse in the literary climate in the late 1830s. In the first place, Donaldson tells that the newspapers got into their stride only with the repeal of the Stamp Act in 1855. Much of the writing that he discusses appeared towards the end of the century when there were many other signs of the recovery of self-confidence. Also, if the best writing in Scotland was driven out of the "London-dominated booktrade" [10] and forced to take refuge in the newspapers, that in itself would be a very telling sign of a loss of status and self-assurance.

In his *Life of Sir Walter Scott*, John Buchan described the Edinburgh in which Scott lived as "a true capital, a clearing-house for the world's culture and a jealous repository of Scottish tradition", [11] David Craig would argue that already Scott and his contemporaries were "deeply conditioned by provincialism". [12] But if provincialism threatened before the 1830s, it became infinitely more destructive afterwards when the drift to the south became a flood. As the symbolic date for the change, we might take 1834 when Carlyle decided that Scotland could not hold him. A generation earlier he would have found sufficient challenge, stimulation and opportunity in Edinburgh. Why did he opt for London in 1834? What had gone wrong?

The classic and contemporary statement of the problem is in Henry Cockburn's *Life of Francis Jeffrey*, published in 1852. Towards the beginning of the book he describes Edinburgh as it was in the early years of the 19th century, shortly after Jeffrey, Scott and Cockburn himself had all passed through the High School and University there. The whole passage is well worth reading in full, but the following are the key sentences:

> The society of Edinburgh was not that of a provincial town, and cannot be judged of by any such standard. It was metropolitan . . . It was the seat of a university famous throughout the world, of the supreme courts of justice, of the government offices, and of the annual convocation of the church formerly no small matter . . .
>
> Many of the curious characters and habits of the receeding age, *the last purely Scotch age that Scotland was destined to see* [my italics] still lingered among us . . . Almost the whole official state, as settled at the union, survived . . . unconscious of the economical scythe which has since mowed it down.
>
> Over all this there was diffused the influence of a greater number of persons attached to literature and science, some as their calling, and some for pleasure, than could be found, in proportion to the population, in any other city in the empire . . . Philosophy had become indigenous in the place, and all classes, even in their gayest hours, were proud of the presence of its cultivators. Thus learning was improved by society, and society by learning.
>
> And all this was still a Scotch scene. The whole country had not begun to be absorbed in the ocean of London . . . The operation of the commercial principle which tempts all superiority to try its fortune in the greatest accessible market, is perhaps irresistible; but anything is surely to be lamented which annihilates local intellect, and degrades the provincial spheres which intellect and its consequences can alone adorn. According to the modern rate of travelling, the capitals of Scotland and of England were then about 2,400 miles asunder. Edinburgh was still more distant in its style and habits. It had then its own independent taste, and ideas, and pursuits . . . This city has advantages, including its being the capital of Scotland, its old reputation, and its external beauties, which have enabled it, in a certain degree, to resist the centralising tendency, and have hitherto always supplied it with a succession of eminent men. But, now that London is at our door, how precarious is our hold of them, and how many have we lost! [13]

No doubt, Cockburn's account of the Edinburgh of his youth is coloured by nostalgia. He was born in 1779 and wrote the *Life of Jeffrey* when he was in his 70s. He was looking back at the great days of his youth "when there were giants in the land" [14], as Scott said of the time of the Scottish Enlightenment. Perhaps Cockburn romanticises the past a little, but he is evidently convinced that during his own life-time Edinburgh and Scotland had lost much of their "independent taste and ideas" and their own "style and habits" because of increasing centralisation from London. He implies that very little independence in these things remained by the time he was writing, that there was increasing pressure from centralisation and that Edinburgh had indeed become provincial.

When Cockburn spoke of the "modern rate of travelling", he meant, of course, the railway and the steamboat. He recorded a similar thought in his *Journal* on 11th August 1844, "Railways and steamers, carrying the southern into every recess, will leave no asylum for our native classical tongue". Here he is thinking of the Scots language (although the same point might be made even more strongly of Gaelic). "Scotch has ceased to be the vernacular language of the upper classes, and this change will go on increasing with the increasing intercourse which rolls the language of the greater (in the sense of more numerous) people over our surface". [15] The erosion of a language is bad enough, but Cockburn was also afraid of an even more fundamental loss, of all independence in taste, ideas, style and habits. If that happened, Scotland would become no more than a geographical expression and there could be no question of a Scottish literature. This erosion has not continued at anything like the exterminating pace which Cockburn feared. Both languages have retreated but they have survived, and confidence in a distinctive national character has recovered. Were there special circumstances which made Cockburn so pessimistic in the 1850s, so soon after a long period of achievement?

The invention of the steam engine, which he mentions, can hardly be the whole story. Certainly, it made a radical difference. Edinburgh and London suddenly became readily accessible to one another for the first time. We have had many drastic revolutions in communications since then, and they have made English voices and English ideas audible in every house in Scotland. Perhaps the first abrupt jump, from the horse to the railway engine, was a greater shock because people were not yet accustomed to rapid technological change. Even so, the languages, literature and culture of Scotland would have been frail plants indeed if the steam engine alone was a threat to their survival.

In fact, the steam engine, and with it the Industrial Revolution, was only one of a number of powerful changes which struck Scotland at about the same time. For one thing, the government in London had started to intervene actively in Scottish affairs. This was quite new. The previous practice of London governments since the Union of 1707 had been to ignore Scotland as completely as possible, except for the suppression of the Jacobite risings and the subsequent destruction of Highland society. In 1761, for example, when James Stuart Mackenzie became the minister responsible for Scottish affairs, he was surprised to find no papers in his office and no sign that any business was being carried on. [16] In any case, the role of governments anywhere at that time were very limited. In Scotland, education and such social services as existed were the concern of the Kirk and the burghs. The Union had left intact the Scottish legal system, the Kirk and the burghs, removing only the Parliament which could have given cohesion and expression to the society as a whole. The consequence was that Scotland had been left "under the guardianship of her own institutions, to win her silent way to national wealth and consequence". [17]

This last phrase comes from Walter Scott's *The Letters of Malachi Malagrowther* of 1826. These three famous letters to the *Edinburgh Weekly Journal*, which were immediately re-issued as a pamphlet, ostensibly dealt with a proposal for the abolition of the Scottish bank-notes. In fact, as is very clear from Scott's *Journal* and from his letters, he seized the chance to raise the whole question of the treatment of Scotland by England. It had been troubling him for years. "I will sleep quieter in my grave", he wrote to James Ballantyne, "for having so fair an opportunity of speaking my mind".[18] England, he argued, had been content to leave Scotland alone as long as she was poor. Now that Scotland by her own efforts had increased in prosperity by a ratio five times greater than England, the government had begun to intervene with a vengeance. Scotland had become "a sort of experimental farm". [19] "A spirit of proselytism has of late shown itself in England for extending the benefits of their system, in all its strength and weakness, to a country, which has been hitherto flourishing and contented under its own".[20] He goes on to write what amounts to the first manifesto of modern Scottish nationalism, a plea for diversity and for Scotland to be free to handle her own affairs in her own way without external interference. "For God's sake, sir, let us remain as Nature made us, Englishmen, Irishmen, and Scotchmen, with something like the impress of our several countries upon each!" [21]

Scott argues that much of the interference in Scottish affairs was contrary to the safeguards in the Treaty of Union and was imposed just for the sake of uniformity in spite of the differences in conditions and attitudes between the two countries. The legal system and the universities were both affected. Lockhart records an episode in 1806 when Scott was deeply disturbed by an attempt to change the procedure in the courts closer to the English model: "Little by little, whatever your wishes may be, you will destroy and undermine, until nothing of what makes Scotland Scotland shall remain".[22] In spite of the outstanding reputation of the Scottish universities, there was pressure on them to conform to English models. The first move in this campaign was in 1826, the year in which Scott wrote *Malachi*. [23]

Writing in 1826, Scott said that this interference, treating Scotland with "absolute contempt" had begun in "the last fifteen or twenty years and more especially in the last ten". [24] In other words, it began at about the same time as the Napoleonic Wars and increased after Waterloo. It therefore coincided with the period when London became the capital of the richest, most sucessful and powerful of the World Powers, which it continued to be for about a hundred years. England was then in a mood of assertive self-confidence, the 'Falkland spirit' writ large and on a much larger scale. It is a mood which has little patience with the divergent ideas and aspirations of a smaller neighbour.

The Napoleonic Wars had other effects within Scotland itself. Even before the war started, the threat of revolutionary ideas from France reduced the establishment to paranoia and panic. Only a few people, like Muir of Huntershill, were actually condemned for sedition; but it was a time when you had to watch what you said. Both Cockburn and Scott, for instance, record that the worthy Dr. Adam of the High School of Edinburgh was "watched and traduced for several years" because "a Latin and Greek schoolmaster naturally speaks about such things as liberty, and the people, and the expulsion of the Tarquins, and republics". [25] Such an atmosphere was obviously destructive of the spirit of free enquiry which had made the Scottish Enlightenment. This is perhaps the main reason why Scottish thought became less innovative and wide-ranging about the end of the 18th century.

The Napoleonic Wars also introduced another element into Scottish life, British patriotism. They were the first wars of the modern kind, wide in scale and involving a self-conscious sense of nationhood among the participants. In Scotland this took an additional turn. The Scots Greys may have charged at Waterloo with a cry of "Scotland for ever", but for the first time Scots also began to share patriotic feelings in common with their neighbours and old enemies across the Tweed. It was expressed by Scott, as in the Introduction to Canto First of *Marmion*. Even Burns, in some moods or under some pressures at least, was capable of expressing it. You find it, for instance, in the song with the significant first line, "Does haughty Gaul invasion threat?":

> Be Britain still to Britain true,
> Amang ourselves united!
> For never but by British hands
> Maun British wrangs be righted!

There is plenty of evidence, of course, that Burns and Scott continued to feel passionately Scottish at the same time.[26] Ever since, most of their compatriots have continued to feel this dual allegiance, at least from time to time and in certain circumstances. This new British consciousness did not destroy the Scottish identity, but it inevitably tended to weaken and confuse it. Probably this was especially true in the early 19th century, when Britishness was a fresh idea and one associated with the triumph of Waterloo.

The confusion was compounded by the disproportionate part which the Scots played in the British Army and in the development of the British Empire. This was a consequence of the vacuum inside Scotland itself without control over her own affairs to provide or stimulate outlets for talent and energy at home. For generations, Scots who were denied opportunities in Scotland turned to the Empire instead. "India", Scott wrote in a letter in 1821, "is the Corn Chest for Scotland where we poor gentry must send our younger sons as we send our black cattle to the south."[27] It is impossible to calculate the effect on Scotland of this drastic haemorrhage over the years of millions of intelligent and enterprising people. As long as the Empire lasted, it accustomed the Scots to think of themselves as partners in a joint British endeavour.

At the same time, Scotland was being radically transformed by the Clearances in the Highlands, which destroyed a whole way of life, and by the Industrial Revolution in the Lowlands. Workers for the new industries were sucked away from the countryside to congregate in urban slums. The parish system of the Kirk had served the rural communities, but it could not cope with the scale and intensity of the new social problems in the towns. As these new stresses developed, the Kirk was preoccupied with its own internal controversies. They came to a head in the 'Ten Years Conflict' which began in 1832, but they had their origin in an Act of the British Parliament of 1712. The Patronage Act, passed in that year in violation of the Union settlement, gave rights to the heritors (or landowners) in the appointment of ministers. This had become increasingly intolerable to the Evangelicals who gained control of the General Assembly in 1834. They passed the Veto Act in the Assembly to give an absolute right to the congregations to refuse a minister presented by the heritors. When the Court of Session and the House of Lords upheld the authority of State against the Church, the Evangelicals saw no alternative to withdrawal from the established Church. In the Disruption of 1843, 470 of the 1,200 Church of Scotland ministers abandoned their manses and their salaries and walked out of the General Assembly to form the Free Church.

This wholesale sacrifice of status, home and income for the sake of principle was, in the words of Cockburn, "one of the rarest occurrences in moral history. I know no parallel to it . . . It is the most honourable fact for Scotland that its whole history supplied".[28] It was magnificent, but it was also disastrous. The Kirk had been "the great unifying institution of the Scottish nation"[29] and a bulwark of of the national identity. Since 1707 the General Assembly of the Church had been a substitute for a Parliament, where representatives of the whole people could meet and discuss great national issues. The parish organisation embraced the whole country and most of the population. The Kirk embodied, fortified and expressed many of the strengths, as well as the weaknesses, of the distinctive Scottish attitude to life. When the English divine and wit, and one of the founders of the *Edinburgh Review*, Sydney Smith, arrived in Edinburgh in 1798, he remarked on the influence of the Clergy:

> In England I maintain that (except amongst Ladies in the middle class of life) there is no religion at all. The Clergy of England have no more influence over the people at large than the Cheesemongers of England have. In Scotland the Clergy are extreemly active in the discharge of their functions, and are from the hold they have on the minds of the people a very important body of men. The common people are extreemly conversant with the Scriptures, are really not so much pupils, as formidable critics to their preachers; many of them are well read in controversial divinity, They are perhaps in some points of view the most remarkable nation in the world, and no country can afford an example of so much order, morality, oeconomy, and knowledge amongst the lower classes of Society. Every nation has its peculiarities, the very improved state of of the common people appears to me at present to be the phoenomenon of this country. [30]

Smith was right to speak of the ministers and the national character together like this because the two were inextricably intermingled.

With the Disruption, this great force f or the cohesion of Scottish society was shattered in two. In every parish in the country there were now two congregations and soon two church buildings. The new building was financed by the contributions of the people and few of the supporters of the Free Church were wealthy. It was yet another sacrifice for the sake of principle, but a distraction from the other work of the Church, including education. Eventually, the Church gradually overcame its divisions and by 1929 it was re-united, apart from a small minority. By then, conditions had radically changed. Life in general had become more secular and the Government had assumed responsibility for education and social welfare. "Religion was no longer the very pith and core of Scottish life". [31] The Church of Scotland never regained its importance as the central institution in Scottish life which it lost in 1843. It was particularly incapacitated as a custodian of the Scottish identity in the period from the beginning of the conflict in 1833 until the schism began to heal towards the end of the century.

Remarkably enough, this decline in the influence of the Kirk coincides precisely with the period of literary decline. There is, of course, no simple, direct relationship of cause and effect between the two, but the decline of the Kirk affected all aspects of Scottish life. It meant that Scotland was deprived of an important line of defence and force of cohesion at a time when strong pressures were tending in any case to undermine national identity and self-confidence and reduce the country to a provincial backwater. The other two great institutions left intact when political independence was lost in 1707, the law and the universities, were simultaneously under pressure. If the Kirk had not been distracted, the General Assembly might have provided a focus for resistance. As it was, there was no natural centre to hold things together. Under the force of all the circumstances, it is hardly surprising that there was a loss of collective nerve and a weakening of the will for national survival. Perhaps without such nerve and such a will there can be no distinctive literature. Perhaps the best that a writer can do in such a case is, like Carlyle, to seek elsewhere the tradition, the community and the atmosphere which has disappeared at home.

If there is substance in these propositions, one would expect a literary revival only with a recovery of national self-confidence and a general assertion of identity. This is, in fact, what happened. Literary, political and institutional developments all reappeared at the same time. In the 1880s the Scottish Home Rule Association was formed and the Scottish Liberal Party adopted a policy of Home Rule for Scotland. The Government revived the office of Secretary of State for Scotland in response to Scottish pressure. The Scottish National Portrait Gallery, the Scottish History Society and the Scottish Text Society were established. Stevenson wrote *Kidnapped* and *The Master of Ballantrae*. By 1895 Partrick Geddes in his periodical, *The Evergreen*, was speaking about a Scottish Renaissance, long before the term was associated with Hugh MacDiarmid. In spite of the gloom of the mid-nineteenth century, the Scottish tradition had not after all ended with a whimper. It still had a long struggle ahead, but that is the theme of the next volume of this history.

Bibliography

Although all the standard histories of Scottish Literature necessarily record the decline between the 1830s and the 1880s, there has been no sustained attempt to consider the factors which may have contributed to it. For literature there is no equivalent book to George Elder Davie's classic work on the universities, *The Democratic Intellect* (Edinburgh, 1961 and reprinted as a paperback in 1982). There are valuable comments on the general problem of cultural pressure in Michael Hechter's *Internal Colonialism: The Celtic Fringe in British National Development 1536-1966* (London, 1975). My own Saltire Pamphlet, *In Bed with an Elephant* (Edinburgh, 1985) is a brief account of the Scottish experience.

The main primary text is Sir Walter Scott's *The Letters of Malachi Malagrowther* (Edinburgh, 1826). It is included in the various collections of Scott's miscellaneous prose and there is a recent reprint which is mentioned in the References. The works of Cockburn and Lockhart. also mentioned in the References, throw light on the literary climate at the beginning of the period of decline.

References

1. George Elder Davie, *The Democratic Intellect: Scotland and her Universities in the Nineteenth Century*, (Edinburgh. 1961)p .337.
2. Kurt Wittig, *The Scottish Tradition in Literature*, (Edinburgh & London, 1958) pp. 253,254.
3. Roderick Watson, *The Literature of Scotland*, (London, 1984) pp. 467,468.
4. William Power, *Literature and Oatmeal: What Literature has Meant to Scotland*, (London, 1935) p. 117.
5. David Craig, *Scottish Literature and the Scottish People. 1630-1830*, (London, 1961) pp. 12,13.
6. John Gibson Lockhart, *Peter's Letters to his Kinsfolk*, 3 vols(Edinburgh, 1819) II p. 356. Letter LV. In selection edited by William Ruddick (Edinburgh. 1977) p. 145.
7. J.H.Millar, *A Literary History of Scotland*, (London, 1903) p. 615.
8. John Gross, *The Rise and Fall of the Man of Letters; English Literary Life since 1800* , Pelican Edition (Harmondsworth, 1973) pp. 19-20.
9. William Donaldson, *Popular Literature in Victorian Scotland*, (Aberdeen, 1986) pp. xii, 71.
10. Ibid, p. xii.
11. John Buchan, *Sir Walter Scott*, (London, 1932) Edition of 1961, p. 210.
12. As 5, p. 13.

13. Henry Cockburn, *Life of Francis Jeffrey* Edition of 1822 Edition of 1872 (Edinburgh) pp. 150,154.
14. Sir Walter Scott, *The Lives of the Novelists*, Everyman's Library Edition (London 1928) pp. 294-295.
15. Henry Cockburn, *Journal* 2 vols (Edinburgh, 1874) II p. 89.
16. Alexander Murdoch· *The People Above: Politics and Administration in Mid-Eighteenth Scotland*, (Edinburgh, 1980) p. 106.
17. Sir Walter Scott, *The Letters of Malachi Malagrowther*, (Edinburgh, 1826). Edited by P.H.Scott (Edinburgh, 1981) p. 10.
18. *The Letters of Sir Walter Scott* edited by H.J.C. Grierson. 12 vols (London 1932-37) Vol. IX (1935) p. 437.
19. As 17. p. 10.
20. Ibid. p. 9.
21. Ibid. p. 143
22. John Gibson Lockhart, *Life of Sir Walter Scott (1837-8)* Edition of 1900 (London) S vols. I p. 460, Chapter XV.
23. George Elder Davie, *The Democratic Intellect: Scotland and her Universities in the Nineteenth Century*, (Edinburgh, 1961), Chapter 2.
24. As 17, p. 4.
25. Henry Cockburn, Memorials of his Time, Edition of 1872 (Edinburgh) p. 5
26. On Walter Scott's attitude, see my *Walter Scott and Scotland*, (Edinburgh. 1981), especially Chapter 7.
27. As 18, Vol. VI (1934) p. 489.
28. As 15, Vol II pp. 30, 32.
29. Sydney and Olive Checkland, *Industry and Ethos. Scotland 1832-1914* (Vol 7. of *The New History of Scotland*), (London, 1984) p. 122.
30. *The Letters of Sydney Smith*, Edited by Novell C. Smith, 2 vols (Oxford, 1953) I pp. 21-22.
31. William Ferguson, *Scotland: 1689 to the Present* (Vol IV of the Edinburgh History of Scotland) (Edinburgh & London 1968).

2.13

R. L. Stevenson and the Scottish Revival.

Address to the Robert Louis Stevenson Club,
Edinburgh, 10th November 2001.

I propose this toast with particular pleasure because I have been an enthusiast for RLS for, quite literally, as long as I can remember. It has been my habit since I was at school to keep note-books in which I record the books I have read. From them I can see that, by the time I was 15, I had read almost all of his novels, essays, travel books and poetry in Scots. Many of them I have read again very frequently. Probably it is because so much of his writing is intimate and personal, even before the great body of his letters became available to us, that we all tend to look on Stevenson as a personal friend.

I think that this intimacy is particularly true of his poetry in Scots where he is at his most natural and relaxed. Stevenson said himself that his verse in Scots was better than in English because it had "more marrow and fatness". (5/336 and 6/34) It also has more feeling and more sheer gusto and fun about it. For Stevenson, as for many of his countryfolk still, Scots is the language of childhood, of close friendship, of the heart, the instinctive, as opposed to the studied and acquired. It was, he said in one of his poems,

> Dear to my heart as the peat-reek,
> Auld as Tantalon.

He used Scots, of course, in prose as well as in verse. The most memorable passages in *Kidnapped* and *Weir of Hermiston*, like those in the best of Walter Scott's novels, are in Scots. Stevenson said of two of his own short stories: "*Tod Lapraik* is a piece of living Scots; if I had never writ anything but that and *Thrawn Janet*, still I'd have been a writer."

At the same time, he was afraid that the language was dying. He has a note at the beginning of the poems in Scots in *Underwoods:*

> The day draws near when this illustrious and malleable tongue shall be quite forgotten; and Burns's Ayrshire, and Dr MacDonald's Aberdeen — awa, and Scott's brave metropolitan utterance will all equally be the ghosts of speech. Till then I would love to have my hour as a native makar, and be read by my own country-folk in our own dying language: an ambition surely rather of the heart than of the head, so restricted as it is in prospect of endurance, so parochial in bounds of space.

Of course, Boswell in the 18th century and Cockburn in the early 19th also predicted the death of Scots, but its no deid yet, for a that. Or, as George Bruce says in his poem about the funeral of the Scots tongue:

> She jinkit again the bitch! Said the man wi the spade.

I am sure that Stevenson would have been delighted to hear that the century which has followed his death has been one of the richest for poetry in Scots, that whole novels have been written in it, that Sydney Goodsir Smith and Robert Garioch, like him, have recaptured the very spirit of Fergusson, and that a cross-party group in the Scottish Parliament aims to restore the language to its proper place in the life of Scotland.

We can feel closely in touch with Stevenson also through his letters, especially now that we have the admirably edited and comprehensive eight volumes of the Booth and Mehew edition. We had to wait until 1994 and 1995 for them, but they have enlarged the available opus of Stevenson and enriched our literature. As Jenni Calder said in a review "These letters are among the best things which Stevenson wrote." Reading right through them is a delightful experience, the next best thing to knowing Stevenson in life. There is a selection in one volume, but I strongly recommend the complete eight. Any selection reflects the taste and interests of the editor and they may be very different from your own.

Stevenson's use of Scots and his love of the language is one of his bonds of affinity with the Scottish literary tradition and, in particular, with Robert Fergusson, Robert Burns and Walter Scott. These are the writers he mentions most frequently and with most enthusiasm in his letters. He says that he had "a great sense of kinship" with Fergusson and that he was "so like himself" and "I believe Fergusson lives in me". (8/290; 7/11 0) He thought of placing an inscription on Fergusson's grave in the Canongate kirkyard to link the names of the three Roberts, Fergusson, Burns and himself, (8/290) something which the Saltire Society did on his behalf many years later. He says of Burns that his interest in him is "perennial" (7/109), that his essay about him was "the darling of my heart" (3/31) and "the best thing I ever did."(3/61)

Even so, Stevenson had reservations about Burns. Just after he had been writing that essay, he discussed Burns in a letter of July 1st 1897 to Edmund Gosse. He said that he had been making "a chronological table of his various loves and lusts" and had been "comparatively speechless ever since. I am sorry to say it, but there is was something in him of the vulgar, bagmanlike, professional seducer. I could kick his bottom for it." But he goes on to say that, "since he was only a Scotchman after all", he liked nothing so well as the "Twa Dogs". He ends with a playful quotation from an imaginary encyclopaedia which defines the English as "a dull people incapable of comprehending the Scottish tongue". (2/328)

The same disapproval of Burns's sexual exploits appears in the essay itself. You may find this strange in the light of Stevenson's fondness for the flesh-pots of the Lothian Road and Leith Walk; but he was writing at the height of Victorian prudery and he had a conventional, strict, Presbyterian upbringing. In a letter of 1891 he refers to his "old Presbyterian spirit — for mind you,I am a child of the Covenanters — whom I do not love, but they are mine after all, my fathers and my mothers — and they had their merits too, and their ugly beauties, and grotesque heroisms, that I love them for."(7/1 11) R.L.S. was, I think, divided between this influence and the pull of his instincts. In one of his last letters of September 1894 he wrote to his cousin, Bob Stevenson: "If I had to begin again . . . I believe I should try to be more chaste in early youth, and honour sex more religiously. The damnest thing of our education is that Christianity does not recognise and hallow sex". (8/365) We are familiar with the concept of a Presbyterian atheist; Stevenson was a Presbyterian Bohemian.

He had his own difficulties with the Edinburgh establishment, but he is generous to them in his essay on Burns:

> The Edinburgh magnates . . . behaved well to Burns from first to last. Were heaven-born genius to revisit us in similar guise, I am not venturing too far when I say that he need expect neither so warm a welcome nor such solid help. Although Burns was only a peasant, and one of no very elegant reputation as to morals, he was made welcome to their homes. They gave him a great deal of good advice, helped him to some five hundred pounds of ready money, and got him, as soon as he asked for it, a place in the Excise. Burns, on his part, bore the elevation with perfect dignity . . . His powerful sense never deserted him . . . It was, in short, an admirable appearance on the stage of life—socially successful, intimately self-respecting, and like a gentleman from first to last.

There is much that is perfectly just about this, even if there are also echoes of Heriot Row, especially in that last phrase. I am not sure about the good advice; much of it was bad and Burns had the sense to ignore it. I have always felt that they might have found him something more appropriate than a place in the Excise.

The real surprise about the essay, however, is Stevenson's attitude to Burns's work on the songs — this national treasure of some 300 songs, which Burns partly wrote, partly collected and partly adapted, a great enhancement of our social pleasure and cultural experience, something of which any country would be proud. Scotland, and the rest of the world for that matter, would be a poorer place without them. RLS, I am sorry to say, dismisses all of this as a sorry decline from Burns's early work. It is melancholy, he says, that "a man who first attacked literature with a hand that seemed capable of moving mountains, should have spent his later years in whittling cherry-stones".

Because of this, Stevenson' conclusion is that Burns "had failed in life". This view of the songs is, I think, Stevenson's one major collapse in critical judgement. It is oddly similar to Hugh MacDiarmid's contempt for folk-song. But Stevenson fully redeems himself in his praise of the rest of Burns's work. "Like most great artists" he says, "Burns proceeded from a school and continued a tradition; only the school and tradition were Scotch, and not English." To English authors he had read, Burns "owned nothing but a warning". On every subject, Burns "could find language to give it freshness, body and relief . . . and make every stroke a triumph . . . If Burns helped to change the course of literary history, it was by his frank, direct and masterly utterance". I think that we can only ask in response to all of that: if this is failure, what would success have been like?

Towards Walter Scott, Stevenson did not have this sort of ambivalence. No question of failure there. For Stevenson, Scott was the inspiration, a great model to be followed, even if he could not hope to equal it. In February 1886 in a letter to Edward Purcell he wrote:

> For God's sake, dear sir, do not compare me to Scott . . . I know Scott's novels to be full of sawdust, but they are full besides of organic blood and built for posterity . . . It lies in the genius, human, quiet, solid, smiling, unperturbed of Sir Walter . . . It lies also . . . in the fact that Sir Walter was a good man . . . whereas I am only a man who would be content to be good if I new what goodness was." (5/213)

In a letter to George Saintsbury from Vailima in February 1892 he said that he had just read "five Waverleys . . . with all the old exquisite delight and admiration". (7/236) Then about a month later to Elizabeth Fairchild: "That is what I have always envied and admired in Scott. With all that immensity of work and study, his mind kept flexible, glancing to all points of material interest. But the lean hot spirits, such as mine, become hypnotised with their bit occupations". (7/253) Even so, Stevenson felt that the novels which he and Barrie had written were fit to be compared to those of Sir Walter and would have earned his approval. He wrote to Barrie in December 1892: "I am proud to think that you are a Scotchman . . . whose work is to me a source of living pleasure and heartfelt national pride. There are two of us now that the shirra (who was Sir Walter, of course) might have patted on the head". (7/447)

In 1883 he found Lockhart's *Life of Scott* "heartbreaking," (4/251) I think because of its account of Scott's last days, and he advised his father not to read it for that reason. (4/221) Some years later it became one of his favourite books. In a letter, again to Saintsbury he says, "to whom do I owe more pleasure than to Lockhart" and he adds: "the Scot leaps out in me; I am proud indeed that the two finest biographies extant were the work of Scotsmen". (7/1 25) The other was, of course, Boswell's *Johnson.*

Stevenson proposed to write a history of Scotland, but despaired of competing with Scott. (7/1 83) He thought too of books on the history of the Union and of the Highlands (3/ 78,100, 126-7, 1 28, 1 36, 146, 148) and for that purpose briefly intended to learn Gaelic. (3/1 28) He said that Scottish history was the only history he knew and the only history reasonably represented in his library. (7/183) In 1881 he applied, with very questionable qualifications, I fear, for the Chair of History and Constitutional Law at Edinburgh University. (3/1 96-8)

I have quoted enough, I think, to show that Stevenson was very conscious of his Scottishness and like Fergusson, Burns and Scott — another point of affinity between them— was a passionate Scottish patriot. Why is it then that in a number of his letters he refers to himself as English? In an early letter to his mother from Germany in August 1 872, for instance, he said that the landlady of the village inn where he was staying asked if he was an Englishman. When he said "yes", she enquired further if he was not also a Scotchman. (1/237) It seems from this that both Stevenson and the German lady were using English to mean British. In a letter of October 1883 to Arthur Martin he makes the point specifically: "I am not an Englishman remember, which already makes a wider difference than people usually count: I am a Scot: one of a people imperially one; domestically different: in a back-kitchen way still managing its own affairs; and in in every point, by law, faith, habit and tradition clinging to its not very beautiful ancestral pattern. (4/193)

"Imperially one", says Stevenson. Linda Colley in her book, *Britons*, remarks that the Empire was a joint English-Scottish enterprise and she continues: "The language bears this out very clearly. The English and the foreign are still all too inclined today to refer to the island of Great Britain as England. But at no time have they ever customarily referred to an English Empire. When it existed, as in retrospect, the empire has always been emphatically British." (p.1 30) But here is Stevenson, at the height of the imperial age, using the word "English" in precisely that sense and he is not alone among his contemporaries. It was, of course, a time when the power and influence of England was at its zenith. We should not read too much into the point, however. In reading through the eight volumes of the letters, I noted seven occasions when Stevenson referred to himself as English, but 30 when he insists, often with emphasis and passion, that he was Scottish, or as he said in a letter, "pure Scotch". (5/258)

One of his frequent themes, in fact, as in the letter to Arthur Martin, was the great difference between Scotland and England. It is the subject, as you will remember, of one of his most popular essays, *The Foreigner at Home*. When he was on one of his first visits to England, in July 1873, he wrote to his mother: "I cannot get over my astonishment, indeed it increases every day, at the hopeless gulph that there is between England and Scotland, and English and Scotch. Nothing is the same; and I feel as strange and outlandish here, as I do in France and Germany." (1/283) Twelve years later, in December 1885, he wrote to Sir Henry Taylor: "No two countries that I know are so unlike as England and Scotland, above all morally". (5/1 60)

Stevenson's disapproval, even hatred, of imperialism is perhaps one example of this moral difference. He displayed it in his support for the Samoans against the imperial powers. Mehew tells us in a footnote of a Foreign Office minute about this, in a tone which I well recognise: "Mr Stevenson would do better if he stuck to novel writing and left politics alone". (8/21) In his letters Stevenson sometimes expressed his feelings on the subject in very strong terms. He wrote to W. E. Henley in 1881: "This is a damned, dirty foul job of ours in the Transvaal . . . God forgive this rotten old England." (3/1 60) And to John Addington Symonds in 1885: "England stands before the world dripping with blood and daubed with dishonour". (5/81) Billy Kay has remarked that Scots, because of our own historical experience, tend to sympathise with people who are struggling against external domination. Stevenson was an example.

Towards Scotland and Edinburgh Stevenson's feelings were not entirely unmixed. At certain times and in certain moods he disliked both the weather and the rigid standards of Presbyterian respectability; but these were transient feelings. It is abundantly clear from his letters that he took a deep love of Scotland and Edinburgh with him wherever he went. I quote a few examples:

To Charles Baxter in December 1881:

> Pray write to me something cheery. A little Edinburgh gossip, in heaven's name. Ah! what would I not give to steal this evening with you through the big, echoing, college archway, and away south under the street lamps, and to dear Brash's, now defunct . . . O for ten Edinburgh minutes—sixpence between us, and the ever glorious Lothian Road, or dear mysterious Leith Walk! (3/263-4)

To Samuel Crockett in April 1888:

> Don't put "N.B." on your paper: put *Scotland*, and be done with it . . . The name of my native land is not *North Britain*, whatever may be the name of yours. (6/1 56)

To J. M. Barrie in November 1892:

> It is a singular thing that I should live here in the South Seas under conditions so new and so stricking, and yet my imagination so continually inhabit that cold old huddle of gray hills from which we come. (7/412)

Finally, to Sidney Colvin in May 1893:

> I was standing out on the little verandah in front of my room this morning, and there went through me or over me a heave of extraordinary and apparently baseless emotion. I literally staggered. And then the explanation came, and I knew I had found a frame of mind and body that belonged to Scotland, and particularly to the neighbourhood of Callander. Very odd these identities of a sensation, and the world of connotations implied; Highland huts, and peat smoke, and the brown swirling rivers, and wet clothes, and whisky, and the romance of the past, and that indescribable bite of the whole thing at a man's heart. (8/91)

I know of no more powerful expression of nostalgia and love of country, in the whole of literature, than that last passage.

Stevenson shared this strong feeling about Scotland, this passionate patriotism, with Fergusson, Burns and Scott. He read their work, thought about them and wrote about them throughout his life. He followed Fergusson and Burns in writing poetry in Scots and Scott in his historical novels. It is often said that we owe an immense debt to Burns and Scott for the part they played in the consolidation and expression of our cultural identity which might otherwise have disappeared as a consequence of the Union of 1707. I think that we owe the same debt to Stevenson.

There is a theory that Scotland suffered a cultural, and especially a literary, decline after the deaths of Scott, Galt and Hogg and the departure of Carlyle for London in the 1830s. This is not altogether true. The Enlightenment was still very much alive with such innovators as Hamilton, Brewster, Clerk Maxwell, Frazer and Kelvin. William Donaldson has unearthed a lively literature in Scots in the pages of the Scottish local newspapers. Still there was a loss in that imperial age of self-confidence in Scotland itself and a need, in George Davie's phrase, of a "burst of reviving energy". When did that come? Many people, who should know better, sometimes speak of it as a phenomenon of the last twenty years or so. Others, rather better informed, attribute it to the Scottish Renaisance of which Hugh MacDiarmid was the central figure. It has much deeper roots than that for it goes back to the 1880s and it has been virtually continuous since then. In that decade the Scottish Home Rule Association, the Scottish National Portrait Gallery, the Scottish Text and the Scottish History Society were all established; William McTaggart was painting and R. L. Stevenson was writing. *Kidnapped*, that essential Scottish novel, was published in 1886. That was when the reviving energy began which has led to the achievements of the present and Stevenson was one of those who inspired it.

For that reason, and for all the pleasure which he has given to generations of readers, I invite you, ladies and gentlemen, to drink to the memory of our fellow citizen, Robert Louis Stevenson.

2. 14

George Davie and the Democratic Intellect

'The Scotsman', 17th July 1999

The Saltire Society has many awards, but the most prestigious of them all is the Andrew Fletcher of Saltoun Award for services to Scotland. Last year it was awarded jointly to the three party leaders, Donald Dewar, Alex Salmond and Jim Wallace, for their part in the decisive result of the Referendum of 11th September 1997. This year the recipient will be a man who is not nearly as well known as he should be, George Elder Davie. For many years he was a lecturer in Logic and Metaphysics in Edinburgh University and he is the author of a very important and significant book, *The Democratic Intellect*, first published in 1961. By a fortunate coincidence, Edinburgh University Press has just reprinted for the third time the paperback edition of 1981.

George Davie is an unostentatious but potent influence on contemporary Scotland, both through this book and through his teaching and conversation. A recent article by Bill Findlay in the Scottish Literary Journal (November, 1998), for instance, showed how pervasive it is. He was writing about Robert Garioch's translations in Scots of George Buchanan's Latin plays, but he refers repeatedly to the influence of Davie's ideas on Garioch and on Hugh MacDiarmid and Sorley MacLean as well. Aspects of the work of the poets of the Scottish Renaisance were a reflection in poetry of the thought of George Davie. For this reason, Alexander Moffat, who painted portraits of the group, wanted to include Davie. He is now doing that as part of the Andrew Fletcher Award.

The subject of Davie's major book may seem unlikely as a source of such fascination and influence. It is a study, which mangages to be both scholarly and passionate at the same time, of a prolonged debate in 19th century Scotland about the nature and content of university education. The Scottish universities believed in a wide, general approach, including philosophy and science as well as languages, either as a preliminary to specialisation or as an education in itself. In England the two universities specialised from the start, in the classics at Oxford and in mathematics at Cambridge. On both sides the debate was conducted with force and intelligence; but the Scots were gradually forced to accept conformity with England, especially as the Government would not otherwise provide finance. In Davie's words, it was a tortuous, dark revolution wherby a nation noted educationally both for social mobility and for fixity of first principle gradually reconciled itself to an alien system in which principles traditionally did not matter and a rigid social immobilism was the accepted thing.

When the book first appeared, it was reviewed in the *New Statesman* by C. P. Snow, the novelist and advocate of the reconciliation of the two cultures of science and the arts. He said that he had been thinking and writing about such issues for years, but had to admit that there was very little that he had to say about the subject which the 19th century Scots had not said before.

The book is also notable for the sheer vigour and precision of the language which makes it a great pleasure to read. Davie generously gives the credit for this to his late wife, Elspeth, who was an accomplished novelist and writer of short stories. It is due to her, he says in the Foreword, "if here and there the narrative begins to move forward with a speed and lively humanity worthy of its theme". That is exactly what it does throughout.

The Democratic Intellect is one of the major influences behind the recovery of Scottish intellectual and cultural self-confidence. This is because he demonstrated so thoroughly and convincingly that Scotland has an intellectual tradition of real value which is worth defending against assimilation. The book is also a challenge as well as an encouragement because it implies that we should try to recover some of the qualities which made our education pre-eminent in the past.

2.15

Scottish Literature: 20th century attitudes

Contributed to 'Dear Maurice' edited by Lester Borley, East Linton, 1998 in honour of Maurice Lindsay

In the 1920s and 30s there was a succession of books which deplored the social, economic and cultural decline of Scotland. One of these was George Malcolm Thomson's *Caledonia or the Future of the Scots*, published in 1927. He dismissed the state of Scottish literature in a short paragraph: "There is no literature in Scotland. The country has produced none in the twentieth century, or, to be exact, since the year 1901, when the House with the Green Shutters was reared in the midst of a kailyard gone to seed. The publishing of books has been dead in the country for a very much longer period". (p.61)

Thomson may have been right about many things when he wrote this book. It was a time when many serious observers were pessimistic about the survival of Scotland as anything more than a geographical expresion. He was, however, quite wrong about literature. Hugh MacDiarmid published his first books of verse in Scots, *Sangshaw* and *Penny Wheep*, in 1925 and 1926. His major work, *A Drunk Man Looks at the Thistle*, appeared in 1926 and all of these were from a Scottish publisher, Blackwood's of Edinburgh. Neil Gunn's first novel, *Grey Coast*, was published in 1926. By 1927 Naomi Mitchison had already published five novels and Eric Linklater and Lewis Grassic Gibbon were at work on their first. Scottish literature was not dead in 1927 but in vigorous life.

Even so, there is some excuse for Thomson. It was, and is still, perfectly possible for intelligent people to grow up in Scotland and be quite unaware of Scottish literature of any period, with the possible exception of a hazy idea of a few lines of Robert Burns. For many years before 1927, and for many afterwards, the schools and universities paid very little attention to anything which had been written in Scotland. In the schools, history and literature were mainly English. This used to be true all over the British Empire while it existed, but old habits have been slow to die in Scotland.

Does this matter? After all, England has produced much fine literature and the English language is the predominant means of international communication. I think that it matters very seriously for several reasons. Firstly, there is the loss of the particular pleasure and understanding that comes from reading about the life that surrounds you and its evolution in these familiar places. Our literature is our recorded experience, our collective memory. Without it, you are a stranger in your own land. We are fortunate in having a rich and inexhaustible literature in all of our languages and it would be a sad deprivation to be left in ignorance of it. I think that you are likely to have a better appreciation of other literatures if you begin with your own. Also, if our children are encouraged to believe that every important book has been written somewhere else, and that every important event happens to other people in other places, they are being persuaded that they and their friends, family and compatriots are inferior. There are signs that this result is not uncommon.

Of course, the picture has never been entirely black. Not all teachers have succumbed to the pressures of all-embracing Englishness. I was fortunate. In the High School of Edinburgh we were not allowed to forget that we had such illustrious predecessors as Robert Fergusson and Walter Scott. One of our schoolmasters was Alexander Law, who edited Allan Ramsay for the Scottish Text Society and who was a great enthusiast for Scottish literature, especially of the 18th century. We had Gaels too, the remarkable Hector MacIver and a brother of Sorley Maclean. The school was generous with book prizes. Among mine were W. M. Mackenzie's edition of William Dunbar and Agnes Mure Mackenzie's book on Scottish literature up to 1714. At Edinburgh University, where I studied what was, and still is, called English, the Professor, Dover Wilson, was quintessentially English. At the same time, some of the lecturers, like George Kitchin, conveyed an enthusiasm for

Scottish literature. I remember the thrill of discovering Robert Henryson in Henry Harvey Wood's edition of 1933. In the early days of the second World War, the rediscovery of Scottish literature was already well under way.

George Davie in his great book, *The Democratic Intellect* (1961) said that the history of Scotland was marked by an "alternation between catastrophe and renaissance in which the distinctive national inheritance was more than once brought to the very brink of ruin only to be saved at the last minute by a sudden burst of reviving energy". (p. xvi) For literature there was such a burst in the early 18th century when Allan Ramsay, whose anthology, *The Evergreen* of 1724 revived awareness of the mediaeval makars, and he was followed by Fergusson and Burns.

Later in that century the philosophers of the Scottish Enlightenment, despite their great achievements, often seemed to forget Scotland in an atmosphere of abstract rationality. Scott, Galt and Hogg early in the next century again restored a consciousness of Scotland.

Thomas Carlyle's departure for London in 1834 symbolised another brink of ruin. William Donaldson[1] has shown that the Scottish spirit and the Scots language continued to find expression in the pages of the 200 or so newspapers which then existed, but there was clearly another burst of reviving energy in the 1880s and 90s. Patrick Geddes in his periodical, *The Evergreen*, a conscious echo of Allan Ramsay, spoke of a Scottish renaissance. It was the period of Stevenson in literature, MacCunn in music and MacTaggart in painting. The recovery of national self-confidence was evident also in political developments and in. the formation of new institutions. The Scottish Text Society published the first of its volumes of early Scottish literature in 1883 and the Scottish History Society the first of its collections of historical records in 1886. The Scottish National Portrait Gallery was opened in 1889. An Commun Gaidhealach, for the promotion of Gaelic language, literature and history, was founded in 1891. In politics, the Government responded to agitation about the neglect of Scotland by reviving the office of Secretary of State in 1885. The Scottish Home Rule Association was founded in 1886 and the Scottish Liberals first adapted Home Rule as a policy in 1888.

From some statements in the press and elsewhere, you might suppose that the revival of Scottish literature and of interest in it has been the work of the last few years. In fact, like the campaign for Home Rule, it has been a continuous process for more than 100 years with some interruption by two World Wars. Substantial academic books on a subject are a good indication of a serious interest. T. F. Henderson's *Scottish Vernacular Literature* was publised in 1898, J. H. Millar's *Literary History of Scotland* in 1903 and G. Gregory Smith's *Scottish Literature: Character and Influence* in 1919.

The first World War delayed the recovery of the Scottish Parliament because a Home Rule Bill had passed its second reading in 1913. What did it do to Scotish literature and to attitudes towards it? Apart from much poetry, the War inspired at least one major work, Lewis Grassic Gibbon's *Sunset Song*. It also seems to have been partly responsible for forming, or strengthening the ideas of Hugh MacDiarmid about Scotland. His biographer, Alan Bold, describes how he returned from the War with a determination that Scotland should have a future. (p.95) He meant by this that the right of self-determination, proclaimed as the purpose of the Allies, should apply also to Scotland, that our literary tradition should be recognised and enhanced, and that Scots and Gaelic should be revived for serious literary use. MacDiarmid was, of course, not alone; but because of the force of his poetry, his energy and determination, he gave a powerful stimulus towards the achievement of all of these political and cultural objectives. On his death in 1978, David Murison said that "after MacDiarmid, as after Knox, Scotland will never be the same again". [2]

From about the time of MacDiarmid's early poetry in Scots in 1925 and 1926, we have been living through one of the great ages of Scottish literature in Gaelic, Scots and English. I do not have the space to discuss, or even to list, all of the poets, dramatists, novelists and other prose writers who have contributed. With apologies to many others, I mention only a few: in Gaelic, Sorley MacLean and Derick Thomson; in Scots, apart from MacDiarmid himself, William Soutar, Sydney Goodsir Smith, Robert Garioch, Robert McLellan, Lewis Grassic Gibbon, and Alexander Scott; in English, Norman MacCaig, Neil Gunn, Eric Linklater, Naomi Mitchison, Robin Jenkins, Edwin Morgan, Allan Massie, Alasdair Gray and A.L.Kennedy.

My present subject is not so much the literature itself but attitudes to it in Scotland and elsewhere. These attitudes have changed radically in the last hundred years or so. At the end of the first World War, MacDiarmid still found it necessary to assert that Scotland had a literary tradition. That has been obvious for centuries, but in some circles it was obscured by an anglo-centric preoccupation and it has taken a long campaign to slacken its grip. By now, the reality and vitality of the Scottish tradition is beyond dispute. Scottish literature is now taught in universities in Scotland and in some in America, Canada, France and Germany. Scottish schools are increasingly paying more attention to Scottish languages and literature than in the past. Apart from many books on particular writers, histories of Scottish literature have been written by Kurt Wittig (1958), Maurice Lindsay (1977), as an alphabetical 'Companion' by Trevor Royle (1983) and in four volumes edited by Cairns Craig (1987-8). The ten volumes of the *Scottish National Dictionary* were published between 1927 and 1976. Work continues on the *Dictionary of the Older Scottish Tongue. The Concise Scots Dictionary*, based on both of the two larger works, was published in 1985. A major work in Scots prose, William Lorimer's translation of the New Testament, was published in 1983. Gaelic has been more succesful than Scots in securing Government recognition and support and an established place in television programmes.

A number of organisations have helped to secure these advances. The Saltire Society was founded in 1936 in response to the concern over the apparent decline in Scottish life and culture. Its object was the encouragement of all the arts in Scotland and to restore the country "to its proper place as a creative force in European civilisation." One of its first actions was to publish a series of cheap editions of early Scottish literature at a time when no other editions were available. These 'Saltire Classics', along with programmes of readings, introduced many people to a literature of which they had heard nothing at school. New writing is encouraged and recognised by the Saltire Book Awards. The Society has also been involved in the creation in August 1997 of the Makars' Court in Edinburgh, a visible sign of the public acclaim of Scottish literature.

Shortly before the Referendum of 1979 on Home Rule, the Saltire Society invited some 200 organisations involved in the cultural life of Scotland to form a joint think-tank, the Advisory Council for the Arts in Scotland (AdCAS). The intention was to draw up suggestions on policies towards the arts which would be put to the new Scottish Assembly, but AdCAS continued although the Assembly was denied by the 40% rule. One of its first campaigns was for paperback reprints of important Scottish books of all periods because most of them were out of print. They persuaded the Scottish Arts Council to introduce a scheme to which several publishers responded. This was the origin of the Canongate Classics which for ten years has been producing fine editions of precisely the kind needed. This was a vital step because unless the books are available, no literature can exist.

Another powerful reinforcement was the formation in 1971 of the Association for Scottish Literary Studies (ASLS) which brought together university and school teachers of Scottish literature along with other enthusiasts. With the financial support of the Scottish Arts Council, it publishes a number of quarterly journals on literature and language, an annual anthology of new poetry and short stories and an annual volume which has ranged from Dunbar to MacDiarmid. It organises conferences and exercises constant pressure to enhance the place of Scottish literature in the schools and elsewhere.

For most of this century there have been a number of literary reviews. Many have come and gone, but those which have been well established for some years are *Chapman*, *Cencrastus*, *The Edinburgh Review*, *Lines Review*, *Gairm* in Gaelic and *Lallans* in Scots.

Maurice Lindsay has been involved in most of these activities, quite apart from his own poetry . His changing attitude to Scotland and its literature is reflected in his autobiography, *Thank You for Having Me* (1983). He says that after the War he was "totally obsessed by a desire to return to Scotland and play some part in reshaping it along, as I thought, the brave lines of MacDiarmid's vision of independence". (p.85) At first he wrote poetry in Scots, but later he thought that the language had receded so rapidly under the impact of television that it had been "reduced to a mere matter of local accent . . . a poor, wasted and abandoned speech". (p.171) In fact, the autobiography is strongly marked by a disillusionment with Scotland generally. He speaks of its "continuing decline" and "all-too-evident national failure in political and economic terms". (pp.212, 203) He thought that Scotland "gave up the struggle for nationhood soon after the First World War". (p.199) The bitterness of these words suggests to me that they were written in the spirit of despair which many people felt after the frustration of the Referendum of 1979. I wonder if he would still say the same after the impressive display of national resolve in the Referendum of 11th September 1997.

In an earlier book, *By Yon Bonnie Banks: A Gallimaufry* of 1961, Lindsay had expressed a more qualified pessimism over the future of Scotland. The last chapter is headed, "The death of Scotland?" and it suggests that Scotland is dying "mainly because it no longer has any real desire to live". It ends with this paragraph:

> So for me the love affair is over. The fervour, the obsession with Scottishness for its own sake, the strongly emotional response to whatever carried even the faintest Scottish overtone, all these things have faded to a gentle but regretful affection; an affection, however, which, I fancy, will persist to the end of my days.

I quote this partly because the definition of the love affair is the best one I know of the way many people, including myself, feel about Scotland, and from which we have no wish to escape. If it has ended for Lindsay, as he says, then we are fortunate that his "gentle affection" has been strong enough to spur him to endeavours on Scotland's behalf which look to me very much like labours of love.

The most substantial of these is his *History of Scottish Literature* (1977), which I have already mentioned. This is a book of about 500 pages of which, he says in the Introduction, the main purpose is to encourage readers to share the "enthusiasm and delight" which the literature of his own country has given him. His anthologies clearly share the same spirit. The earliest of these, *Modern Scottish Poetry: An Anthology of the Scottish Renaisance, 1920-1945*, first published in 1946, has travelled with me in many countries and has been one of my favourite books for half a century. *Scotland: An Anthology* (1974) contains prose as well as poetry and amounts to a generous sample of the whole of Scottish literature. It is a wonderful bed-side book and so is *Scottish Comic Verse.* (1981) Lindsay has written a book about Robert Burns and also his indispensable *Burns Encyclopedia.* (1959, 1979, 1980) This is an admirable work of reference, but it is much more than that. Lindsay in the Introduction again speaks of helping his readers to find "pleasure and delight" in the poems and letters of Burns. That is surely the right approach to literature.

In addition to all this writing and editing (and there is much more about the Scottish countryside, architecture, music and painting) Lindsay has supported the Saltire Society, has been President of the ASLS and editor of the *Saltire Review*. He presented radio and television programmes about literature and the other arts in Scotland for more than 20 years. In his book, *Francis George Scott and the Scottish Renaissance* (1980) Lindsay says of the Saltire Society: "A measure of the success of its pioneering efforts in the early days is the vastly improved state of all these concerns half a century later". (pp. 127-8) You might say exactly that of Lindsay himself. His contribution to Scottish literature, and to its reputation, influence, and appreciation, has been prodigious.

The greatly enhanced status and confidence of Scottish literature in the last 100 years or so is not unconnected with the long sequence of events which led on 11th September 1997 to the emphatic expression of the desire for the restoration of the Scottish Parliament. Scotland has recovered the will to survive which Lindsay feared that it lost. In his *Scottish Journey* of 1935, Edwin Muir said that Scotland was falling to pieces because there was "no visible and effective power to hold it together". (Ed. of 1979, p. 25) Now that we have met the challenge of that risk, we have every reason for confidence that Scottish literature will go from strength to strength.

References

1. William Donaldson: *Popular Literature in Victorian Scotland* (Aberdeen, 1986) and *The Language of the People* (Aberdeen, 1989)
2. David Murison quoted in Paul H. Scott, *Towards Independence* (Edinburgh, 1991 and 1996) p. 137.

2.16

Scotland, Slovenia and a New Renaissance

'Scottish Affairs', No. 38 Winter 2002

Since the 1960s the Slovene Centre of PEN, the international organisation of writers, has held an annual International Writers' Meeting to which other PEN Centres, including the Scottish, are invited to send representatives. I have been lucky enough to have taken part in three of these meetings and this year Laura Fiorentini came with me.

The idea behind thse events is to provide an opportunity for writers from many countries to have a frank exchange of views, not only about literature, but about the current state of the world. Over this period and in this tormented region, although happily Slovenia has been largely spared the worst, this has been a brave venture. It has also been remarkably successful. These meetings are an oasis of friendly co-operation and good sense, even when they involve people from countries at war or close to it. During the whole period of the dissolution of the former Jugoslavia, writers from all the constituent countries have taken part. So have others from such areas of conflict as Israel and Palestine. They have shown that sensible and well-intentioned people can find common ground even in the most unpromising circumstances. These discussions are not futile because writers may be able to take back something of the spirit of the meetings and have some influence on public opinion in their own country.

Part of the secret of the success of these meetings lies in the informality and warmth of Slovene hospitality. Also the sheer beauty of the place and the comfort of the hotel probably help to establish an appropriate atmosphere. For several years the meetings have been held in Bled, on the edge of a magnificent lake in the foot-hills of the Alps. There is a baroque church on an island and the most fairy-tale like of all fairy-tale castles on a precipitous cliff.

The water of the lake is clean and transparent and this is a country which still has wild flowers and butterflies. All of this is not hopelessly remote, but on the borders of Italy and Austria. Marshall Tito showed good judgment in making his summer headquarters in a villa on the lake-side. It is now a five star hotel where the President of the Republic gives his reception for the participants in the Writers' Meeting.

One of the main literary themes this year was on the question whether history and the books of the past still have relevance for us in our rapidly changing world. This is a familiar idea in this country where the Blairite adoration of modernity has tended to suggest that the past can and should be ignored; 'modern good, heritage bad'. (David Black in his recent book about the Parliament building, *All The First Minister's Men*, suggested that this was the reason for Dewar's stubborn rejection of the obvious site on the Calton Hill.)

In the paper which I had prepared for the meeting I took the opposite line and had the feeling that I was stating the obvious. After all, you cannot hope to understand the present without some idea of how we arrived at our current ideas and institutions. Also, literature and the arts generally are not like science which builds on and replaces the achievements of the past. The new is not necessarily better. Would anyone now claim to equal Shakespeare, Mozart or Burns, or Vergil for that matter? We still find pleasure in the arts of the past and can still learn from them much that is in danger of being forgotten.

I was reinforced in my feelings about this last point by a book which I happened to be reading on the train journey from Venice to Ljubjana, J. H. Plumb's *Book of the Renaissance*. In this he discusses the qualities which Castiglione in the 16th Century thought were necessary for the complete human being. Apart from a courteous and easy manner, without pedantry or excessive professionalism, they included: "a knowledge of the classics, an acquaintance with history and philosophy, an appreciation of music, painting, architecture and sculpture". It struck me that, if you add science and mathematics, this is the ideal at which education has aimed for centuries, but no longer.

Anyone who now advocated Castiglione's standard would probably be received with derision. The conduct and attitudes which used to be approved as good manners and proper consideration for others are now spurned as eccentric and old fashioned. Greed, self-assertion and violence are now more likely to be admired than condemned. Instead of the active, enquiring, sceptical mind, intellectual laziness is encouraged by the avoidance of difficulty and the search for the easy option. Instead of thought and analysis, we now have sound-bites and propaganda. The ideal of the Renaissance, and of the Scottish educational tradition of the Democratic Intellect, of a wide, general approach to thought and learning, is displaced by narrow specialisation. Of course, it will be said that these views are typical of an older generation who always think that the country is going to the dogs. Also, there have been gains in increased personal freedom and a higher standard of living, at least for the employed. In face, however, of the deplorable statistics of poverty in Scotland and of the high rates of illiteracy and inumeracy, there is no room for complacency.

The Renaissance of 14th century Italy was stimulated by the recovery of the intellectual and artistic values of ancient Greece. Similarly, Hugh MacDiarmid's Scottish Renaissance aimed at the restoration to Scottish poetry of the language, range, intelligence and international awareness of our own medieval poetry. It seems to me that we now need a new and more general renaissance to recover some of the moral and intellectual values of the comparatively recent past.

This need is not confined to Scotland or to Britain. It is true that the decline of standards has been fostered by British Governments in the last twenty years, the Conservatives by their encouragement of competitiveness and greed, Labour by its obsession with modernity, and both by their submission to commercialism. In Scotland we are fortunate to have an alternative to the British parties. But the problem is now widespread throughout the world. The globalised economy and its voices in television and the internet are spreading the infection like a vicious virus. The formal discussions and the conversations in Bled were full of concern for precisely the same dangers as those which threaten us. Cultural and linguistic diversity are important defences against universal globalisation, uniformity and Americanisation. That is why the independence and cultural vitality of small countries like Slovenia, or Scotland, are valuable for the cultural health of the world.

The discussion of these issues in Bled involved consideration of the nature of nationalism. There are those who use the word in a purely negative sense to mean aggressive xenophobia or expansionism, fascism, imperialism, the suppression of national or personal freedom. This usage is very common in Continental Europe, but it is not unknown in this country, especially, oddly enough, among those who are assertively British. Confusingly, the word is also used to mean the exact opposite, the rejection of imposed uniformity or political control, the defence of national and personal liberty. This is the sense in which the word is used in Scotland. As the late Cardinal Winning said in a famous speech in Brussels in 1998, the Scottish nationalism of the SNP is not aggressive or violent, but "mature, respectful of democracy and international in outlook". This is also the attitude of the Slovenes. In Bled I have always found a close intellectual rapport.

This is not surprising because there are similarities between Scottish and Slovene historical experience. We have both lived next to a larger, more powerful and expansive neighbour. Slovenia was the earliest Hapsburg possession and it was for centuries part of the Austro-Hungarian Empire. The Slovenes, like the Scots, are egalitarian, unpretentious and welcoming. They share too our respect for books and education, as is evident in the support which all levels of government give to the Writers' Meetings. Not only the President of the Republic but the mayors of both Bled and Ljubjana gave receptions for the participants.

The population of Slovenia is about 2 million, less than half of that of Scotland. Unlike Scotland, it does not have centuries of experience as an independent state; but it is now far ahead of Scotland in status. It declared independence on 26th June 1991, after a plebiscite in which 88.2% of the people voted for it. In May 1992 it became a member of the United Nations and negotiations for membership of the European Union are in an advanced stage. The satisfaction, optimism and self confidence which independence has created is evident in almost every conversation with a Slovene and in everything that you see around you. As in other countries, I have the impression that the psychological and cultural satisfactions of independence are even more gratifying than increased prosperity. There is no doubt that independence has done wonders for Slovenia. I have often been asked why Scotland, a larger and more highly developed country and one of the oldest nations in Europe, has not yet followed their example. I could only reply that we are on our way.

Notes on History

3.1

Why have we forgotten Berwick?

'The Herald', 30th March 1996

I have been asked why so terrible and destructive an act as the English sack of Berwick in 1296 has made so little impact on our collective consciousness that it is now largely forgotten. At the time Berwick was our largest and wealthiest town, in the words of the historian, Hill Burton "the key of Scotland, and the centre of its commercial riches." This was a massacre on a scale which even then caused horror and revulsion. It was also the sudden violation of a long-standing peace between the two countries and the provocation of the resistance which created the Scottish nation. Berwick never fully recovered from 1296, just as Scotland as a whole never fully recovered from Flodden.

The first, and saddest, reason for our forgetfulness is quite simply that events of this kind were not uncommon in the repeated English attempts over 300 years to subdue Scotland. Edinburgh was similarly sacked seven times. As late as 1544 the instructions of Henry VIII's Privy Council to the Earl of Hertford told him:

> Put all to fyre and swoorde, byrne Edinborough towne, so rased and defaced when you have sacked and gotten what you can of it, as there remayn forever a perpetual memory of the vengeance of God . . . sack Lythe [Leith] and burne and subverte it and all the rest, putting man, woman and childe to fyre and swoorde without exception . . . turne upset downe the Cardinalle's town of St Andrews . . . sparing no creature alive within the same.

Hertford carried out these instructions with such zeal that he was able to report that he had destroyed 7 monasteries (they included the great Border Abbeys), 16 castles, 5 market towns and 243 villages.

The 19th century English historian, J. A. Froude, summed up the consequences of these 300 years in these words: "The English hated Scotland because Scotland had successfully defied them: the Scots hated England as an enemy on the watch to make them slaves." In the 18th century Daniel Defoe wrote: 'Never two nations, that had so much affinity in circumstances, have had such inveteracy and aversion to one one another in their blood."

In the light of this history it is remarkable that the English Government was at last able to achieve its objective of asserting control over Scotland through the Union of 1707 without the use of military force. Scotland was then weak constitutionally and militarily because of the effects of the Union of the Crowns and economically because of the Darien disaster and the accident of several successive years of bad harvests. A majority of the Scottish Parliament succumbed, entirely against the popular will, to a sophisticated blend of intimidation, bribery, propaganda and ingenious drafting.

The second reason for our forgetfulness of Berwick is one of the conseqences of 1707. In the 19th century the Empire became a substitute for achievement at home. The Union, on which the imperial connection depended, became, like the monarchy, part of an orthodoxy that was beyond question. The history of independent Scotland, and its prolonged defence against heavy odds, was incompatible with the orthodoxy. Our schools and universities taught a history that was called British, but was in fact largely English. Although our universites in recent years have done excellent work in Scottish history, this has still hardly reached the schools. The second reason therefore is simply general ignorance of the facts.

This evasion continues, of course. Not long ago there was an exhibition in the Museum of Antiquities in Edinburgh which included some photographs of the ruins of the Border Abbeys. The captions said that they had been destroyed in the Reformation. I pointed out to one of the organisers that it was Hertford and not John Knox who was responsible. "That's true', he said, "but it would not be tactful to admit it."

I think that there is still a third reason for our forgetfulness. We are, contrary to some wide-spread ideas, an astonishingly docile and forgiving people. The English radical reformer, William Cobbett, toured Scotland in 1832. He was a shrewd and experienced observer. One of the things which struck him was "the docile and cheerfully submitting labourers of Scotland" whom he contrasted with "the glum and stubborn chaps in the South." That still seems to me to be true, when you think of the comparatively muted and restrained response to to the repeated injuries and humiliations inflicted on Scotland. Without going too far back in the past, I mean such things as the run down of the Scottish steel industry, the virtual theft of the TSB from its depositors, the violation of the undertakings to Rosyth, the use of Scotland as a site for nuclear-armed submarines and the reprocessing of nuclear waste, the present destruction of our local government and educational system. Our docility is excessive. Perhaps it is a result of low expectations because of our long experience of injuries inflicted on us by a powerful and aggressive neighbour, and of their indifference to our wishes since they achieved control.

Our patient tolerance and suffering in silence may be Christian virtues, but they are also invitations to our masters in Whitehall to exploit us and treat us with contempt. Sir Walter Scott in his *Letters of Malachi Malagrowther* (which everyone concerned with Scotland should read) said: "there is no harm in wishing Scotland to have just so much ill-nature . . . as may keep her good-nature from being abused." That is a lesson which we still have to learn; but with moderation.

In many other parts of the world, old injuries are used as an excuse for new revenge. In Scotland we are fortunately free from this spirit and this is something in which we should take pride and which we should maintain. The compelling and persuasive case for independence which is made by the SNP does not look back, but forward. It is based on the need for democratic responsibility for our own affairs because we cannot otherwise realise our potential economically, culturally and socially and make our own

3. 2

Scotland in Europe

Paper for Conference in the University of Glasgow, October 1999. Published in 'Cencrastus', No. 67, 2000

In the Introduction to his *Scotland: A New History* (1991) Michael Lynch says that the adoption by the SNP of a policy of independence in Europe "re-establishes one of the most important threads of continuity in Scottish history". Scotland's close involvement with Europe for many centuries is indeed a familiar theme.

At the end of the 18th century, for instance, Dugald Stewart said; "from time immemorial a continual intercourse had been kept up between Scotland and the Continent". He suggested that this might be one of the causes of the phenomenon which we now call the Scottish Enlightenment:

> The constant influx of information and liberality from abroad, which was thus kept up in Scotland in consequence of the ancient habits and manners of the people, may help to account for the sudden burst of genius, which to a foreigner must seem to have sprung up in this country by a sort of enchantment after the Rebellion of 1745.

In the middle ages Scotland had a compelling need to look for friends and allies in continental Europe. From the end of the 13th century and for the next 300 years we were subjected to repeated English invasions in an attempt to reduce us to submission and their population was even then several times larger than our own. Since England had similar ambitions in France, and was successful in Wales and Ireland, it was natural for Scotland and France to become allies. This became one of the longest and closest alliances in European history. It was so close that the citizens of each country had all the rights of citizens of the other. For centuries the body guards of the kings of France were Scottish. In 1510 Andrew Forman,

Bishop of Moray, was the Scottish Ambassador to France, but he was also appointed French Ambassador to the Holy See for negotiations affecting the peace of Europe. The association was not only military and diplomatic, but also intellectual and commercial. Between its formation and the Reformation at least 17 of the Rectors of the University of Paris were Scots. Michel de Montaigne was a pupil of George Buchanan, whose plays in Latin were performed all over Europe.

Michel Duchein in his *Histoire de L'Ecosse* (1998) says of Scottish literature of the 15th century; [I translate]

> French influence was strong which is easily explained by the close intellectual links between the two countries. But the important point is precisely the openness of Scottish literature to the rest of the world; this was by no means an isolated literature, shut up in itself. In this domain as in diplomatic (and more modestly in the economic) Scotland of the 15th century was an integral part of what we now call Europe and which at that time was called Christendom.

English hostility also meant that Scotland had to look overseas for trading partners and, in any case, transport by sea was then much easier by sea than by land. Scottish trade was not only with France, but also with all our neighbours across the North Sea, with Flanders and the Low Countries, Scandinavia. Poland and Russia. To give only one example, only a month after the battle of Stirling Brig, Andrew Moray and William Wallace wrote to the Senate and Commoners of Lubeck and Hamburg to say that trade could be resumed "because the Kingdom of Scotland has, thanks be to God, by war been recovered from the power of the English".

Scotland's relationship with other European countries was so close, and Scots were evidently so highly regarded that they were often entrusted with tasks of the highest responsibility of the kind which governments usually reserve for their own citizens. I have already mentioned Andrew Forman's appointment as an ambasador of France. In the 18th century George Keith, tenth Earl Marischal of Scotland, and his brother, James, were Jacobite exiles after the

'15. James became a Russian general and then a Field Marshal of Prussia under Frederick the Great. George became Frederick's ambassador to Paris and Madrid and the governor of Neuchâtel, where he was the friend and protector of Rousseau. Under Peter the Great, Patrick Gordon became a general who reformed the Russian army and Admiral Samuel Greig did the same for their navy.

Differences of language seem to have caused little difficulty. There is a good deal of mutual intelligibility between Scots and Dutch, German and the Scandinavian tongues. French has influenced both Gaelic and Scots. Clerics, academics and educated people generally had Latin as a lingua franca over the whole of Europe. The land which became Scotland was only partly, precariously, and for a short time, occupied by the Romans. But, although we had not been part of the Roman Empire, Scots afterwards adopted Latin with particular enthusiasm. George Buchanan was generally regarded as the finest post classical Latin poet, 'poetarum sui seculi facile princeps', as they said at the time. His memorial window in Greyfriars Kirk in Edinburgh says that Scotland marked the border of the Roman Empire, but was the last refuge of Latin eloquence. Even in the 18th century, although it was somewhat eccentric by that time, John Clerk of Penicuik wrote his history of the Union in Latin. Men like James Boswell seem to have learned French and Italian with ease, probably because of their solid grounding in Latin. It continued to be the central subject in Scottish high schools up to the time of the Second World War. Because of our international connections, Scots needed Latin in the past, just as people all over the world now feel the need to learn English.

Scotland then for many centuries was a very active participant in the affairs of Europe, in diplomacy, trade, the universities and the armies and navies. The departure of James VI to London in 1603 made a radical difference. Kings were then the effective heads of government and foreign policy and the making of peace and war were part of the royal prerogative. Scotland had lost her international identity and no longer had her own voice in the affairs of Europe. in the words of Hume Brown, Scotland in 1603 had become "severed and a withered branch, and her people knew it." Through the shared monarchy, Scotland contributed men and taxes to England's wars against our traditional trading partners and allies. No Scottish interest was served by these wars and no account was taken of Scotland in the peace treaties.

Political assimilation went further when Scotland was deprived of her Parliament by the Union of 1707. Increasingly Scottish energies were diverted away from Europe and from Scotland towards the Empire. Scotland played a disproportionate part in the administration and defence of the Empire and an alarming number of people emigrated. There were some two million emigrants between the 1820s and the First World War and emigration resumed at an increasing rate after 1918. To many people, Scotland seemed to be bleeding to death. In 1935 Edwin Muir said in his book, *Scottish Journey*. that Scotland "was gradually being emptied of its population, its spirit, its wealth, industry, art, intellect and innate character".

Even during this imperial phase in our history, connections with Europe did not cease. After the Reformation, Scottish students still went to universities on the continent, but Holland took the place of France. Montesquieu, and French thought generally, were a major influence on the Scottish Enlightenment and Dutch medicine on the development of the Edinburgh medical school. In the other direction, James Macpherson's *Ossian* was received rapturously all over Europe. Goethe put him on a par with Homer and Napoleon took a copy with him on his campaigns. The novels of Walter Scott were international best sellers for at least a century, translated into most European languages, imitated by Balzac, Manzoni, Pushkin, Tolstoy and countless others, and made the subject of hundreds of plays, operas and paintings. An idea of Scotland derived from Macpherson, Burns and Scott and from Scottish song influenced Haydn, Beethoven, Schubert, Mendelsohn, Brahms, Chopin and other European composers. Byron, "born half a Scot and bred a whole one", as he said of himself, was a consumate European and a major force in European romanticism. In the 18th century Scottish painters and architects, such as Allan Ramsay, Henry Raeburn and Robert Adam, studied in Rome. In the 19th MacTaggart, Peploe, Hunter and Fergusson were responsive to French impressionism and the style and atmosphere of France and French painting.

These are only a few examples of the close and continuous cultural and intellectual interchange between Scotland and the rest of Europe in previous centuries, but it has continued to the present. Hugh MacDiarmid campaigned for the restoration of Scottish vernacular literature to the mainstream of European letters. Douglas Young, Robert Garioch, Edwin Morgan and others have translated poetry from many European languages and much modern Scottish poetry has been translated into them. Since 1994 the BOSLIT project at the National Library of Scotland has been compiling a database of translations of Scottish writing. So far, it has recorded over 21,000 translations into more than 100 languages. There are many admirable translations of Moliere in Scots. David Purves has recently written one of Checkov's *Three Sisters* and Liz Lochhead is working on another.

To quote Michel Duchein once more, he says of contemporary France and Scotland: "Il demeure entre les deux peuples une sympathie profonde dont temoigne l'image positive de l'Ecosse en France et de la France en Ecosse".

Within the countries of the European Union there is a general recognition of the value of the diversity of European cultures and a conviction that, whatever else may be harmonised, cultural diversity must be preserved and enhanced. In Scotland this is not a new idea, probably as a consequence of our long appreciation of other cultures and our experience of the pressures towards the suppression of our own from a larger and expansive neighbour. Andrew Fletcher of Saltoun in *An Account of a Conversation*, published in 1704, proposed that Europe should be organised into groups of small autonomous states, co-operating to secure peace and "the common good of mankind". As far as I know, this is the first proposal for an association of European states and one of its purposes was the encouragement of cultural diversity. Fletcher said that large states, where the governments are distant from the people, are violent, unjust and unnatural". A diversity of small states, on the other hand, would "highly tend to the improvement of all arts and sciences . . . as the ancient cities of Greece did".

David Hume clearly had a high regard for Fletcher, whom he described in his *History of England* as "a man of signal probity and fine genius". In his essay, *Of the Rise of the Arts and Sciences*, Hume made precisely the same point as Fletcher about the advantages of the "cluster of little principalities" in ancient Greece:

> Each city produced its several artists and philosophers, who refused to yield the preference to those of the neighbouring republics; their contention and debates sharpened the wits of men; a variety of objects was presented to the judgement, while each challenged the preference to the rest; and the sciences, not being dwarfed by the restraint of authority, were enabled to make such considerable shoots as are even at this time the objects of our admiration.

In the following century. Walter Scott's *Letters of Malachi Malagrowther* of 1826 was a strong protest against the interference of Westminster in Scottish affairs and against their efforts, as he said, to reduce everything in Scotland to the English model. It was also an eloquent statement of the value of cultural diversity:

> Let us love and cherish each other's virtues — bear with each other's failings — be tender to each other's prejudices — be scrupuously regardful of each other's rights. Lastly, let us borrow each other's improvements, but never before they are needed and demanded. The degree of national diversity between different countries, is but an instance of that general variety which nature seems to have adopted as a principle through all her works, as anxious, apparently, to avoid, as modern statesmen to enforce, anything like an approach to absolute 'uniformity'.

Scotland can claim to be the oldest of European nations since the Declaration of Arbroath of 1320 is the first expression of the ideas of national identity and national independence. We have a long history of close association with the rest of Europe to our mutual benefit. For these, reasons, it is particularly inappropriate, to use a mild term, that Scotland of all places should not be a member in its own right of the European Union. Under devolution we still have no international identity and international relations are reserved to Westminster. That includes relations with the European Union, although decisions which it takes affect virtually all aspects of Scottish life, including those which are within the province of the Scottish Parliament.

The policies which British ministers follow in Brussels are British policies. Certainly, the Scottish Parliament and Executive can make their views known when these policies are being formulated, but they are decided in London. Where Scottish interests or Scottish opinions differ from those of England, it is those of England which will prevail and they alone will be expressed in the European Councils of ministers. Scottish ministers may at times be permitted to attend and speak at these meetings, but only if they are invited by the London Government and only if they follow the agreed British line.

Labour and Conservative unionists argue that Scottish interests have more weight in Brussels if they are expressed by Britain as one of the larger states with more votes. This is clearly untrue. If the Scottish view or interest is not the same as the British, it will not be expressed at all. If the Scottish and English view or interest coincide, they will have more weight and not less, if the Scottish voice and votes are added to these of England.

The representation of Scotland by Britain has another disadvantage. Successive British Governments of both parties have been reluctantly European. They have alternated between the arrogance of assuming that they are entitled to the leadership of Europe to acting the odd man out in a minority of one. Some prominent English Conservatives now even advocate withdrawal from Europe. This is not the way to win friends and influence people. In consequence, Britain is unpopular among other European Governments and can expect no favours. On the other hand, there is much evidence of general goodwill towards Scotland. We have many old alliances to renew.

Our whole status in the world would be transformed by independence. In Europe we would have our own voice and vote in the Councils of Ministers, our turn in the rotating presidency, the right to nominate a member in the European courts and a share in appointments to the European Commission and the civil service. In the world at large, we should emerge from a submerged province to recognition as a full member of the international community. The logic of the longest thread of continuity demands no less.

3.3

The Disaster of 1603

'Sunday Herald', 29th December 2002

Some months ago there was speculation in the press that there would be a grandiose official celebration in 2003 of the three hundredth anniversary of the Union of the Crowns in 1603 when James VI of Scots became also James I of England. Then, shortly before the summer recess, this was denied by a discrete announcement in the House of Lords. Perhaps the planners had discovered that it might be embarrassing to draw attention to the consequences of the 1603 Union. But Jack McConnell rushed in where angels fear to tread with a proposal, or an instruction, to VisitScotland that the execution of Wallace and the Union of the Crowns should be celebrated. It is certainly a good idea that major events in Scottish history should be celebrated; but we should choose achievements (such as Bannockburn and the Declaration of Arbroath), not catastrophes, outrages or disasters. There is no doubt that the Union of the Crowns was disastrous for Scotland.

The emotions of the Scottish people when James left for London on 3rd April 1603 are described in a notable passage of deep melancholy which concludes Patrick Tytler's *History of Scotland.* This history was written between 1826 and 1843 and has long been superseded by modern scholarship but this passage is still of value as a description of feelings which Tytler evidently shared. He ended his book with the departure of James; he thought that this was the end of Scottish history since Scotland had lost the independence which she had defended for centuries. The end of border warfare was welcome, but the loss of independence was a matter of deep unease and unhappiness.

This might seem a surprising reaction. It was a Scottish king who was taking over England, not the other way round; but the Scots were realists. James's succession to the English throne was a consequence of the marriage in 1503 of James IV, just 12 years before the Battle of Flodden, to Margaret Tudor, a daughter of Henry VII. When the marriage was being negotiated, (as the chronicler, Polydore Vergil, records) some of Henry's advisers opposed it because they saw that it might mean the succession of a member of the Scottish royal line to the English throne. Henry told them not to worry. If that happened, it would be the accession, not of England to Scotland, but of Scotland to England. The greater would always absorb the less, as England had drawn Normandy under her sway. He was right.

In the early 17th century the King was much more than only a symbol of national independence; he was the effective head of government. When James flitted to London, Scotland was still nominally independent. The internal machinery of government continued much as before, but it was now subject to a distant King, surrounded by English advisers. In particular, foreign policy was essentially a matter of royal prerogative. Scotland by losing her own separate monarchy had also lost her international identity. Hume Brown wrote of this:

> The Union of the Crowns brought many disadvantages to Scotland, but the result of it that most vitally affected her was her severance from the nations at a period when new principles and ideas were guiding their policy. Throughout the entire century Scotland was a severed and withered branch and her people knew it.

The Scottish royal Court had been the main source of patronage of poetry, music, painting, architecture and the theatre. The subject of much of the poetry of William Dunbar was the life of the Court of James IV. The first great Scottish play, David Lyndsay's *Ane Satyre of the Three Estaitis*, was first performed for James V and his Court in Linlithgow palace, which, considering the force of its satire, shows a high degree of enlightenment and tolerance. James VI also encouraged the theatre, wrote poetry himself and formed the Castalian Band of poets. All of this encouragement of the arts vanished when the king left for London. The theatre went into a long period of darkness.

The Scots language lost its status as the language of Court, government and law. *Basilicon Doron*, a book which James had written in Scots, appeared in print in English and this became the usual practice. The translation of the Bible which James authorised was also in English and for at least three centuries it was the most widely read and influential of all books in Scotland. Scots were therefore made to feel that their own speech was inferior. The damage which this inflicted on self-confidence and self-expression is apparent, even today.

England was a larger country than Scotland with greater wealth and more people (although, significantly, the disparity in population was much less than it has become). It had a more highly developed government machine, including an intelligence service. The monarch was treated with much greater pomp and deference than in Scotland and he had a considerable army and navy at his disposal. He was the head of the Church of England; in Scotland Melville had told him that of the Kirk of Scotland he was "nocht a king, nor a lord, nor a heid, but a member and God's sillie vassal". When he flitted to London James moved into a completely new situation, one that flattered his vanity and encouraged his inflated views of kingship. "The state of monarchy", he told the House of Commons, "is the supremest thing upon earth. For kings are not only God's lieutenants upon earth and sit upon God's throne, but even by God Himself they are called gods". And about Scotland he said: "Here I sit and govern by my pen, I write and it is done, and by a clerk of the Council I govern Scotland now, which others could not do with the sword".

These were dangerous illusions. James had acquired a keen sense of political reality in the hard school of his years of experience in Scotland, and in spite of the extravagance of his language he was careful not to push things too far. His son however, who succeeded to the two thrones as Charles I, was only three when he left Scotland and was educated entirely in the atmosphere of the English Court. His high-handed attitude firstly towards the Church in Scotland and then to the Parliament in England led to the miseries of 13 years of civil and religious wars in both countries and to the invasion and occupation of Scotland by Cromwell.

With the Restoration of Charles II in 1660 Scotland again became nominally independent, but it was an independence severely limited by the join monarchy. Scotland still had her own Parliament, but the officers of state (or, as we should now say, ministers) were appointed and instructed by the King or his English advisers. Government finances were collected and distributed by London. Lauderdale and then the Duke of York (the future James VII and II) were appointed, as Michael Lynch says, "virtual viceroys of Scotland". It was a period of rigid control of the Scottish Parliament and of the "unprecedented repression" of the Covenanters, the "killing time".

The "Glorious Revolution" of 1688/9 liberated the Parliaments of both Scotland and England to a certain extent. The Scottish Parliament could now discuss and decide whatever it wished, but its legislation was still subject to royal assent, which was not automatic, and the officers of state were still appointed and the finances controlled by London.

Daniel Defoe argued that an advantage of a Union with Scotland as that it would provide "an inexhaustible treasure of men" which would enable England to make a greater impact in Europe. Scotland was already treated in this way during the 17th century. In Hume Brown's words: "From the Union of the Crowns the sole business of Scotland with foreign countries was to contribute men and money towards whatever policy her predominant partner might choose to adopt". These policies involved wars between England and Scotland's traditional trading partners in Europe, to the great detriment of Scottish trade. After 1688 King William moved so many Scottish troops to Holland that Scotland itself was left with hardly any defence at all.

By the end of the 17th century the cumulative effect of a century of civil war and of indirect control had reduced Scotland to a pitiful condition, made worse by a succession of poor harvests. The Scottish Government attempted to seek a remedy in overseas trade by establishing a trading post in Darien. William gave royal assent to the Scottish Act; but, in response to English commercial interests, then did everything he could to frustrate it. Partly because of this, and partly because the venture was badly managed, Darien was a complete failure. In a great patriotic endeavour many Scots had invested all their funds in it and now faced ruin. Bruce Lenman does not exaggerate when he says in his *Economic History of Modern Scotland* "Late seventeenth century Scotland passed through a decade of indescribable anguish, both physical and psychological. By 1700 there was universal agreement in Scotland that the Union of the Crowns of 1603 was a proven disaster".

This was the situation which faced the Scottish Parliament elected in 1703, to the limited extent that parliaments were elected at that time. Andrew Fletcher of Saltoun, known since then as "the patriot", addressed the essential problem in a series of powerful speeches, "the miserable condition to which this nation is reduced by dependence upon the English court":

> All our affairs since the Union of the Crowns have been managed by the advice of English ministers, and the principal officers of the kingdom filled with such men as the court of England knew would be subservient to their designs.
>
> . . . So long as Scotsmen must go to the English court to obtain offices of trust or profit in this kingdom, these offices will always be managed with regard to to the court and interest of England, though to the betraying of the interest of this nation, whenever it comes into competition with that of England.

As it happened, Scotland had been presented with an opportunity to escape from the Union of the Crowns. On 30th July 1700 the last of Queen Anne's 18 children died and there was now no obvious heir to the throne. The English Parliament, without consultation with Scotland, passed an Act of Succession in 1701 offering the throne to Sophia, the Electress of Hanover and her descendants. Scotland was now free to make her own decision. Accordingly, and in accordance with Fletcher's proposals, the Scottish Parliament passed the Act of Security in August 1703. This provided for the settlement of the Scottish crown, on the death of Queen Anne, on a successor different from that of England, unless the sovereignty of Scotland, "free from English or any foreign interference" had been otherwise secured. When this clear declaration of independence was refused royal assent, the Scottish Parliament passed it again in 1704. This time assent was given.

But this did not mean that England was prepared to allow Scotland to escape from control. England was engaged in almost perpetual war with France and the risk that an independent Scotland might again revive her traditional policy of the Auld Alliance was unacceptable. The English Parliament passed an Act which amounted to an ultimatum. Unless Scotland adopted by 25th December 1705 the same succession as England, Scots would be treated as aliens and incapable of inheriting property in England and the import of the main articles of Scottish trade would be prohibited. The same Act provided for the appointment by the Queen of commissioners to "treat and consult" concerning the union of the two kingdoms, provided that the Scottish parliament did the same.

The word, 'union' , was at that time a vague expression which usually meant an agreement of any kind. Since there were many outstanding issues, the Scots were perfectly ready to talk; but when they arrived in London they found that the English insisted on discussing only their own draft for an "incorporating union". They had evidently decided that the joint monarchy was no longer sufficient to guarantee English control and that the troublesome Scottish Parliament should be abolished. The Scottish Parliament was eventually induced to accept this Treaty of Union by means of an elaborate campaign of propaganda, bribery (including the repayment of the Darien investments) and military intimidation. As John Clerk of Penicuik said at the time, the Union was better than the alternative, an English invasion and the imposition of worse terms.

Some historians have said that the Union of the Crowns of 1603 led inevitably to the Parliamentary Union of 1 707. This is true only in the sense that the 1603 Union reduced Scotland to such a condition that she was too weak to resist the English demands in 1707.

3.4

An English invasion would have been worse: why the Scottish Parliament accepted the Union

A revised version of a paper for the Conference of the 18th Century Scottish Studies Society, Edinburgh University 3rd to 6th July 2002

'Scottish Studies Review'

When the news of the Treaty of Union reached Paris, Saint-Simon recorded in his *Memoirs* the reaction of the Court of Louis XIV:

> It passes understanding how so proud a nation, hating the English, well acquainted with them through past sufferings and moreover so jealous of their own freedom and independence should have submitted to bow their necks beneath such a yoke. [1]

This was a very natural reaction. As France, the ancient ally, was fully aware, the Scots had defended their independence for 300 years against a larger and more powerful neighbour at a very heavy cost. As recently as 1703 and again in 1704 the Scottish Parliament had made a firm declaration of independence in the Act of Security. This decided that the Scottish Parliament on the death of Queen Anne would appoint a different successor to the Scottish throne than the English unless other means had been settled to secure the sovereignty of Scotland against English or any foreign interference. Why then did the same Parliament with the same members accept only three years later not only the same monarch as England, but the abolition of the Scottish Parliament itself? And this in spite of the clear opposition of the great majority of the Scottish people.

In trying to answer this question, I think that the first point to bear in mind is that Scotland at the time was, despite the brave words of the Act of Security, in a very weak bargaining position. She had already lost a very large part of her independence when in 1603 James VI accepted also the English throne and flitted to London. Monarchs then were the actual, and not merely the theoretical, heads of government. Foreign policy, peace and war, state expenditure, the appointment of state officials, including even the ministers in charge of Scottish affairs, were all made in their name and carried out under their direction. An immediate effect of James's removal to London was that Scotland no longer had a foreign policy or even an international identity. As far as the rest of the world was concerned, Scotland had ceased to exist.

James VI understood the Scottish situation and the ways of thought of the Scottish people. His successor, Charles I, left Scotland when he was three and did not visit the country again until thirty years later. He was so far out of touch with Scottish susceptibilities that his attempt to impose an English pattern on the Scottish church provoked a civil war. He and his successors carried on wars with Scotland's traditional trading partners, but money and men were raised in Scotland to help in their conduct. Scotland itself was left with virtually no military forces. In the words of Hume Brown, "from the Union of the Crowns the sole business of Scotland with foreign countries was to contribute men and money towards whatever policy her predominant partner might choose to adopt." [2]

In a speech to the Scottish Parliament in 1703 Andrew Fletcher described the Scottish situation: "All our affairs since the union of the crowns have been managed by the advice of English ministers and the principal offices of the kingdom filled with such men, as the Court of England knew would be subservient to their designs . . . We have from that time appeared to the rest of the world more like a conquered province than a free independent people". [3]

In Scotland the 17th century was one of religious war and persecution, the ruination of foreign trade and economic decline, all as a direct consequence of the Union of the Crowns. Towards the end of the century there were additional disasters. Between 1695 and 1699 bad weather and poor harvests caused widespread starvation. The Darien Scheme, in which many Scots in a great patriotic endeavour had invested most of their savings, was a complete failure. This was partly due to English opposition. King William as King of Scots gave assent to the Scottish Act establishing the Darien Company; as King of England he did his best to sabotage it.

After the abdication of James II (in the English version) or the deposition of James VII (in the Scottish) the settlement of 1689 restored parliamentary freedom. The Scottish Parliament could again discuss and decide whatever it pleased; but (and it is a substantial but) their Acts required royal assent from London and the members of the Scottish Government were still appointed by the King on the advice of his English ministers.

A Scottish Parliament was elected in 1703, to the limited extent to which Parliaments were then elected from a minute fragment of the population. They had to face the complex of problems caused by the joint monarchy. There seemed, however, to be an opportunity to escape from it.

All of Queen Anne's many children had died and she was now too old to have more. The English Parliament, without consultation with Scotland, had passed in 1701 an Act of Succession which conferred the English throne on the Electress Sophia of Hanover and her descendants. Scotland was therefore now free to choose a different successor and the Scottish Parliament declared this intention in the Acts of Security of 1703 and 1704.

It soon became plain that this was something which England was not prepared to tolerate. They had become accustomed to the ability to control and exploit Scotland which the joint monarchy had given them for a century and would not surrender it willingly. There was always the possibility that if Scotland recovered her independence she might renew her alliance with France with which England was repeatedly at war. Accordingly both Houses of the English Parliament in 1705 passed the Aliens Act which amounted to an ultimatum. Unless Scotland had accepted the same succession to the throne as England by 25th December, Scots would be treated in England as aliens and incapable of inheriting property, and exports from Scotland of the main items of trade would be prohibited. The same Act proposed the appointment of commissioners by the Queen to "treat and consult" with Scotland "concerning the union of the two kingdoms", if Scotland took similar action. This was an invitation which Scotland was perfectly prepared to accept. There were many outstanding grievances between the two countries and union at that time was a vague term meaning no more than agreemant of any kind on any subject.

In the Scottish Parliament the Duke of Hamilton professed to lead the opposition, but he had a secret agreement with the English Government and several times frustrated his own side at crucial moments. [4] One of the most serious of these was during the debate on the English proposal. Late in a sitting, after many members of the opposition had left, he unexpectedly moved that the appointment of the Scottish commissioners should be left to the Queen. It meant that both teams were in effect appointed by the English Government.

When the negotiations began in London in April 1706 the English made it clear that they insisted on an "incorporating union" in which the two kingdoms would be united into one with the same Parliament. The Scots made an alternative proposal that the two Parliaments should continue with the same succession and a reciprocal exchange of rights and privileges and with free navigation and trade. This was a substantial concession since it accepted the joint monarchy which had been so unfavourable to Scotland; but the English were not prepared to discuss it. The Earl of Mar, the Scottish Secretary of State, wrote to Carstares in Edinburgh: "You see what we are to treat of is not in our choice, and we see the inconveniences of treating on an incorporating union only". [5] Another of the Scottish Commissioners, Clerk of Penicuik, explained the situation years afterwards in his *History* of these events: "You cannot force your will on those stronger than yourself". [6]

With the Scottish team consisting almost entirely of men accustomed to acting on instructions from London, this was not so much a negotiation as a *diktat*. Even so, they had to produce a document which stood a chance of acceptance by the Scottish, as well as the English, Parliaments. The Treaty therefore contained provisions ingeniously designed to appeal to the self-interest of the members of the Scottish Parliament, the lords, the lairds and the representatives of the burghs. The lords were to lose their right to sit in Parliament (because only 16 representatives were to have seats in the House of Lords) but otherwise they were to have all the privileges of the English peers, including freedom from arrest. Heritable offices and jurisdictions and the rights and privileges of the royal burghs were to continue. So were Scots law and the legal system and many members of the Scottish Parliaments were lawyers. Above all there was the Equivalent, the payment to Scotland of 398,085 pounds and 10 shillings in compensation for accepting liability for a share for the English national debt. This was a piece of creative accounting typical of the parsimony and skill of the English Treasury. It had to serve many purposes, and it was to be repaid by the Scots accepting liablity to pay English customs and excise duties. Walter Scott who wrote the only frank account of the Union transaction that appeared in the 19th century (strangely enough in a book written for children, *The Tales of a Grandfather*) said of this arrangement: "In fact, the Parliament of Scotland was bribed with the public money belonging to their own country." [7] An important part of this was the undertaking in the Treaty itself to use part of the Equivalent to repay investments, plus interest at 5% per annum, in the Darien company. Since many members of the Parliament had lost most of their savings in that venture, this was a powerful inducement. There was also straightforward bribery, as George Lockhart subsequently proved through an enquiry by the new British parliament.

So I return to the question with which I started. Why did the Parliament which asserted Scottish independence in 1703 and 1704 agree three years later to its surrender? Certainly bribery was a factor. As Burns said:

> We're bought and sold for English gold,
> Such a parcel of rogues in a nation!

Or Walter Scott again: "Men of whom a majority had thus been bought and sold, forfeited every right to interfere in the terms which England insisted upon". [8]

But, apart from that, is there any other and more creditable reason? In the 1850s when T. B. Macaulay was writing his *History of England* he was puzzled by this and he sought help from the Scottish historian, Hill Burton. His suggestion was that "a simple solution might be found in the urgency of Scots for participation in the English trade." [9] This has become the orthodox view. It seems plausible; and it offers a face-saving explanation both to the Scots, who did not like to think of even a completely unrepresentative Parliament succumbing to bribery, and the English who did not like be seen as a larger country bullying a smaller. Unfortunately. it is a theory which does not stand up to the contemporary evidence.

A few people argued at the time that there would be advantage for Scotland in legal access to the trade with the English colonies, which had been banned to Scottish ships under the English Navigation Act. Some Scottish merchants had been engaged in it in defiance of the Act in any case. There could be no objection on the Scottish part to its legalisation; but it was not a major factor. It had been included as a Government amendment to the Act of Security, but no one in the Scottish Parliament seems to have noticed or objected when it was deleted from the version of the Act which received royal assent in 1704.

Andrew Fletcher discussed the point in his *Account of a Conversation*, written just after the 1703 session of Parliament. One of the participants was the Earl of Cromarty (who seems to have been about the only man in Scotland at the time who was a genuine enthusiast for an incorporating union). He said that liberty of trade to the plantations "must be of incalcuable advantage to the Scots nation". Fletcher denies it and points out that Wales, united to England for 300 or 400 years and with one of the best ports, is "the only place of the kingdom, which has no considerable commerce".[10]

The Royal Burghs, who represented the merchant community, petitioned against the Union on the grounds that the imposition of taxes, designed to meet English conditions, would be harmful to Scottish trade. They were right. The immediate effect of the Union was to inflict damage on the Scottish economy and it took about 60 years to recover. Daniel Defoe had acted as as an English spy and propagandist during the Union transaction and had argued in his pamphlets addressed to a Scottish audience that it would be economically beneficial to Scotland. Twenty years later when he wrote his *Tour Thro' the Whole Island of Great Britain* he admitted that he had been wrong. There had been no increase of trade "but rather the contrary and that the people were poor and looked poor. [11]

Adam Smith in a letter of 4th April 1760 said of the Union:

> the immediate effect of it was to hurt the interest of every single order of men in the country . . . Even the merchants seemed to suffer at first. The trade to the Plantations was, indeed, opened to them. But that was a trade which they knew nothing about; the trade they they were acquainted with, that to France, Holland and the Baltic, was laid under new embarrassments which almost totally annihilated the two first and most important branches of it . . . No wonder if at that time all orders of men conspired in cursing a measure so hurtful to their immediate interest. [12]

Walter Scott said much the same (and remember that Walter Bagehot said of him: "You might cut paragraphs, even from his lighter writings, which would be thought acute in the *Wealth of Nations*.") [13]:

> Scotland was only tantalised by a Treaty which held out to the Kingdom the prospect of a free trade, when, at the same time, it subjected them to all the English burdens and duties, raising the expenses of commerce to a height which Scotland afforded no capital to defray so that the apprehension became general that the Scottish merchants would lose the separate trade which they now possessed, without obtaining any beneficial share in that of England. [14]

I think that the most convincing proof that trading considerations were not a major factor in influencing members of the Scottish Parliament to vote for the Union is to be found in the elaborate apologia of Sir John Clerk of Penicuik. He was reluctant to accept appointment as one of the Scottish Commissioners for the Union because of the "great backwardness" of the Scottish Parliament to any such idea. He finally agreed, as he frankly admitted in his *Memoirs*, because the Duke of Queensberry threatened to withdraw his patronage. [15] He became responsible on the Scottish side for questions of finance and trade, and after the Union he was rewarded with the remunerative post of a Baron of the Court of Exchequer. But his conscience seems to have troubled him. He spent the next 40 years writing a *History of the Union* in Latin to explain and justify his part in bringing about the Union, as well as a "Testamentary Memorial" for his "children, brothers and friends" and *Observations* of 1730 on the same subject.

Since he was anxious to make a case for the Union, and finance and the economy were his special responsibility, he would certainly have claimed that it brought advantages for Scottish trade, if that had been possible. Even in 1730 he makes no such claim, but he is emphatic about the detestation of the Union among the people at large. In the *Observations* he says that at least three fourths of the population were opposed and in the *History* that not even 1% were in favour. [16]

If the Union was vastly unpopular and harmful to "every single order" of the people, there must have been some other very compelling reason to explain the majority vote in Parliament. Bribery alone can hardly be the explanation. Clerk is honest about this. In the *History* he says that as soon as the Scots "aspired to better things" (that is sought to escape from the joint monarchy), it became a necessary English policy "either to destroy us or to force us into union on well-defined terms"; and in the *Observations* that it was a "moral certainty that England wou'd never allow us to grow rich and powerfull in a separate state". The alternative to Union therefore was that Scotland "would fall under the Dominion of England by right of conquest". [17] A majority voted for the Union because it was preferable to an English invasion and the imposition of worse terms.

There is other evidence which supports Clerk's explanation. In July 1703 the English minister, Godolphin, sent to Seafield, the Chancellor of Scotland, a polite, but unmistakable, threat of military force, in which he pointed out how much greater England now was in wealth and power than Scotland. [17] The Earl of Roxburgh in a letter of 26th December 1704 said that if Scotland did not very soon accept either the same succession or a union, "Conquest will certainly be upon the first peace". (He evidently meant as soon as Marlborough was free from military engagement on the Continent)[18] It was the great disparity in military strength that made Scotland so vulnerable. The joint monarchy had left her with hardly any army at all, but the implied threat was, in the words of T. B. Smith, "invasion by one of the great captains of history at the head of a veteran army, backed by the military resources of one of the most powerful states in Europe." [19] In fact, England moved both cavalry and infantry units to the Border when the Treaty was under discussion in the Scottish Parliament.

So much then for the causes of the Union; what was its nature? Its purpose was essentially an English strategic purpose, to reduce Scotland to political impotence so that it could not be a distraction in England's wars with France. As Linda Colley says in her book, *Britons: Forging the Nation*, Britain was "an invented nation . . . forged above all by war." [20] When this had been achieved, England lost interest in Scotland. During the rest of the 18th century and most of the next, British Governments hardly intervened in Scotland. Almost the only exception was the ruthless suppression of the Highlands after the '45.

The Union did not make Britain a unitary state. Scotland was deprived of its Parliament, but most other institutions carried on as before. They included the law, the kirk, education and local government, all of which had far more influence on everyday life and habits of thought than the remote and inactive British Parliament. There was a serious weakness in that Scotland had no means of making necessary changes in the law, but the country remained very largely autonomous. Autonomy was diminished by increasing Goverment intervention in the 19th and 20th centuries. This was accompanied by demands for the recovery of the Scottish Parliament, which was eventually achieved after a century of agitation.

The major effect of the Union was that it helped England to persue her European and imperial ambitions with more confidence. This was one of the arguments used by Defoe in one of his pamphlets of 1706 in favour of the Union addressed to an Englsh audience. The advantage of the Union, he said, is "wholly on England's side", the power of which by the addition of Scotland "would be so fortified" that it could "make a different figure in all the affairs of Europe . . . Scotland is an inexhaustible Treasure of Men". [21]

Scots played such a predominant part in the discovery, development, defence and administration of the Empire (as Michael Fry has amply demonstrated in his book, *The Scottish Empire*) that it is questionable if it would have been possible without them.

The expansion of the Scottish economy in the second half of the 18th century has often been attributed to the Union; but it was mainly due to revolutionary change in industrial and agricultural techniques. In the 19th century participation in the Empire became a major factor in Scottish life. It provided innumerable opportunities for careers of all kinds and a captive source of raw materials and a market for many Scottish industries. Pride in the Empire displaced pride in Scotland. The net effect was probably to the disadvantage of Scotland itself because of the distraction of attention and the loss of a large part of its most active and enterprising citizens through massive emigration. A comparison of present day Scotland with other countries in western Europe of a comparable size which have remained or recovered independence suggests that they have followed a more fortunate course. The quality of life in all of them is superior to Scotland by any standard of measurement.

Even so, for most people in Scotland for most of the 19th century the monarchy, the Empire and the Union, by virtue of which Scotland was a partner in the Empire, became almost sacred symbols which it was sacrilegeous to criticise. That is why, I think, a mythical view of the Union became holy writ: that it was a sensible agreement freely and even eagerly negotiated by Scotland for the sake of economic advantage and that all good things flowed from it. You still find this doctrine repeated as if it were undeniable truth. Even Neal Ascherson does so in his recent book, *Stone Voices*.[22] The Union of 1707 was an event which had important consequences, not only for Scotland and England, but for Europe and the rest of the world. It is surely time that we took an uninhibited look at its nature and its consequences.

References

1. Duc de Saint- Simon, Memoirs (41 vols. Paris, 1901) Quoted by John S. Gibson in *Playing the Scottish Card: The Jacobite Invasion of 1708* (Edinburgh, 1988) p. 103.
2. P. Hume Brown, *History of Scotland* (3 vols. Cambridge, 1912) Vol ii p. 240.
3. Andrew Fletcher of Saltoun, *Selected Political Writings and Speeches*, edited by David Daiches. (Edinburgh, 1979) p. 70.
4. See my *Andrew Fletcher and the Treaty of Union* (Edinburgh 1992 and 1994) especially pp. 138-144.
5. As 4. p. 151.
6. Sir John Clerk of Penicuik, *History of the Union of Scotland and England*, translated by Douglas Duncan (SHS, Edinburgh, 1993) p. 162.
7. Sir Walter Scott, *Tales of a Grandfather* (Edinburgh, 1889) p.769.
8. As 7. p.770.
9. This correspondence is quoted in the Introduction to *Thoughts on the Union* by A. V. Dicey and A. S. Rait (London, 1920) pp. 2-3

10. As 3. pp.119-420.
11. Daniel Defoe, *A Tour Thro' the Whole Island of Great Britain* (London, 1727), Vol III, p. 33.
12. Adam Smith, *Correspondence*, edited by E. C. Mossner and I. C. Ross (Glasgow, 1994) p.68.
13. Walter Bagehot. *Collected Works* (London. 1995) pp. 416-419.
14. As 7. p.733.
15. Sir John Clerk of Penicuik, *Memoirs* edited by John M. Gray (SHS, Edinburgh, 1892) p.58.
16. Sir John Clerk of Penicuik, 'Observations on the Present Circumstances of Scotland' in *Miscellany of the Scottish History Society*, Volume X (Edinburgh, 1965) p. 192; *History*, as 6. p. 118
17. *History*, as 6. p.173; *Observations*, as 16. p. 118.
18. In *Correspondence of George Baillie of Jerviswood* (Bannatyne Club, Edinburgh, 1842) p. 28.
19. T. B. Smith, "The Union as Fundamental Law" in *Studies Critical and Comparative* (Edinburgh, 1962) p. 9.
20. Linda Colley, *Britons: Forging the Nation* (Yale, 1992) p. 5.
21. Daniel Defoe, *An Essay at Removing National Prejudices* (London, 1706) p. 28.
22. Neal Ascherson, *Stone Voices: The Search for Scotland* (London, 2002).

3.5

The Secret Service of Daniel Defoe

'Scotland's Story', 2000, Part 30, pp 7-9

The fame of Daniel Defoe now rests almost entirely on his novels, especially *Robinson Crusoe*, one of the best known books ever written. In fact, he turned to novel writing only in the last ten years of his life when he was in his 60s. You might say that this was a peaceful occupation in his retirement, after a precarious life of survival on his wits. Before that he had been through bankruptcy and imprisonment and had written millions of words on a great variety of subjects. He was one of the founders of modern journalism as well as of the novel. No fewer than 545 titles, ranging from satirical poems and political and religious pamphlets to substantial volumes, have been ascribed to him. For several years he was employed by the English Government as a spy and he was intensely engaged in the promotion of the Treaty of Union. That was the most remarkable episode in a turbulent life, when he had a key, but secret, role in an important event in circumstances worthy of one of his own novels.

Defoe was born in London, probably in 1660, in a Presbyterian family of modest means. He was educated for a ministry in the church, but went into trade for which he had a romantic passion. His business ventures were ambitious, but finally unsuccessful. By 1692 he was bankrupt and he was haunted by debt for most of his life, and he had a wife and seven children to support. He tried to earn his living by his pen, but that too landed him in disaster. In 1703 he published *The Short Way With the Dissenters*, an ironic attack on the high Tories, He was prosecuted for seditious libel and sentenced to stand three times in the pillory, pay a fine of 200 marks and be detained in prison at the Queen's pleasure.

In this extremity Defoe wrote to William Paterson, the London Scot who proposed both the Bank of England and the Darien Scheme, and who was in the confidence of Robert Harley, a leading minister in the English Government. Not surprisingly in the circumstances, this was an abject appeal for clemency, in which Defoe offered to dedicate his life and powers to the benefactor who would release him. Harley, aware of Defoe's brilliance as a controversialist, accepted the offer and ordered his release in September 1703.

Defoe began almost immediately to publish his *Review*, an early political periodical, which appeared at first weekly and then three times a week from 1704 to 1713 and was written mostly by Defoe himself. It was the main mouthpiece of the Government and from the beginning was largely devoted to promoting the "incorporating Union" with Scotland. This had become a vital objective of English policy. Since the Union of the Crowns in 1603 Scotland had been kept under political control through the joint monarchy, but was now threatening to escape. In 1703 and again in 1704 the Scottish Parliament had passed the Act of Security which called for the restoration of Scottish independence on the death of Queen Anne, either through the choice of a different monarch than the English one or by the transfer of all power from the monarch to the Parliament itself. This was a prospect which the English Government was not prepared to tolerate. An independent Scotland might renew its traditional policy of alliance with France, the country with which England was engaged in a long power struggle.

England set about the achievement of the Union with an ingenious and sophisticated battery of policies. Scotland was brought to the negotiating table by a threat of economic sanctions. There it was faced with a demand that it accept a draft treaty which insisted on incorporation, but which included provisions designed to appeal to the self-interest of the classes represented in the Scottish Parliament. This was reinforced by bribery and propaganda. The implied alternative was an English invasion and the imposition of worse terms.

Defoe began his campaign of propaganda, both in the *Review* and in a series of pamphlets, by addressing English opinion. The Union would end the threat from the north and gain for England an "inexhaustible treasure of men" and a valuable new market. It would mean a great increase in the power of England. The only other possible course was war which would be "the most bloody, implacable and cruel, that had ever happened between the nations". England had increased so much in strength that it should be able to crush Scotland, but a war could always have unforeseen consequences.

In September 1706, when the debate in the Scottish Parliament on the Treaty (which lasted three months) was about to begin, Harley ordered Defoe to Edinburgh as a secret agent. There he was not only to report, but do everything possible to help to secure acquiescence in the Treaty. Since many of his reports have survived and have been published (*The Letters of Daniel Defoe*, edited by G. H. Healey, Oxford, 1955), we know far more about Defoe's activities than is usual with secret missions. He was very conscious of the risks if his real purpose had been discovered. Popular feeling against the Treaty and those who made it was very strong. His first letters from Edinburgh have vivid descriptions of violent demonstrations against the Union. "A Scots rabble", he said, "is the worst of its kind". Years later, after Defoe himself had admitted at least part of the truth, John Clerk of Penicuik, who was a leading supporter of the Union in the Scottish Parliament, wrote in his *Memoirs*: "He was a spy amongst us, but not known as such, otherways the Mob of Edinburgh had pulled him to pieces".

Defoe had, however, one great asset; he was a Presbyterian who had suffered persecution in England for his beliefs. Probably for this reason, he was able to ingratiate himself so successfully that he was soon acting as an adviser to Parliamentary committees and the Assembly of the Church. He told Harley that he was "privy to all their folly", but "perfectly unsuspected as corresponding with anybody in England". He was even able to influence the proposals that were put to Parliament. He reported to Harley: "having had the honour to be always sent for to the committee to whom these amendments were referr'd I have had the good fortune to break their measures in two particulars viz the Bounty on Corn and proportion of the Excise."

He continued too with his propaganda, still writing his *Review* and a new series of pamphlets, published, as always, anonymously. He was too good a propagandist to worry about consistency and for Scottish consumption he used quite different arguments, even the opposite, from those he had used in England. In particular, ignoring the English doctrine of the sovereignty of Parliament, he told the Scots that they could have complete confidence in the guarantees in the Treaty. Since the British Parliament would be created by the Treaty, it could not violate it without destroying the foundation of its own existence. Some of his pamphlets purported to have been written by Scots. They continue to mislead even reputable historians who have been known to quote them as evidence of Scottish opinion at the time.

The same is true of a massive *History of the Union* which Defoe published in 1709 and which historians have often accepted as a reliable contemporary account. Defoe does take pains to give it an air of objectivity. He gives some space to the arguments against the Union, but always has the last word. He disposes of the most formidable opponent, Andrew Fletcher of Saltoun, by simply ignoring him. Nor does he say anything about the deviousness of the Duke of Hamilton who was the official leader of the opposition but acted against them at several decisive stages in the debate. He makes no attempt to explain why the same Scottish Parliament which was so assertive of Scottish independence from 1703 to 1703 became so supine in 1706.

It is typical of the lack of generosity of Governments that Defoe received very little award, and of course no recognition, for his services. He did, however, make use of his Scottish experiences in yet another book, his *Tour Thro' the Whole Island of Great Britain*, published in 1727. Here he admitted that the increase of trade and population in Scotland, which he had predicted as a consequence of the Union, was "not the case, but rather the contrary".

3.6

The Scottish Enlightenment

'Scotland's Story', 2000, Part 36, pp. 10-14

The 18th century in Scotland was one of the great periods of human achievement, comparable to the Athens of Pericles or the Florence of the Renaissance. It was rich in innovative thought which introduced fundamental changes in the way people everywhere regarded both the physical world and human society. There were, Walter Scott said, giants in the land, such men as David Hume (1711-76) and Thomas Reid (1710-96) in philosophy, Adam Ferguson (1723-1816) in sociology, Adam Smith (1723-90) in economics and moral philosophy, James Hutton (1726-97) in geology, William Cullen (1710-90) and Joseph Black (1728-99) in chemistry, William Robertson (1721-93) and David Hume again in the writing of history, Henry Home, Lord Kames (1696-1782) in a great variety of subjects from literary criticism and law to agriculture. Many modern academic disciplines virtually take their origin from the work of these men. That was not all. This was also the age of the poetry of Robert Fergusson and Robert Burns, the architecture of Robert Adam, the portraits of Allan Ramsay and Henry Raeburn, the beginning of the Edinburgh medical school, James Boswell's *Life of Johnson* and his comprehensive *Journals*, and of James Watt's work on the steam engine, the power source of the industrial revolution and of the locomotives and steam ships which circled the world in the course of the following century.

The first historian of ideas who attempted to explain this "sudden burst of genius," as he called it, was Dugald Stewart who succeeded Adam Ferguson as Professor of Moral Philosophy in Edinburgh in 1785. He attributed it to the constant intercourse between Scotland and the rest of Europe which had been maintained "from time immemorial". It is certainly true that the

Scottish tradition of studying and teaching in continental universities had kept Scotland for centuries in the mainstream of European thought. But there was a more basic reason, the importance attached to education in Scotland since the Middle Ages and particularly after the Reformation. John Knox's First Book of Discipline of 1561 proposed the establishment of a school in every parish, a high school in every town and a university in the major cities. For the next 200 years the Scottish Parliament and the General Assembly of the Kirk worked to achieve this and before long the mass of the people in Scotland were probably the best educated in the world.

The Kirk in Scotland gave more weight to reasoned discourse than to ritual and this encouraged habits of metaphysical specualation. There was a strong tradition of historical and philosophical writing in Scotland from the Middle Ages. As Vincent Hope says in the *Oxford Companion to Philosophy*:

> The Scottish universities had, until recently a traditional reverence for philosophy, which was compulsory for every degree . . . There was no idea of exclusive specialisation, let alone that the best results require it. The policy of non-specialisation allowed Hume, Smith and Reid, at the tradition's high point, to variously combine psychology, moral philosophy, optics, mechanics, economics, history and jurisprudence. Philosophy and science were taken to be one.

There was, in fact, nothing sudden about the "burst of geniuus". As John MacQueen has written: "The Scottish Enlightenent was the natural, almost the inevitable, outcome of several centuries of Scottish and European intellectual history".

The men who made the Scottish Enlightenment were all products of this educational system. (They were all men because women were still excluded from higher education.) They reflected the wide approach to learning which George Davie described as the Democratic Intellect in his book of the same title. It was democratic in two senses. It was an education open to all and it regarded all aspects of learning as important and inter-related.

The Union of 1707 had left Scotland largely autonomous in everything except the power to make new laws. The institutions which remained Scottish, the Church, the legal and educational systems and local government, affected people much more than a distant and largely inactive Parliament. The literati of the Enlightenment were educated in one of these institutions, the universities, and usually found careers there or in the Church or the law.

David Hume, for instance, began to study for a legal career at Edinburgh University, but then decided to devote himself to literature, by which he meant philosophy and history. He lived for a time in France where he wrote his first book, *A Treatise Of Human Nature*. He returned to Scotland, but failed to secure a chair in Edinburgh University. For a time he was a tutor to a nobleman and then secretary to a general on a military expedition. He again failed to secure a university chair (this time in Glasgow), but he was appointed as Librarian to the Advocates' Library in Edinburgh, a post which was useful for research for his *History of England*. He then, surprisingly, became Secretary to the British Embassy in Paris, where he was much cultivated by philosophical and literary society. For two years he then worked for the Government in London as Under-Secretary of the Northern Department. There he does not seem to have been entirely happy, because in his letters he was given to referring to "the Barbarians who live on the banks of the Thames".

Finally he returned to Edinburgh, where, as he said, he found "every blessing of consequence". He delighted in the society of his friends, including Adam Smith who was close at hand in Kirkcaldy. James Boswell expected to find him, as a sceptic in religion, troubled by the thought of his approaching death, but failed to disturb his composure. When he died Adam Smith said that he approached "as nearly to the idea of perfectly wise and virtuous man, as perhaps the nature of human frailty will permit".

Hume's employment by the Government in Paris and London was exceptional among the literati. Most of them seldom left

Scotland, except those who were engaged as tutors to noblemen on the Grand Tour, as Smith was by the 3rd Duke of Buccleuch. Smith also was exceptional in being educated after Glasgow University at Oxford (which he compared unfavourably to the Scottish universities).

Among the literati who were ministers of the Church of Scotland the most prominent, and indeed the leader of the moderates in the General Assembly, was William Robertson. He was the son of a minister of Borthwick in Midlothian. He studied in Edinburgh University and himself became a minister in Edinburgh and eventually Principal of the university. He published his *History of Scotland* in 1759 and that of *Charles V* in 1769, but his history of the Americas was not finished before his death. It was Robertson's work (as well as his own) which prompted Hume to say that "this is the historical Age and this the historical Nation", and "the People most distinguish'd for literature in Europe".

Thomas Reid was another son of a minister who became a minister himself. He was Professor of Philosophy in Aberdeen and then succeeded Adam Smith to the chair in Glasgow. He was the leading critic of Hume and the founder of the Common Sense school of philosophy, which was widely influential in Scotland and Europe, especially in France. Adam Ferguson, another minister who became a Professor of Moral Philosophy (at Edinburgh) was an adherent of this school. His *Essay on the History of Civil Society* (1767) was the foundation of sociology as an academic discipline. He was a native Gaelic speaker who served as the chaplain to the Black Watch. It was in his house in Edinburgh that Walter Scott as a schoolboy met Robert Burns.

Henry Home was called to the Bar in 1723 and raised to the Bench as Lord Kames in 1752. He was the most conspicuous example both of Walter Scott's doctrine that a good lawyer had to be a man of all-round learning and of the versatility of the Scottish Enlightenment. The range of his books prompted Voltaire's gibe that if you wanted to know the rules of anything from epic poetry to gardening, you had to go to Edinburgh to learn them. He was one of the hosts of Benjamin Franklin during his visit to Scotland and it was to him that Franklin wrote that the six weeks which he spent there were the time of "the densest Happiness" that he had ever experienced.

William Cullen studied medicine at Edinburgh and set up a practice in Glasgow where he lectured on chemistry in the University, the first such post in Britain. He then held chairs in medicine in Glasgow and Edinburgh, but continued to stress the importance of chemistry as a subject in its own right and one that was useful to agriculture and industry. Joseph Black was one of Cullen's pupils and assistants who succeeded him in both the Glasgow and Edinburgh chairs. Black evolved the theory of latent heat. Together these two men established chemistry as a scientific discipline. James Hutton was another student of medicine (at Edinburgh, Paris and Leiden) who turned to chemistry and agriculture and then to mineralogy and geology. His researches revealed that the earth was immensely older than had been supposed and his book, *A Theory of the Earth* (1785) is the basis of modern geology.

These men of the Scottish Enlightenment shared many characteristics in common. They all had the wide approach of the Democratic Intellect and they all believed that advances in knowledge should be applied to the improvement of industry, agriculture and society generally. Because Scotland is a small country they were mostly in close contact and on terms of friendship. Adam Ferguson was a cousin as well as the biographer of Joseph Black. James Hutton was a friend and dining companion of both Black and Smith. Black was Hume's doctor in his last illness and Smith was his literary executor.

They were clubable, convivial and social. Neil McCallum said "this momentous generation was in constant converse with itself", and that James Watt's workshop was "a kind of academy whither all the notabilities of Glasgow repaired, to discuss the nicest questions in art, science and literature'. You could say the same of the clubs which were an important part of the social and intellectual life of Edinburgh. Hugh Blair devoted one of his sermons, "On the Happiness of a Future State", to life after death. It sounds very much like one of these clubs: "The intercourse we here maintain with one's fellows is a source of our chief enjoyments."

It was a very accessible society. As Amyat, the King's chemist, said in a famous passage: "In Edinburgh, the access of men of parts is not only easy, but their conversation and the communication of their knowledge are at once imparted to intelligent strangers with the utmost liberality". This is one of the reasons why the literati were so influential. Their clubs included landowners, lawyers, merchants and ministers as well as the philosophers and men of letters. New ideas and practical experience were in constant interchange.

They were, by and large, a generation that after the '45 concluded that there was no escape from the Union and that there was little alternative to acceptance of a situation which you could not change. That did not stop Hume, Ferguson and Smith expressing discreetly their agreement with Andrew Fletcher that the independence of a diversity of small nations was more conducive to happiness and progress than their assimilation into large states. John Millar noted that small states tended to have a free constitution, but that large ones were liable to become despotic.

3.7

Who owns Scottish History?

That was the question posed at a debate at the third Scottish Book Town Festival in Wigtown on 22nd September 2000. This was the author's response.

One obvious answer to the question who owns Scottish history is no one, or everyone, which is the same thing. It is open to everyone to read the books, study the evidence and come to his own conclusions. Of course, that is not the whole answer. Few people have the time, inclination and ability to undertake research into the original sources, and no one could do that for the whole course of Scottish history. We therefore all depend, to a greater or lesser extent, on the secondary sources, the accounts written by other people and on the conclusions which they have drawn from the evidence.

The question then resolves itself into the simpler one, who writes the books? It is said that history is written by the winners and that is often true. All we know about the Etruscans or the Picts comes from archaeological evidence, because the history has been written by those who conquered and displaced them. These are, no doubt, extreme cases because even the conquered usually can, sooner or later, state their case. A dominant group, however, often attaches such importance to asserting a particular doctrine that it makes it an article of faith which everyone has to believe. For centuries, in many countries, it was impossible, or at least very dangerous, to deny the fundamental doctrines of Christianity. Until very recently, it was almost equally difficult in this country to question the somewhat absurd institution of monarchy.

To impose your will like this, you need wealth and power, wealth to finance propaganda and power, if need be, to use the army or the police to eliminate your opponents. Propaganda is as old as government. One of the greatest of epic poems, Virgil's *Aeneid*, is propaganda for the greatness of imperial Rome. For centuries the Catholic Church employed the best architects, sculptors and painters in the service of its improbable doctrines. You were liable to be burnt alive, if you dared to question them.

To come nearer to home, the Whig view of English, or so-called British, history, is another example of a doctrine imposed by a dominant group, the wealthy land-owners who controlled first the English and then the British state. This was the doctrine that the Glorious Revolution of 1688 created the most perfect of all constitutions and that English history was uniquely the record of an advance to liberty. Norman Davies in his recent great book *The Isles*, pointed out that there was nothing unique about it. Many European countries, including Scotland, had similar institutions. Even so, he says, English historians "positively crowed with nationalistic self-satisfaction"; they had no doubt that England was unique. Their confidence was so impressive, and the control of the ruling majority over patronage so complete, that even the Scottish universities in the 19th century decided to teach English history instead of our own.

In fact, of course, the liberty so triumphantly celebrated was confined to the very small wealthy minority of the population who were entitled to vote. This began to change very slowly with the Reform Act of 1832, but it was not until about the end of that Century that all men over 21 were allowed to vote and women had to wait some decades longer. As Linda Colley say in her book, *Britons*, "the U.K. remained, right up to the First World War, one of the least democratic countries by the standard of eastern as well as western Europe".

The Whig view of history is a telling example of the way in which a group with control over the means of propaganda can persuade a whole people over a long period of time to believe something which is not true and to believe it with such certainty and passion that anyone who questions is regarded as idiotic or sacrilegious.

Another example, or more precisely an aspect of the Whig view, is the completely false, but firmly established, version of the causes, nature and effect of the Union of 1707 between Scotland and England. It is described as a sensible and rational arrangement freely negotiated between the two countries. In fact it was imposed by the English Government, who refused even to discuss an alternative, at a time when Scotland was in a very weak position. We had been weakened by a whole succession of events. Since 1603 we had been nominally independent, but the members of the Scottish Government and all State appointments were made in theory by the King, but in fact by the English Government. Our foreign trade had been ruined by England's wars on the continent and we had been impoverished by the religious and civil wars of the 17th century. Towards the end of that century, there had been a series of disastrously bad harvests which had caused wide-spread starvation. The country had been weakened still more by the failure of the Darien scheme, partly because of English opposition.

Still, how does one explain that the Parliament of a country, which had resisted an English take-over against very heavy odds for 300 years, suddenly vote to abolish, or at least suspend, itself? This is particularly surprising because the same Parliament with the same membership had firmly asserted Scottish independence by voting for the Act of Security in 1703 and again, when royal assent had been refused, in 1704. Also the Parliament was left in no doubt that the Union was vastly unpopular in Scotland. Sir John Clerk of Penicuik, one of the leading figures in the Government which accepted the Union, spent many years writing a history of the affair in the decent obscurity of Latin. He seems to have had a guilty conscience, but he admitted in his history that no more than 1% of the people were in favour. Certainly bribery on a scale which was remarkable even in that age played a part, as Robert Biurns reminds us:

> We're bought and sold for English gold,
> Such a parcel of rogues in a nation.

Clerk, however, tells us that the real reason for the majority vote was that the alternative was an English invasion and the imposition of worse terms.

This was an uncomfortable situation. The Scots did not like to think of their parliamentarians, even if they were thoroughly unrepresentative, yielding tamely to bribery and intimidation. The English, if they thought about it at all, did not want to admit that they acted as an unscrupulous bully. So, with relief, Lord Macaulay and the Scottish historian John Hill Burton, in correspondence between themselves in the 1850s hit on the happy idea that the Union had been a bargain in which Scotland had exchanged independence for access to the English and colonial markets.

This was not a very creditable explanation perhaps; but it sounds rational and it was plausible because it was arguable in the 1850s that Scotland had eventually benefitted from access to these markets. But if this was an effect, it was certainly not a motive for a majority in the Scottish Parliament in 1707. The trading community, represented by the Convention of Royal Burghs, petitioned against the Union, as did many others, and one of the reasons they gave was that the imposition of English customs and excise duties would be harmful to Scottish trade. They were right; it took the Scottish economy about 60 years to recover from the immediate effects of the Union. The English spy and propagandist, Daniel Defoe, in his *Tour Through The Whole Island of Great Britain* of 1724-26 admitted that the economy had been depressed by the Union. Sir John Clerk, although he had been responsible for questions of trade in the Scottish Government, never claimed that it had been a motive for supporting the Union. Adam Smith in a letter of 1760 said that the immediate effect of the Union was "to hurt the interest of every single order of men in the country", even the merchants. "No wonder", he added, "if at that time all orders of men conspired in cursing a measure so hurtful to their immediate interest". I do not suppose that any parliament in the world has ever voted for a measure harmful to their interests, even if there is a possibility that it might eventually be beneficial.

In spite of all of this, the view concocted by Macaulay and Burton survived almost without challenge for about 100 years. It is still widely believed and a respectable academic historian not long ago wrote a pamphlet in support of it. I think that it is a view which still colours the instinctive attitude of many people in Scotland to the Union and to independence even if they are unconscious of the reason. In the heyday of British imperialism in the 19th century there was a strong desire in Scotland to think well of the Union because it was by virtue of it that Scotland was a partner in the Empire and, rightly or wrongly, that was assumed to be desirable. This desire was so strong that any evidence to the contrary was suppressed and ignored.

Let me give a few examples. Lockhart of Carnwath's *Memoirs of the Union* is one of the liveliest and most vivid historical records in our literature and he could speak from first-hand experience because he was a member of the Scottish Parliament from 1703 to 1707 and the only opposition member who attended the talks on the Treaty in London. An edition was brought out by a descendant in 1817, but no other until I persuaded the Association for Scottish Literary Studies to publish one in 1995. Conformist historians have preferred to rely on Defoe's *History of the Union*, although he was known to be an agent of the English Government who was in Scotland only towards the end of the affair. His reliability may be judged from the fact that he made no mention at all of Andrew Fletcher of Saltoun, the most formidable opponent of the Union. Similarly, Walter Scott's *Letters of Malachi Malagrowther*, which is a passionate demand for cultural diversity and an argument against English interference in Scottish affairs, had long been out of print until I edited one for Blackwood's in 1981. When I begun to look into the history of this affair I very soon came across clear evidence that the Duke of Hamilton, who posed as the leader of the opposition in the Scottish Parliament of 1703 to 1707, was in fact in the pay of the English government. I explained this in my book *Andrew Fletcher and the Treaty of Union*. John Gibson, who has written about Scotland in the 18th century told me that his own research confirmed my conclusion and remarked, "how strange that no one has noticed it in nearly 300 years". All the evidence has long been available in published sources. Historians have refused to notice it, because of their Unionist prejudices.

Two more small, but not untypical examples. Hume Brown at the beginning of the last century wrote a history of Scotland which for long was the standard authority and is still useful. He was well aware of the facts about the Union because he edited the letters of the Earl of Seafield, which are an important source. In the appendix to a collection of essays about the Union published in 1914, he gave the text of a letter of 1711 from the Earl of Glasgow, who was in charge of the distribution of £20,000 which had been sent to Scotland to ease the passage of the Union. The letter contains an admission that if the facts had become known at the time, "the Union had certainly broken". This is damning enough, but Hume Brown without any indication that anything has been left out, omits the phrase, "our mob and generality of Scotland being so incensed against the union". This sort of thing continues. Only a few weeks ago, Hugh Milne produced an edition of *The Edinburgh Journals* of James Boswell. In the Introduction, Milne says that Boswell had "occasional reservations" about the Union. This is a gross understatement. Throughout his life, Boswell repeatedly expressed his bitter detestation of the "shameful Union', as he called it, which had "reduced Scotland to a province".

A tactic of the apologists for the Union is to claim the support of anyone likely to influence opinion, such as Robert Burns and Sir Walter Scott. They ignore the fact that Burns throughout his life in his verse and in his letters constantly expressed his strong Scottish feelings and his detestation of the Union. Instead, they triumphantly brandish the few professions of conformity which Burns wrote in self-defence when he was faced with the very serious threat of a Government investigation into his political reliability. Colin Bell has described Scott as a "pragmatic North Briton". Some people go further and claim him as an enthusiast for the Union. Anyone who believes this should read the *Malachi* letters, the *Journal* and above all the chapter on the Union in the *Tales of a Grandfather*, which is almost the only honest account of the affair written in the whole of the 19th Century. It is a passionate denunciation of the "total surrender of their independence, by their false and corrupted statesmen . . . despised by the English and detested by their own country".

The distortions of the views of Burns and Scott is only one example of the misrepresentation of Scottish history and experience in the service of propaganda for a sordid political transaction 300 years ago. A 19th century English historian, Sir John Seeley, said that "history is past politics". It is time that we uncovered the reality of this particular political act.

3.8

The Cultural Deficit

'Sunday Herald', 18th April 1999

An Irish woman, who is training at Moray House in Edinburgh to be a teacher, recently told me about her impressions from visiting Scottish schools. "From the content of the curriculum, you might think you were in England". This applies particularly to history and literature. In private schools, she said, it is even worse because they aim at English 'A' levels, not Scottish Highers. Several academics teaching in Scottish universities have told me that their Scottish students arrive in a state of almost complete ignorance of Scottish history. My own conversations with otherwise well educated people suggest that this ignorance is very wide-spread.

There are several reasons why this is surprising. We have a remarkable history of achievement for many centuries in original ideas, the arts, science and technology. Few, if any, countries of a comparable size have contributed so much to civilisation. In the last 30 years or so Scottish historical scholarship has been a particularly lively branch of our cultural renaissance. More books which throw new light on the Scottish past have appeared since the 60s than ever before. The sales of thse books show that there is a steady demand for them. There is a strong increase in the number of students in the Scottish History departments of the universities. The popularity of the new Museum ot Scotland also shows a hunger for information about our past.

The schools are the weak link. It is still possible to go through them and emerge knowing almost nothing about Scottish history, literature, languages or music. In virtually every other country of the world it is thought natural and essential that the schools should convey a grounding in the history and culture of the country as the basis of understanding of their own society. Not in Scotland. We are still to an extent stuck in the imperial past when our educational objectives were largely influenced by the requirements of the British and Indian civil service examinations. It used to be like this all over the old Empire; but others have seen the error of their ways long before us. Many schools are now giving more attention to Scottish literature, but our history, indeed history of any kind, still has a very inadequate place. Our restored Parliament will begin to make good the democratic deficit from which Scotland has suffered. We still have a very serious cultural deficit in our schools.

Does this matter in the modern world? I have no doubt that it does. If people leave school with no knowledge of the past of their country, they cannot understand the present. Worse than that, they are left with the impression that they are citizens of a backwater where nothing of any consequence has ever happened or is likely to happen. This is a recipe for producing the inferiority complex or even self hate which many people have detected in Scotland. There is quite often evidence of this sad state of mind in the letter pages of our newspapers.

The dangers of this cultural deficit have been widely recognised. The foundation of the Saltire Society was one response to it as long ago as 1936 and much has improved since then. A particualarly encouraging development was the decision of the Scottish Consultative Council on the Curriculum in 1996 to set up a Scottish Culture Review Group to study the problem and make recommendations. Under the direction of Robbie Robertson they undertook an extensive consultation involving more than 400 responses from teachers and others involved in education. In May 1997 they held a conference in Moray House called, optimistically as it turned out, "The Stert O a New Sang'. There they presented evidence that there was a strong desire throughout Scotland for more attention in the schools to Scottish culture and especially to Scottish history. Their full report was eagerly awaited.

But what happened? In June 1998 the SCCC suddenly announced that the publication of the Report was to be delayed. It was generally believed, and it has not been denied, that this was due to Labour Party anxiety (on the model of the Sean Connery knighthood) to avoid anything that might give encouragement to the SNP. Then in February this year they produced an extraordinary document. This summarised the original Report in 9 pages and preceeded it with 19 pages of almost unreadable cliché. The intention of this seemed to be to suggest that a so-called "broader view" of culture as "a way of thinking and feeling about the possibilities of a better life" should take precedence over Scottish culture in what it calls the "narrow sense". It was transparently an attempt to confuse the issue and produce an excuse for no action at all.

All education everywhere is presumably concerned with possibilities of a better life, but the clear problem in Scottish education is the Scottish cultural deficit. This has been a disgrace for decades. In the new Scotland which is emerging it is intolerable. The Scottish Parliament will have to give urgent attention to it.

3.9

The Rediscovery of Scottish History

Marinell Ash was an American who, in her sadly short life, adopted Scotland and became passionately interested in our history. One thing in particular troubled her and she made it the subject of the only book which she had time to write, *The Strange Death of Scottish History*. What had happened to the study of our history in the 19th century? It had a very good start. Not only did we have several centuries of historical writing, but in the early 1800s we were pioneers in the scientific study of the historical evidence. Much of the inspiration for this came from Sir Walter Scott. So far from the romantic of popular imagination, he was an enthusiast for the discovery, publication and study of written records. He encouraged his friend, Patrick Fraser Tytler, to write his *History of Scotland*, which as Ash says was "the first history in the English language based on personal research in the primary sources".

After such a start, why did the Scottish Universities largely disregard Scottish history in the course of the 19th century and replace it with so-called British history, which was the history of England with an occasional scornful glance over the shoulder at Scotland? The answer, of course, is that this was part of the gradual surrender of the Scottish universities to English influence which George Davie described in his great book, *The Democratic Intellect*.

The irony is that when Ash published her book in 1980, the revival of Scottish historical studies was already well under way. This might be dated from 1965, when Geoffrey Barrow's monumental work on Robert Bruce was first published. In the 30 odd years since then, more important books of innovative scholarship on Scottish history have been published than in the previous 100. As a glance at the bookshps will confirm, Scottish historical studies are now very much alive. The opening of the Museum of Scotland will give them a new impulse. It is true that the schools still lag behind the universities, but they must eventually follow.

There is still the occasional attempt, usually emanating from Oxford University, to throw Scottish history back into the dustbin. There was a notable example of this recently in an Edinburgh newspaper by Niall Ferguson who would have us believe that "Scottish history is bunk". He told us that all Scottish politicians are "embarrassed by Scottish history, as if it suits none of them to bring up the past". This is the reverse of the usual complaint that we are too obsessed with the past and are always talking about Wallace and Bruce, Mary, the Covenanters, the Union, the Jacobites, the Clearances and so forth. The SNP, after all, has annual commemorations of Bannockburn, of Wallace and even of Alexander III. The Saltire Society does the same every year for Andrew Fletcher of Saltoun. For the SNP and like-minded people this is entirely natural because Scotland established a national identity, which we believe requires expression through independence, in consequence of our history of many centuries of independent development.

Also it is a history of which we are right to be proud. The distinguished English historian. J. A. Froude, said: "no nation in Europe can look with more just pride on their past than the Scots". There are two reasons for this. The first is the truly heroic resistance for 300 years against the repeated attacks of a larger and more powerful neighbour. The other is our remarkable record of achievement, out of all proportion to our size, in the arts and sciences. We have also been very innovative in political ideas, especially over national freedom and the sovereignty of the people. As Ted Cowan remarked recently on Radio Scotland, the Declaration of Arbroath is at the foundation of modern constitutional thought, preceeding the French Revolution and American Independence by some 400 years. Andrew Fletcher in the 18th century advocated both Scottish independence and European integration. Ferguson's denigration of Scottish history seems to be intended as an argument for the Union; but the examples he quotes point in the opposite direction. James Boswell was a life-long opponent of the Union, despite his fondness for the flesh-pots of London. Indeed, one of the reasons why he was drawn to London was his conviction that the Union had ruined Scotland. Sir Walter Scott's *Letters of Malachi Malagrowther* was the first manifesto of modern Scottish nationalism. John Buchan said in a speech in the House of Commons that he believed that every Scot should be a Scottish nationalist. Linda Colley said that "Great Britain was an invented nation superimposed, if only for a while, onto much older alignments and loyalties".

What are we are supposed to conclude from the fact which Ferguson mentions that the mortality rate for Scottish soldiers in the first World War (26 per cent) was more than double the British average (12 per cent). Does he think that this was a sign of enthusiasm for the Union? It looks to me more like a proof of exploitation.

But is Ferguson saying something serious behind the flippancy of his approach? I think that he is making three points: firstly that Scotland was better off as a partner in the Empire than it would have been outside it; secondly that Scotland has been so changed by the Union that our history before it is simply irrelevant; thirdly, that many Scots in the past embraced the Union enthusiastically and some still believe that they benefit from it.

Ferguson is right to describe himself as an anachronism because this complex of opinions was widely held in the 19th century when the Empire was at its height. As Michael Lynch says in his *Scotland: A New History* the Scots then embraced not the Union but the Empire. It provided an outlet for Scottish exports and many opportunities for careers as soldiers, administrators, teachers, doctors and all the rest of it. Many Scots felt pride in it as a philanthropic venture which spread civilisation and Christianity and was compensation for the loss of control over our own affairs and for the neglect of Scotland itself.

Now that the Empire has long disappeared what have been the consequences of our part in it? Ferguson suggests that we should compare ourselves to the Danes or the Czechs. Well the Czechs are still reovering from their submersion in the Soviet Empire; but the condition of Denmark and of the other small independent northern European countries compares very favourably with our own. That seems to me to suggest that Scotland would now be in a happier condition if the Union had not involved us in the imperial adventure.

Then how true is it that Scottish history before 1707 is irrelevant, or in Ferguson's word (following Henry Ford) bunk? In the middle of the 19th century, when Scottish cultural self-confidence was at a low ebb, the English cultural historian, H. T. Buckle, undertook a detailed study of Scottish and English mental attitudes. His conclusion was that they were as different as if they had never had any influence on each other. Since then, of course, Scotland for the last hundred years has experienced a sustained cultural revival which has consolidated our distinctiveness.

Why have we remained so different in spite of the Union? I think that there are several reasons for this and most of them are historical. In the first place, the characteristics of both the Scots and the English were already firmly established in the centuries before 1707. The English attacks had obliged the Scots to look for allies in the rest of Europe. This meant that Scotland, unlike England, had developed in close association with European thought and practice. Then the Reformation took a very different form in Scotland. The Church of Scotland with its emphasis on equality, education, effort and self-control has had profound effects on the Scottish character which survive even in the largely secular society of today. The Union abolished the Scottish Parliament, but left almost everything else untouched, including the law, the Church and the schools and universities. All of these had far more influence on our lives and ideas than any Parliament, at least until very recent times. Lindsay Paterson in his book, *The Autonomy of Modern Scotland* concluded that Scotland has continued to enjoy more real autonomy than many nominally independent countries. Also, of course, our literature, painting and music have both expressed and helped to form our identity.

Finally, Ferguson says in effect that he is a Unionist because he has "benefited immensely" from the Union by going to an English university, working in England and marrying an Englishwoman. It does not seem to strike him that he could do all of these things even after Scotland becomes independent. In spite of the wild scare stories of Labour ministers, no one is proposing to rebuild Hadrian's Wall. Both Scotland and England will still be members of the European Union, within which people can move, go to universities, take jobs and marry as they please. Indeed after independence our relations with England will be even more co-operative and friendly because the frustrations and resentments which result from subordination will be removed.

The case for independence has nothing to do with hostility to England or its institutions. It is simply that we would prefer to do things in our own way. Equally, I should hope that the case for the Union need not involve an attempt to dismiss our remarkable history as something of no importance.

Cultural Campaigns

4.1

The Saltire Society at 60

'The Scotsman', 22nd April 1996

The Saltire Society was founded in Glasgow on the 22nd April 1936. Where does it stand sixty years later, what has it achieved and what has it still to do?

The Society grew out of a conversation between George Malcolm Thomson, a journalist, and Andrew Dewar Gibb, Professor of Scots Law at Glasgow University. Both had written books about the deplorable state of Scotland at that time. The economy was in drastic decline and the culture of the country seemed to be at its last gasp. Edwin Muir in *Scottish Journey* (1935), another of these death-bed reports, said that Scotland was a nation that was being lost to history. "Scotland is gradually being emptied of its population, its spirit, its wealth, industry, art, intellect, and innate character." Thomson and Gibb decided that something should be done about it and the Saltire Society was the result.

From the begining the Society set itself an ambitious target. It was defined by John Oliver as "remaking a nation". The aim was "to restore the country to its proper place as a creative force in European civilisation." National self-confidence had to be revived on the basis of an awareness of what Scotland had achieved in the past and could do again.

The Society has taken an interest in all aspects of the cultural, intellectual and social life of the country. It has campaigned against the neglect of Scottish history, languages and literature in the schools, for autonomy for Scottish broadcasting, for a national theatre. High standards in design and construction of housing and civil engineering have been encouraged by Saltire awards. The Scottish Book of the Year award sponsored by *The Scotsman*, has recognised established writers such as Sorley Maclean, Norman

McCaig, Edwin Morgan and George Douglas Brown, but also the first books of Alastair Gray and A. L. Kennedy. Recitals of Scottish music and poetry, particularly during the Edinburgh Festival, have introduced many people to a tradition of which they were unaware. Brian McMaster, the Director of the Edinburgh Festival, for instance has said that he first heard early Scottish music at a Saltire performance.

Perhaps the most influential of the Society's activities has been the publication of books. At a time when most Scottish literature was virtually unknown and hardly any texts were in print, it started the systematic publication of cheap editions of important Scottish writers of all periods. This has had far reaching consequences. Scottish literature is no longer ignored by our schools and universities and is enthusiastically studied by universities in North America, France, Germany, Italy and Japan.

There is no doubt that there has been a remarkable revival in our cultural self-confidence and performance since the 1930s. In a book published in 1980 Maurice Lindsay said that "the vastly improved state" of all aspects of Scottish culture was "a measure of the success of the Saltire Society's pioneering efforts." Of course, no one would claim that this achievement is due to the Society alone. Many other organisations and innumerable individuals have made essential contributions. When G. M. Thomson said in his book, *Caledonia*, in 1927 that Scotland no longer had a literature, he had not noticed that Hugh MacDiarmid had already published his early lyrics and *A Drunk Man Looks at the Thistle*. He was a one-man renaissance in himself.

Many of the initiatives of the Society have been taken up and carried forward by more specialised organisations, such as the Association for Scottish Literary Studies. The Saltire Society launched the idea of a joint think-tank between cultural organisations, the Advisory Council for the Arts in Scotland. That, in turn, gave rise to the Campaign for a National Theatre. This is an entirely healthy development. We need diversity. Our national revival cannot be left to any one group of people, however talented and well intentioned.

But that does not mean that we no longer need the Saltire Society. It is the one organisation which covers the whole field, independently of government, and which can take bold, and if necessary controversial, initiatives. One which is current is the commissioning of the sculptor, Sandy Stoddart, to erect a powerful bronze statue of David Hume in the High Street of Edinburgh. This is likely to become a new and inspiring symbol of Edinburgh and Scotland. It would not have happened without the Saltire Society.

Much still has to be achieved. For example, the neglect of Scottish history in our schools is still a national disgrace. The Saltire book, *Why Scottish History Matters*, was a good start, but we need a really vigorous campaign. Has Scotland produced a sufficiently bold and imaginative scheme to put some of the Millennium and Lottery money to good use? The Society could call a conference of organisations interested in a major project. One possibility is the restoration of Linlithgow Palace, the finest Renaissance building in Scotland, as a base for the training and performance of traditional music in all its forms.

The Saltire Society is a unique institution. Anyone can join, help to share its policy and take a full part in its affairs. In fact, as Nigel Tranter once remarked, if more people joined, Scotland would be a better place. On the other hand, it performs functions, particularly in its awards, which in other countries are the responsibility of the state. The absence of our own government has made this necessary. Similarly the National Library and the Scottish National Portrait Gallery (which the Saltire Society helped to save) were founded as a result of private action.

No doubt the Society will change to meet changing conditions; but the commercially driven pressures towards world-wide conformity is likely to give it an important role for at least the next sixty years.

4. 2

The First Ten Years of AdCAS

The introduction to 'A Selection of AdCAS Papers, 1981 to 1991'.

AdCAS is the Advisory Council for the Arts in Scotland

This selection of AdCAS documents is published in June 1991 to mark the 10th anniversary of the formal launch of the organisation and to provide a convenient work of reference for its future activities.

In fact, the origins of the organisation go back more than ten years to a conference which the Saltire Society held in St. Andrews from 16th to 18th September 1977. This was at a time when it was confidently expected that Scotland was about to recover through the Scotland Act a measure of control over its own affairs through an elected Assembly. In this atmosphere of confidence there was a great deal of planning and discussion, about the new opportunities which this offered and about the policies of all kinds which the new Scottish Government should follow. The Saltire Conference was a contribution to this debate with the particular purpose of discussing policies towards the arts and cultural and intellectual matters generally. Although I was working abroad at the time, I was able to attend the Conference and write a paper for it. This proposed that the Saltire Society should consult organisations of all kinds that were concerned with, or interested in, the arts to see if they would be prepared to form a joint body to evolve ideas on cultural policy and press for their achievement. A resolution to this effect was adopted.

Accordingly, a Saltire Society committee, with Professor John MacQueen as Convener and A. C. Davis as Secretary, drew up a list of about 180 organisations, statutory, professional and voluntary. Professor Kenneth Alexander (as he then was) sent them a questionnaire to invite their views and ask if they would be interested in attending a Conference to set up some form of joint organisation. 82 organisations responded favourably. They were invited to a Conference in Edinburgh on 17th February 1979, which approved a Manifesto for the Arts in Scotland. Among other points, this called for the establishment of an Advisory Council.

Shortly after this, the atmosphere changed radically with the Referendum of March 1979 and the subsequent election of a Conservative Government which repealed the Scotland Act. Even so, Professor MacQueen's committee carried on with their preparations and requested an interview with the Secretary of State. Representatives of the Saltire Society and the Chairman and Director of the Scottish Arts Council were received by Mr Alex Fletcher, Minister for Industry and Education, on 14th December 1979. He declined Government participation in the proposed Advisory Council, but said that the Government "would recognise the value of its advice". A National Conference to set up the new organisation was held in Saltire House in Edinburgh on 13th June 1981 with Sir Kenneth Alexander in the Chair. Representatives of 72 organisations took part. They approved the Terms of Reference of the new organisation, elected its first Executive Council and agreed that a Conference should be held every three years.

The first ten years of AdCAS have therefore been conducted against quite a different background from the one which we had all assumed during the preparatory phase from 1977 to 1979. Instead of a new Scottish Government, which would be likely to share our assumptions and, understand our aspirations, we were faced with a Conservative adminstration which took a very different point of view. For the whole of the decade, majority Scottish opinion and the Government opposed one another across a gulf of mutual distrust and hostility. In these circumstances, there was little hope of progress on our more ambitious projects, such as a National Theatre and autonomy for broadcasting and the Scottish Arts Council and the formation of a body to promote cultural exchange with other countries. These will probably have to wait for a change of Government.

On the other hand, there has been real progress towards other objectives. In the early years of AdCAS we devoted much effort to achieving the publication of paperback editions of important Scottish books. With the help of the Scottish Arts Council and through the agency of a number of publishing firms, this is now flourishing. There has been a marked improvement in the position of Gaelic (although not yet Scots) broadcasting on television, and this with Government financial assistance. The Edinburgh Festival under Frank Dunlop acquired more Scottish, as well as a more widely international, character. There is now a general recognition that Scottish arts in all aspects, as opposed to arts in Scotland, are in a flourishing state. A body like AdCAS can do no more than encourage a favourable climate of policy and attitude, and draw attention to obstacles and hinderances. This is an ancillary, but a useful, function.

For some years, our major effort has gone into campaigning for a National Theatre because we believe that there is an urgent need for it and that nothing would do more to reinvigorate the whole cultural life of the country. This has been an aspiration in Scotland for about 70 years, but when it is eventually achieved, the Conference which AdCAS held on 30th May 1987 will probably be seen as a decisive turning point. This was probably the most representative meeting ever held of people involved in the theatre in Scotland or concerned with it. After a full, impressive and eloquent debate, a Resolution was passed unanimously which recognised that there was a pressing need for a Scottish National Theatre Company. As Sir Alan Peacock, the Chairman of the Scottish Arts Council, wrote after the Conference: "Anyone concerned with the Arts in Scotland could hardly fail to be impressed by the support shown for a National Theatre".

Since the Conference in 1987 we have had working parties on the proposal for a National Theatre which have produced two reports. The publication of the first of these on 30th November 1987 coincided with the dissolution of the Scottish Theatre Company because of inadequate financial support. This was a serious setback but a further report, taking account of the new situation, was published in 1990 and presented at a further Conference. Work continues.

A. C. Davis and I have been involved in the work of AdCAS from the beginning. After more than ten years we feel that its time that we took a less active role. We have put this compilation of documents together in the hope that it may be of use to our successors.

Note

AdCAS continued until the Scottish Parliament was restored in 1999. It was then decided that the Parliament itself, and the multiplicity of lobbying bodies, meant that it was no longer necessary, but that the Saltire Society would call special conferences as the need arose.

4.3

Edinburgh International Festival

Letter to Tom Morgan, Lord Provost of Edinburgh, 15th October 1982

Dear Lord Provost,

At the Edinburgh International Festival Conference on *The State of the Arts* on 3rd September 1982, one of the speakers was Mr Sergio Romano of the Italian Ministry of Foreign Affairs. One of the points which he made was that a festival of the arts can only have real significance if it has deep roots in the place where it is held.

We believe that this is a very valid point and one which has disturbed many people in Scotland from the early years of the Edinburgh Festival. There has been little dispute that the Festival has performed a valuable function in bringing productions of the highest quality from other countries to Scotland. There is much less confidence that the contribution invited from Scotland itself has been sufficiently sustained or adequately representative. We consider that the Scottish contribution has been unsystematic and sporadic and has tended to diminish in recent years.

We accept, of course, that it is of the first importance that the Festival should continue to aim at the highest international standards, but we also believe that it is essential that there should always be an adequate representation of the best which Scotland has to offer. There are several reasons for this. Without it, as Mr Romano suggested, the Festival will increasingly tend to be seen as an artificial manifestation transplanted from the outside, lacking both roots and a distinctive character of its own. We lose the opportunity which the Festival offers of stimulating the arts in Scotland by inviting comparison with international standards before an international audience. We deprive the foreign visitor of an opportunity to see and hear something Scottish which he is unlikely to encounter elsewhere.

It is true, of course, that events on the Fringe have compensated to some extent for the absence of an adequate Scottish contribution to the official programme. But this is not a satisfactory answer. By its nature, the Fringe is undiscriminating and includes performances at all levels of attainment from the highest to the lowest. The visitor is liable to take as representative something which fall far short of the best that is available. Omission from the official programme implies that Scotland can not offer anything worthy of it.

In fact, Scotland has a great deal to offer. It is arguable that the most original contribution which, the Edinburgh Festival ever made to any of the arts, as opposed to merely importing something which already existed, was the revival after four centuries of David Lyndsay's *Ane Satyre of the Thrie Estaitis.* (There is a good deal to be said for festivals having an element of continuity, like *Everyman* at Salzburg, as well as novelty. Revivals of this play every few years would offer such a continuity.) That is only one example. There is a very substantial body of work for the Scottish theatre in this century in the plays of Bridie, Reid, Kemp, MacLellan and others. The contemporary theatre is very much alive. The Festival could repeat its success with the *Thrie Estaitis* and exercise a creative function both by commissioning new plays and by searching out existing, but neglected, material. There is no shortage of acting and directing talent. It certainly costs less to use a Scottish Company than to bring one in from outside.

In opera, the Festival might consider the encouragement of Scottish Opera to look at the possibility of a series over a number of years of some of the operas based on the works of Walter Scott. The authority on this subject, Jerome Mitchell, has suggested three among those which are well worthy of revival. These are, Boieldieu's *La Dame Blanche*, Carl Loewe's *Emmy* and *Le Revanant* by José Melchore Gomis.

Musically, the distinctive Scottish achievement is in the field of folk music, which is unsurpassed by any other country. There is a wealth of material in folk song, music for the pipes, fiddle and clarsach, and no shortage of skilled performers. We suggest that recitals of this kind in St Cecilia's Hall should form part of the programme every year. Poetry should also form part of these recitals, on the model of Tom Fleming's reading of MacDiarmid's *A Drunk Man Looks at the Thistle* some years ago. The poetry of Robert Henryson and William Dunbar, for example, would lend itself admirably to this. Other examples are recent readings by Edith MacArthur of the Border Ballads and the recitals which the Saltire Society has given on the Fringe during every Festival since the beginning.

The Scottish Arts Council have already launched a series of exhibitions by contemporary Scottish painters. We suggest that these should be supplemented by a series of the work of Scottish painters of the past such as Raeburn, Wilkie, MacTaggart and Gillies.

We are not suggesting anything very drastic, expensive or difficult, merely that every Festival should have a Scottish element, which might be no more than one play, one exhibition and a few recitals in St Cecilia's Hall.

There is another important point. From, time to time, the Festival has organised symposia or discussions such as *The State of the Arts* and the Writer's Conference in 1980. Invariably these conferences have given the impression that they have been held in Edinburgh only geographically. The Chairman and the majority of British members of the panels have been imported from London. Their contributions have been directed for the most part to English, and not Scottish, conditions. This is clearly inappropriate in Edinburgh, with its great literary, philosophical and scientific traditions and before an audience which is predominently Scottish. An inevitable consequence is that the discussion from the floor has been unnecessarily distracted by protests against this English bias. We suggest that events of this kind should be seen as an opportunity for a direct dialogue between Scotland and the rest of the world, not as something largely transported from London. There should be a Scottish chairman and an adequate, not merely a token, Scottish representation on the panel.

We consider that the damaging and limiting impression that the Edinburgh International Festival has no real roots in the country where it is held is largely a consequence of the fact that it is organised from a London office. This imposes its own form of parochialism, which is seen most obviously in the conferences discussed in the previous paragraph. There is a tendency for the Festival to be out of touch with developments in Scotland and to be unduly influenced by current London fashion. We know that this is a point which has often been discussed in the past, and that the present Director has a strong preference for operating from London. We do not propose that the present arrangement should now be disturbed, although we suggest that the Director should have a Scottish assistant or advisor in close touch with artistic developments in Scotland. We do urge that, when the time comes for the appointment of a successor, the new Director should be resident in Scotland and operate from an Edinburgh office.

We are convinced that these proposals offer a basis not only for the Festival to cultivate genuine roots and distictive character, but also to offer the visitor an experience which he cannot find elsewhere and, perhaps most important of all, to stimulate the arts in Scotland itself.

We are sending copies of this letter to Mr John Drummond, and to Mr Gerald Elliot, the Chairman of the Scottish Arts Council,

Your sincerely,

P. H. Scott,
Chairman
AdCAS

4. 4

An Open Letter to the Anglocrats

'Scotland on Sunday', 13th November 1988

Chris Bauer in his article, 'The Incomers', in 'Scotland on Sunday' on 6th November 1988 coined the word Anglocracy to describe the Englishmen (they are all men) who have captured almost all the top jobs in the Scottish cultural establishment. P. H. Scott, the Convener of AdCAS which began to look into this problem more than a year ago, addressed an open letter to the Englishmen who play such an important part in the life of Scotland.

Dear Anglocrats,

Congratulations and thanks for speaking so frankly in your interviews with Chris Bauer. This whole subject was taboo for too long. Open discussion is much better for all of us than embarassed silence on one side and unexpressed resentment on the other.

Let me say at once that there is nothing personal in all of this. I have the pleasure of knowing many of you and am well aware of the worth-while jobs which you are doing in Scotland. Take Frank Dunlop, for example. He has put fresh life and vigour into the Edinburgh Festival and has also greatly increased its Scottish content. He is ahead of many Scots in realising that the cultural life of Scotland will not be satisfactory until it "creates a truly top-class National Theatre which owes its allegiance to Scotland and is funded on the same level as comparable institutions the world over".

What then is all the fuss about? I notice that most of you in your statements agree about two things. First, you agree that Scotland has a distinct cultural identity, in Tim Clifford's words, "the strongest, proudest and most clear-cut" in the United Kingdom. Second, you do not see why we think that this is under threat or understand, as Richard Mantle said, "what people think they are losing by not having a Scot in this job".

I suggest that it is a question of degree. None of us would worry about having a few Englishmen in some top jobs, although it would be better if some were women and some came from other parts of the world. What worries us is the fact that there has been a virtually complete English take-over in many aspects of our national life, including especially the top jobs in the arts. Can this really be healthy in a country with a long and valuable cultural tradition of its own? Would any other country stand for it? To be honest, it seems to us that many Incomers who take up jobs in Scotland, where they are supposed to defend or represent part of our cultural tradition, know very little about it when they arrive here.

There are, I think, several very serious disadvantages in this situation. It creates a colonial atmosphere with all that implies in the breeding of an inferiority complex, alienation, irresponsibility and a sense of helplessness. We do not, at present, have political control of our own affairs. What are we to feel when we lose control also of the cultural life which is supposed to be a distinctive expression of our identity?

What are we to do about it? Some time ago AdCAS (which is a think-tank representing a wide range of organisations involved in the cultural life of Scotland) made three proposals:

1. Vacancies for jobs of this kind should be advertised in the Scottish press.

2. A sound knowledge of the Scottish background, aspirations and conditions should be included among the essential requirements for the post.

3. A conscious effort should be made to recruit a suitable Scottish candidate.

Most people would assume that these things already happen as a matter of course, but the strange fact is that they do not. Would you agree to adopt them in your own organisation and press for them to apply to the appointment of your successor when that time comes?

Yours sincerely,

Paul H. Scott
Convener
AdCAS

4.5

The BBC: the Anglosaxophone

'The Herald', 6th April 1993

In response to the Government White Paper, *The Future of the BBC*, the organisation itself has produced its own glossy booklet, *Extending Choice*, a title which betrays an anxiety to align themselves with Conservative dogma. In it they achieve the unlikely feat of displaying an even more centralist and London knows best attitude than the Government does in its recent publications. I have been comparing the documents with increasing incredulity.

Let us look first at the paper, *Scotland in the Union*, in which the Government gives us the results, such as they are, of its "stock-taking" exercise. The first 9 chapters set out proposals for some tinkering with the existing machinery, but the 10th and final chapter comes closer to an acceptance of the reality of Scotland. It acknowledges that a more concerted recognition of Scotland's status as a nation is necessary and that the Scots "want their Scottishness to be recognised, understood and respected". It assures us that the Government will not hesitate "to create, when appropriate, new bodies to take account of the distinctive Scottish identity". We have yet to see the Government acting in full accordance with these principles, but the fact that they have been stated so clearly is significant.

Of course, a self-respecting nation, as the Government has now accepted that we are, wants above all the right to accept responsibility for its own government. The Government are misguided enough to deny that to us, but they seem to have accepted the need for cultural, if not yet political, self-determination. The transfer to Scotland of reponsibility for university funding and the Scottish Arts Council are steps in that direction. We have already most of the institutions of a distinctive culture, apart from the all important exception of a Parliament. The "new bodies", in the Government's phrase, which are still lacking are a National Theatre and a genuinely autonomous corporation for public service broadcasting. Towards the first of these, the Scottish Arts Council have announced a feasibility study. The revision of the charter of the BBC, which expires in 1996, offers an opportunity for a new approach to broadcasting in Scotland.

J. M. Reid, in a book published as long ago as 1959[1], said that the position of broadcasting in Scotland was anomalous. "When regular broadcasting began in 1922, Scottish self-confidence was at its lowest ebb. It is impossible to believe that at any other time, a people who had long had most other cultural media in their own hands — Church, schools, newspapers — would have accepted a monoply in a new form of communication over which they had no sort of control". The distinguished historian, Geoffrey Barrow, has said that the failure to establish a Scottish public service broadcasting was "the most serious cultural disaster which Scotland had suffered in this century". For decades, many individuals and organisations, such as the SNP, the Saltire Society and the Advisory Council for the Arts in Scotland, have been campaigning for autonomy in broadcasting.

In its White Paper, *The Future of the BBC*, the Government has responded to this demand. It says (p. 37): "The special needs and interests of Scotland, Wales and Northern Ireland will need to be reflected in any new organisational structure for the BBC. The BBC services in the three countries could be given a larger measure of autonomy . . . It is essential that there should be sufficient radio and television programmes for each country, which reflect its culture, needs and interests".

The BBC, I am sorry to say, have ignored this clear lead. There is no mention of autonomy for the three countries in the whole of their document of 88 pages. On the contrary, the recent establishment of a Resources, Engineering and Services Directorate under direct London control is a serious curtailment of the limited freedom which BBC Scotland already enjoys. It is true, of course, that the BBC paper makes a gesture towards what they choose to call regional broadcasting. It tells us (p. 47) that "the BBC is the *British* Broadcasting Corporation, not the *London* Broadcasting Corporation. It should remain in touch with the views and priorities of its audience thoughout the UK . . . It should reflect . . . the regional and cultural diversity which so enriches Britain".

Apart from a few passages like these, the paper uses language throughout which shows that the authors do not understand the question at issue. Where the Government speaks of the "three countries", the BBC speaks constantly of one nation, Britain or the UK, as if it were one homogeneous unit, and not an artificial construction in decline and with a very uncertain future. They declare in fact that they act, and propose to continue to act, as a propagandist for a controversial view of Britain which a large part of the Scottish population do not accept. They even speak repeatedly of "British culture" in the singular, although not one but several cultures are involved. The matter is further complicated by the almost universal practice in England of using British and English as interchangeable terms. The confusion is very obvious at one point in the paper where they refer to "national institutions like Test Match Special".

I admire many things about the BBC and I think BBC Scotland does a remarkable job on very restricted resources. London control, however, has distinct disadvantages. It has an attitude of metropolitan arrogance. Asa Briggs, the historian of British broadcasting, says, it assumes that the best talent resides in London and that "local culture" is inferior to the "universal culture" of the metropolis. It also keeps an unfair proportion of the funds raised in Scotland from the sale of licences. In 1990-91 the audience in Scotland paid over £110 million. Less that half of this, £51 .5 million, came back to finance programme making in Scotland.

Market research by the independent television companies has shown that the Scottish audience wants more Scottish programmes. An autonomous, Scottish Broadcasting Corporation, with the £110 million could meet that demand. This would mean more jobs for broadcasters and technicians in Scotland, enhanced self-confidence and self-expression, more patronage of the arts, entertainment suited to the Scottish taste and more analysis of Scottish events. Of course, we should buy some programmes from England and other countries, but the choice would be ours. I think that they would be unlikely to include coverage of the test matches or the Oxford-Cambridge boat race.

No doubt we shall be told that a small country like Scotland cannot afford to run its own broadcasting. All the small, independent countries in Europe, comparable to Scotland in size and other respects, manage perfectly well. Switzerland even maintains separate full-time services in three languages and part-time in a fourth.

The BBC proposals fail to come to terms with our need to stand on our own feet in this vital matter. The decision, of course, rests with the Government. It will be a test of the sincerity of chapter 10 of their paper on the Union.

Reference

1. J. M. Reid, *Scotland: Past and Present* (Oxford, 1939), p. 167

4.6

How the Scottish National Portrait Gallery was Saved

'Scottish Affairs', No. 10, Winter 1995

In 1991 and 1992 there was an intermittent debate in the Scottish press about the news that the Trustees of the National Galleries were considering plans for a new National Gallery of Scottish Art on the grounds that their collections had outgrown their exhibition space. At first, discussion focussed on the general concept. Was it desirable for the major part of the Scottish collection in the National Gallery and the Gallery of Modern Art to be removed from their international context and isolated in a separate building? This would mean a violent break from the established idea of the National Gallery that it should aim at showing the development of the Scottish school against a background of examples from other important schools. Scottish painting has always been intimately related to the painting of the rest of Europe with constant influences in both directions. It would therefore be very difficult to find any artistic or academic justification for its isolation. This was the general conclusion reached in the debate in the press between artists and art historians. In Duncan Macmillan's telling phrase, a National Gallery without the Scottish collection would be a National Gallery of nowhere.

The objection to isolation could to some extent be met if the new Gallery was within a few minutes walk or bus ride. Glasgow, however, launched a determined bid to secure the new Gallery and for many months the Trustees seemed deliberately to encourage a guessing game, Edinburgh or Glasgow, as though that were the only issue. From then onwards much of the press and media focused on that one simple point, to the general confusion of the public.

In the course of 1992 a rumour started to circulate that the new plans would involve the closure of the Scottish National Portrait Gallery. I heard the rumours but, like many people, I found them impossible to believe. The SNPG is, in the words of the late Marquess of Bute, "one of Scotlands major cultural institutions". It is distinct from an art gallery because its purpose is to illustrate Scottish history. The focus of interest is on the subjects of the portraits, not on the painters. It was gifted to the Scottish people for this purpose by a former proprietor of *The Scotsman* over a hundred years ago. Since then it has become not only one of the most successful galleries of its kind in the world, but an expression of Scottish identity. As subsequent events were to show, it also enjoys the deep affection and respect of a great many people in all parts of Scotland. Apart from all of that, the building (which is a masterpiece of the Gothic revival) was in the final phase of a restoration which had spread over 10 years and cost more than £10 million. The space available for portraits was about to double because of the transfer of the Museum of Antiquities to the new Museum of Scotland in Chambers Street. In view of all these circumstances, could any sane person seriously propose that the SNPG should be closed and its collections included in a gallery which had a completely different purpose?

This happy state of innocence was shattered in January 1993. Nigel McIsaac wrote to me (and to the Saltire Society and the Scottish Arts Club) to draw attention to an article by Timothy Clifford, the Director of the National Galleries. This was in the Winter, 1992, issue of *The Art Quarterly* of the National Art Collection Fund. One sentence in it was clear confirmation that the rumours were right after all: "We do, however, have to remember that it is intended that the Scottish Gallery of Art and History subsumes all existing material in the Scottish National Portrait Gallery".

We discussed this alarming development in the Advisory Council for the Arts in Scotland (AdCAS) early in January. They approved a letter which I sent on 12th January 1992 to Angus Grossart, the Chairman of the Trustees with copies to the press.

This pointed out that the SNPG had been a personal gift to the nation for a specific purpose and questioned whether any one had the right to dispose of its assets for any other purpose. Such an action would be "an act of cultural barbarism" and would destroy one of the most valuable and interesting of our Scottish institutions. We asked for an assurance that "whatever steps are taken over a gallery of Scottish art, the SNPG will be maintained intact". This letter was prominently reported in *The Scotsman*, *The Herald*, and *Scotland on Sunday*.

Since no assurance was forthcoming, AdCAS arranged a joint protest in April 1993 against the proposal with the support of the Saltire Society, the Cockburn Association, the Scottish History Society, the Association for Scottish Literary Studies, the Heritage Society of Scotland and the Scottish Centre of International PEN. The Scottish Arts Club made a strong protest on similar lines. This was again widely reported, but it was evidently still difficult for people to believe that there was a real prospect that the Portrait Gallery would be closed. A correspondent wrote to me at the time: "I have tried to persuade myself that the proposal is a kind of bad dream that will fade away and be forgotten".

The dream was encouraged for a few months longer by a stubborn silence on the part of the Trustees, although such powerful voices as Duncan Macmillan, Basil Skinner, Duncan Hall and Geoffrey Barrow affirmed their support for the Portrait Gallery. At an AdCAS Conference in October 1993 Colin Bell said that in his experience the great majority who had any interest in artistic matters in Scotland were utterly opposed to any suggestion that the SNPG might be absorbed in a Gallery of Scottish Art or in any other way impaired or diminished. On 21st October I wrote again to Angus Grossart to draw his attention to these views and to ask once more for an assurance that the SNPG was safe in the hands of the Trustees. He acknowledged this very politely on the 29th, a month before the Trustees at last made an announcement on the 30th November, St Andrew's Day. This was to the effect that the Trustees had decided to establish a National Gallery of Scottish

Art in a new building in Kelvingrove Park in Glasgow and would for this purpose close the Portrait Gallery and transfer its contents to the new site.

The Trustees had evidently accepted the argument of the Glasgow lobby. As inducements, Glasgow had offered to provide some of their own pictures on permanent loan to a gallery in Glasgow but not in Edinburgh and suggested that they might be able to obtain funding from European sources. The Glasgow lobby argued that Glasgow as a major centre of population deserved a share of the national collection and that a new gallery there would have more visitors. The second of these arguments needs more research. The Trustees seem to have accepted visitor statistics to the Kelvingrove Museum and Art Gallery as evidence, but, since that building serves several purposes, we need to know how many of these visitors look at the pictures. A fine exhibition of the best of Scottish paintings in the McLellan Gallery in Glasgow last year had only 23,000 visitors in 3 months, in spite of a supporting television series presented by Billy Connolly. A similar exhibition in Edinburgh in 1990, with no such television support, had 158,000 visitors in the same period of time.

The campaign by a Glasgow lobby did not mean that Glasgow opinion as a whole was in favour of the proposals of the Trustees. Many influential Glasgow voices, such as Alasdair Gray, Elspeth King and Michael Donnelly, spoke out against the closure of the Portrait Gallery and the idea of a Gallery of Scottish Art. Others were opposed to any new building in Kelvingrove Park. The lobby was led by some leading politicians in the District Council and their Director of Galleries and they were supported by the press and media in Glasgow. They frankly admitted that they were concerned with the prestige and prosperity of Glasgow and not with the aesthetic objections to the proposals themselves. A dialogue of the deaf became inevitable.

Few events in recent Scottish history have produced such a passionate reaction. The Glasgow lobby saw it with satisfaction as another successful bid, like the National Orchestra or Opera or

Ballet companies, the Garden Festival and the City of Culture to snatch a prize from Edinburgh. The headline in *The Herald* was "Pessimism turns to picture of joy" and beneath it Keith Bruce said that the success was "all the sweeter because victory over Edinburgh's bid was so unexpected". *The Scotsman* congratulated Glasgow on "good marketing, native cunning and sheer bravado" (a barbed congratulation, perhaps); but said it was 'the wrong decision, taken for the wrong reasons . . . (it) runs against all the rationale which governs the great collections of other capital cities".

Apart from the Glasgow lobby, the fury and indignation (and these words are not too strong) aroused by the Trustees' announcement had almost nothing to do with simplistic east-west rivalry. The main issue after as before the announcement, was the threat to the Portrait Gallery. It has always had a warm place in my affections and I was dismayed by the idea that it might be closed. I had not realised that so many people felt in exactly the same way. Perhaps it is because it is such an embodiment of the Scottish identity that an attack on it is an attack on our identity itself. Letters of protest dominated the correspondence columns of *The Scotsman* for weeks and the Saltire Society received more letters on this subject than on any other in its entire history. People of all kinds joined in this protest, including two Conservative Ministers, Malcolm Rifkind and Lord James Douglas Hamilton, and such prominent people as the Countess of Rosebery (a former Trustee of the National Galleries), Ludovic Kennedy and Sir Steven Runciman.

In response, I called a meeting in the Saltire Society of the organisations who had joined in the original AdCAS protest. We formed a 'Save the Portrait Gallery Committee', although we knew that the wider issue of the well-being of the National Galleries as a whole was at stake. Basil Skinner (a former Assistant Keeper of the SNPG), Duncan Macmillan (the leading authority on the history of Scottish Art), Lady Rosebery, and Shand Hutchison (the President of the Scottish Arts Club) have been members of the Committee from the beginning. We decided to call a public meeting on the 18th January 1994 to discuss the whole issue and invited the trustees to take part. They declined to appear, but Timothy Clifford and Julian Spalding (Director of the Glasgow Museums and Galleries) agreed to present the case for the proposals. Basil Skinner, Duncan Macmillan, George Rosie, Alasdair Gray and Lord Perth (who was to open a debate in the House of Lords in the following week) were also to speak, and I was to take the chair.

At first, we had supposed that the Talbot Rice Gallery in Edinburgh University would be large enough to hold the meeting, but as the evidence of the level of public concern grew, we gratefully accepted the offer of the Governors of the Edinburgh College of Art of a large lecture theatre with arrangements to transmit the proceedings to any overflow in the corridors and central hall. In fact, well over a thousand people came on a cold and wet winter evening. They were probably the most remarkable crowd ever to assemble for a demonstration in Edinburgh. They were remarkable both for their diversity — earls and law lords rubbed shoulders with civil servants, businessmen, painters, students and people of all descriptions — but also for their demeanour. They listened politely to Clifford and Spalding but their firm determination to preserve the Portrait Gallery was never in doubt. Eric Robinson of Scottish Arts Lobby Voice (SALVO) was the only speaker from the floor who suggested that it was a question of east-west rivalry and the meeting bristled with disapproval. The atmosphere was electric. You felt that no one could resist such a formidable expression of public resolve. A resolution was passed unanimously calling on the Secretary of State to reject the proposals and on the Trustees either to re-open the question on the basis of public consultation or to resign.

After the public meeting I wrote on 24th January on behalf of the Saltire Committee to the Secretary of State for Scotland and to the Trustees to say that the discussions both in the press and at the meeting suggested that there would be general approval for a solution on the following lines:

- The Scottish National Portrait Gallery would remain in its present site and might expand into the part of the Findlay building at present occupied by the Antiquities, the York building and the Scottish Equitable building. This would enable it to develop its role as an historical archive by including more pictures recording aspects of Scottish life and topography.

- The National Gallery of Scotland and the Scottish National Gallery of Modern Art would continue to follow the policy of exhibiting the "full range and diversity of the Scottish School" (to quote one of the pamphlets published on 30th November) along with outstanding examples of the schools of other countries.

- The National Galleries would explore means of circulating parts of the collections to municipal and other galleries throughout Scotland.

- A new Gallery of Art, Architecture and Design would be established in the old Sheriff Court in Glasgow. This would concentrate on the Glasgow School, but would include examples from other parts of Scotland and from other countries. This would help to solve the problem of the large proportion of the Glasgow collection which is at present in storage.

- The restoration of the Royal Scottish Academy building is now urgent and must therefore have priority. The future use of this building is vital to the whole question. The rights of the RSA in this matter should be confirmed.

In the debate in the House of Lords on 26th January 1994 most of the speakers defended the Portrait Gallery. Lord Fraser replied for the Government. He confirmed (as we had argued from the start) that the proposals of the Trustees required the approval of the Secretary of State for Scotland and that a change in the use of the Portrait Gallery would require the agreement of both Houses of

Parliament. This statement was, of course, a direct repudiation of the Trustees' announcement of 30th November which was couched in language which suggested a final and binding decision.

On 9th February the Trustees issued a statement which seemed to be an attempt to save face and at the same time admit defeat over the Portrait Gallery: "The trustees remain committed to the policy of building a National Gallery of Scottish Art in Glasgow. They are now conducting a further detailed appraisal to consider how, consistent with that objective, the Scottish National Portrait Gallery can be maintained within its present building". This statement was, in fact, self-contradictory because the proposal of 30th November depended on the closure of the Portrait Gallery both as a source of pictures and of the running costs for the new gallery. In one of the four pamphlets which the Trustees issued at the same time, they said that the SNPG "is envisaged as the engine of the new National Gallery". They could not have both.

The original proposals of the Trustees had now been wounded beyond all hope of recovery. It remained for Ian Lang to deliver the coup de grâce. This he did with surgical precision on 9th May. Having regard to the views of the "art professionals, the wider art community and the general public" he was not prepared to support the proposals of the Trustees for a gallery of Scottish art and history or to approve the transfer of the collection from the SNPG building. On the other hand, he was prepared to fund a new £ 1.4m, picture store in Edinburgh and give priority to expenditure on the RSA and SNPG buildings. He would be prepared to look at a proposal for a new gallery, provided that "wide and open consultations by the Trustees" showed that the proposal "commands broad public support".

Ian Lang had therefore publicly rejected the proposals of the Trustees (appointed by himself) and broadly accepted the arguments of the public protest articulated and expressed by the Saltire Committee. This is a rare concession by a Government which is notorious for its indifference to public pressure. Why did they act differently in this case? In the first place, the proposals of the

Trustees were ill-conceived and it was tactically unwise of them to present them as a fait accompli. They had miscalculated the attitude of the public to the Portrait Gallery. The strength of the opposition was overwhelming not only because it was so effectively argued but because it was supported both by the leading authorities on the subject and by prominent supporters (and even members) of the government itself. Even so, I think that a blow has been struck for the principle of open government and against the secretive power of a nominated quango. We pressed for consultation from the start and now the quango has been openly instructed to undertake it.

As I write, the Trustees have said that they are about to make new proposals, but this time in the form of options for "wide and open consultation".

4.7

Some Portraits by Raeburn

'Sunday Times Scotland', 27th July 1997

R. L. Stevenson wrote an essay, 'Some Portraits by Raeburn', about an exhibition that was held in what we now call the Royal Scottish Academy just over a century ago. There have, of course, been many Raeburn exhibitions since then; but, surprisingly, the one which opens in the same rooms on 1st August is the first major exhibition of his work since 1956.

Stevenson tells a story about a lady who came back to Edinburgh after an absence of 60 years. She was sad to find none of her old friends, but she went to the Raeburn exhibition and there they all were. Raeburn was a prolific painter of portraits in Edinburgh from about 1787, when he came back from two years study in Rome, until his death in 1823. Stevenson was close enough to the age of Raeburn to be able to say that his subjects "are not yet ancestors, they are still relations." It was, he said, "a complete act of the human drawing room comedy: Lords and ladies, soldiers and doctors, hanging judges and heretical divines, a whole generation of good society". For some 40 years Raeburn painted pretty well everyone in Edinburgh who had any claim to fame or fortune, and many visiting lairds and others as well.

Walking into a room full of Raeburns, as you can in this exhibition, is like walking into one of these drawing rooms. Raeburn conveys character so powerfully that it is like meeting the living men and women. Meeting them, moreover, on terms of unembarrassed and unguarded frankness and familiarity. As Stevenson says, all the people in the portraits give the impression that they are quite unconscious that they are sitting for a picture. Duncan Macmillan in his book, *Scottish Art*, suggests that this is because Raeburn was a good conversationalist who shared the interests of his sitters. He was clearly at ease with them as they were with him.

It is therefore not surprising that that the lady in Stevenson's essay felt that she was meeting old friends, the kenspeckle figures of the Edinburgh of her youth. Even if she did not know the individuals, she would recognise the familiar cast of features. There are Scottish, and even I think Edinburgh, faces which you can see both in Raeburn's portraits and on the streets of Edinburgh every day. I have noticed this when you come across a Raeburn in a gallery in some distant place, as has happened to me in Ottawa, Paris and Budapest (for no important gallery is complete without one). Your eye is caught by something which is familiar both in the style of the painter and the features of the subject.

Raeburn's ease with his subjects is matched by his command of his medium. He was a painter of accomplished skill and fluency. His portraits are works of beauty in themselves, even if the subjects are not always handsome. He has range and variety. He can be the supreme painter of masculine power and authority, as with *Lord Newton*, but also of feminine grace and delicacy, as with *Isabella McLeod*. He can convey a relationship as clearly as the individual characters in his conversation pieces such as *Sir John and Lady Clerk of Penicuik*. The dress of his subjects may be lightly suggested or displayed in splendid detail as it is in *MacDonell of Glengarry*. He can surprise us with the incongruity, but also the grace, of *The Reverend Robert Walker skating on Duddingston Loch*.

If the features of Raeburn's sitters are familiar, there is an atmosphere and style about them which is strikingly different from the present age. Stevenson noticed it: "Some disparaging thoughts upon our own generation could hardly fail to present themselves". For Raeburn's lifetime (1756-1823) embraced the great ages of the Edinburgh of the Enlightenment and of Walter Scott. He was too late to paint David Hume (who died in 1776), but he painted Scott several times and one of these paintings is among the best known of Scottish icons. This was a time when Edinburgh was first of all at the forefront of innovative ideas in philosophy, science and technology and then at the heart of a literary movement which had a profound influence on the literatures of the rest of Europe and of north America. Both of these movements were concerned with human personality and human society. As Duncan MacMillan has persuasively argued there is a close connection between this philosophy and literature and Raeburn's own response to character.

Raeburn's lifetime also coincided with the building of the New Town of Edinburgh to which David Daiches has applied Carl Becker's phrase, "the heavenly city of the eighteenth century philosophers". He describes it as "ordered, elegant, rational, optimistic". The same adjectives apply to Raeburn and his sitters. They radiate a self-confidence based on a conviction that they belonged to this elegant and rational world. New Town Edinburgh is an environment which flatters its inhabitants because it is so obviously based on these qualities and created for the exercise of them. Raeburn's portraits also flatter us because they similarly assume that we belong to a place and a people that are capable of reason, elegance and optimism.

If Stevenson in about 1880 doubted if his age could measure up to this challenge, we are in an even sorrier state. We are still recovering from the effects of two world wars, innumerable horrors, waves of economic depression. We are confronted with the current problems of drugs, crime, destruction of the environment and global commercial vulgarity. Who today can look at the world with the calm self-assurance of Raeburn's Lord Newton?

That is why the timing of this Raeburn exhibition is so apposite. The works of Raeburn are one of our great national treasures, but they are also a challenge. They are a powerful reminder of what we have achieved in the past and can do again. This is what Scotland needs as we are about to enter a new age of increased responsibility and increased opportunity. We should look to Raeburn and the whole range of his self-confident subjects as an inspiration for the future.

4.8

A Stage for Scotland

'The Herald' Essay, 27th May 1995

A Scottish National Theatre has been a cherished aspiration for most of the present century. Our leading dramatists, directors and actors have campaigned for it, such people as Tyrone Guthrie, James Bridie, Duncan Macrae, Robert McLellen, Tom Fleming, Edith Macarthur, Gerda Stevenson, Bill Bryden, Hector Macmillan, Donald Campbell, Peter Brook, Kenny Ireland. Several times we have been very close to it with the Scottish National Players, the Glasgow Citizens, the Lyceum and the Gateway in Edinburgh and, most recently, the Scottish Theatre Company. In May 1987 a conference was called by the Advisory Council for the Arts in Scotland (AdCAS). This was widely representative of the theatre community in Scotland and it resolved unanimously that there was a pressing need for a Scottish National Theatre. It launched a campaign which still continues.

This campaign has enlisted substantial support, particularly of Scottish Equity, which represents the acting profession. In 1991 the Scottish Arts Council (SAC) began a detailed enquiry into the future of the arts in Scotland. The findings were summarised in a report by Joyce McMillan, *Arts for a New Century*, which recognised that "the growing confidence in Scotland's indigenous culture is reflected in a strong campaign for a Scottish National Theatre". In response the SAC set up a feasability study by the consultants, Bonnar Keenlyside, of which I shall say more later. Their report was accepted in principle by SAC last December. They announced that they would "now undertake further work to establish the practicability of a Scottish National Theatre initiative."

So far, nothing has been heard ot this "further work", but clearly the time for action has arrived after years of discussion and hope.

During the last General Election campaign arts spokesmen for all four of the main parties in public meetings in Edinburgh and Glasgow committed themselves to a Scottish National Theatre. More recently, the Lord Provosts of both cities have pledged their support.

There are many reasons why so many people are anxious to achieve a National Theatre for Scotland. Joyce McMillan referred to one of them in her report: "the case . . . rests on the contention that it is absurd for Scotland, which has little indigenous tradition in ballet and opera, to support major national companies in these areas, while having no National Theatre to protect and express our much richer inheritance of Scots drama and theatrical tradition".

This in a very fair point. We are delighted to have Scottish Opera and Scottish Ballet, but it has to be admitted that there is very little which is Scottish about them, apart from the geographical location and the names. This could, and I think , should, change. There are, after all, a few Scottish operas and we have composers capable of writing more. There are many others which have Scottish affinities, such as the great number derived from the Waverley novels. The ballet could draw on our own vigorous dance tradition, as Covent Garden did in *Donald of the Burthens* many years ago. Unfortunately neither company has so far shown much interest in aspiring to even an element of Scottishness. This is a pity because diversity is better than uniformity and originality than imitation.

In drama the position is quite different. During most of the 19th century there was in practice a thriving national theatre, based mostly on adaptation of Scott's novels. In this century hundreds of plays have been written, but usually they were given a few performances and never heard of again. Many of them are well worth reviving, as the National Theatre campaign demonstrated in a very successful series of readings in the Festival Theatre in Edinburgh last year. There is also a Scottish style of acting which has very deep roots as you can see in any production of David Lyndsay's *Ane Satyre of the Thrie Estaites.* What we do not have is a company committed as a principle, but not exclusive, objective to the developent of this repertoire and tradition, both in revivals and in new work. John Linklater rightly said in an article in this newspaper on 9th August 1993 that the systematic neglect of our heritage of plays is a national disgrace.

Scottish drama today is very much alive. It would be very easy to draw up a list of recent productions which delight, illuminate and linger in the mind. But this is another reason why we need a National Theatre, and not why we should rest contented with what we have. The productions in our theatres are hampered by severe financial restraint. They can afford only small casts and short rehearsal time. If we are to see, and let the rest of the world see, the best that our theatre is capable of producing, we need a national company which can give to our best plays the resources which they need.

There is another even stronger, if less obvious, reason. It was well expressed at the AdCAS conference in 1987 by David Daiches, our most distinguished critic and historian of literature.

> Without a National Theatre the arts tend to fall apart. To focus Scottish literary culture, to redefine it, to develop its relations with other cultures and to enable its languages and the literary imagination to be nourished with a new kind of richness, we need a Scottish National Theatre.

At the same conference the directors of the National Theatres of Iceland and Finland (suitable models for a small northern country) agreed with Daiches. Their experience like that of many other countries, has shown that a National Theatre is a great stimulus to artistic self-confidence and expression. A theatre directed to the life, conditions and ideas mainly of its own country is a powerful aid to the understanding and enhancement of that society.

As Hamlet told the players, the function of drama is "to hold, as t'were, the mirror up to nature; to show virtue her own feature, scorn her own image, and the very age and body of the time his form and pressure". We can only do this when we hold the mirror to our own face, in other words, when the plays are mainly directed to our own condition and experience. Of course, we also want to see plays concerned with other places and other times, but it is disorienting to see nothing else. We are familiar with this from our television screens. They are usually occupied with programmes made elsewhere about other people, but they suddenly become relevant when we hear a Scottish voice talking about a Scottish subject.

We also have obligations to the rest of the world. We are contributing nothing, or very little, to the total of human diversity when we merely imitate others. As John Ramsay of Ochtertyre said in one of his letters, "professed copying ever implies inferiority". That is what we are doing when we try to reproduce a production from Broadway or Shaftesbury Avenue. If we are to produce work that the rest of the world will want to see, it has to be distinctive. The intelligent tourist too wants to see something which he is unlikely to see at home.

We are well provided with major cultural institutions, National Galleries, Museums, Library, Opera, Ballet, Orchestras, Universities and so forth. A National Theatre is the only component which is missing, but it is a vital one. Why has it taken so long? In the days before state sponsorship of the arts, there was little prospect of funding. In 1945 when a Scottish sub-committee of the Arts Council of Great Britain began to sponsor the arts, little consideration seems to have been given to the particular conditions of Scotland. It may have seemed more important to those responsible for policy to bring to Scotland art forms which hardly existed there at all than to encourage indigenous creativity. They made little distinction between art in Scotland and Scottish art. The SAC became an autonomous organisation responsible to the Scottish Office in April 1994 and for some time it has been giving more attention to indigenous work, but it is restricted by financial limitations and established commitments.

Under present conditions the SAC does not have the funds to satisfy the present clients, let alone new developments. It has even felt obliged to withdraw the comparatively small amount of revenue funding from the Brunton Theatre, although it has made an outstanding contribution to Scottish drama. All the other companies which depend on SAC funding are naturally anxious about their own future. It is no surprise that some of their directors resist the idea of a National Theatre because they see it as a threat to their own funding.

For the present at least, money from the Lottery offers very little help. Both the allocations through the SAC and through the Millennium Commission are restricted to capital expenditure. The trouble is that for the arts it is not so much new buildings which are needed as funding for the activities inside them.

Is there a way out of this impasse? This is where I should like to refer again to the Bonnar Keenlyside report. This suggested that there were three options: a new touring company or an existing building based company or a fund to finance national productions. In fact, these are not really options, but complementary characteristics, all of which would be required in any satisfactory solution. A National Theatre would certainly have to tour within Scotland and to other countries. But it must also have available to it a theatre building or buildings, for practical purposes, to give it a visible identity and develop audience, loyalty and, above all, so that it can stage its own productions without having to persuade any other organisation to accept them. (The lack of their own theatres undermined both the Scottish National Players and the Scottish Theatre Company) Finally funds would certainly be needed to finance work of the scale and quality that is needed, and this must not be at the expense of the existing companies.

There is a way in which progress towards the objective could be made almost immediately. The SAC already help to fund seven building-based companies. Five of them (Citizens, Dundee, Perth, Pitlochry, Lyceum) are fairly large theatres with a capacity of about 500 or more. Their directors, and perhaps of some of the other companies as well, could co-operate on joint national productions which would tour round the theatres. There have already been tentative moves in this direction. Such productions would need special grants to reduce the usual financial restraints. The group of directors would form the management of the National Theatre and they would gradually establish a team of actors specialising in Scottish drama. In this way the National Theatre would evolve, as it should, out of co-operation between the existing companies and all would benefit in the process.

Where, you might ask, would the money come from? Since these theatres are already funded, the extra required would be much less than the cost of forming a new company from scratch. The Scottish Office could be asked to find it from its budget. In 1949 the government spokesman at the second reading of the Act which established the National Theatre in London said that he hoped that Scotland and Wales would soon follow the English example. Nearly 30 years later the government should accept an obligation to find the money. Then there is the Millennium Fund. At a meeting in the Royal Society of Edinburgh last October the Earl of Dalkeith, the Scottish member of the Commission, held out some hope that exceptions might be made to the rules about capital expenditure. It would be difficult to think of a better celebration in Scotland of the new millennium than the adequate endowment of the National Theatre.

At the conclusion of the AdCAS Conference in 1987 Tom Fleming said "A nation must have a theatre if it is to have a heart. The Scottish style of acting is appreciated throughout the world. Do not be put off by lack of money. The will has to be shown and the rest will happen. There will be a Scottish National Theatre, but what we have to decide is, does it happen when we are all alive? Is it to be in this generation? It will happen one day. I am sure of that".

Now is the time to show the will.

4.9

The Scottish National Theatre: an aspiration whose time has come

'The Herald', Essay, 13th November 1999

In May 1995 I was asked by the editor to write one of the first of these *Herald* essays about the prospects for a Scottish National Theatre. I think that he did this because, like many people and with good reason, he thought that this long-standing aspiration was about to be achieved.

Since about the beginning of the century many of our best dramatists, actors, theatre directors, as well as members of their audiences, have hoped, argued and worked for it. The Scottish National Players, the Citizens in Glasgow, the Gateway and the Lyceum in Edinburgh and the Scottish Theatre Company have at various times come close to achieving it. In the 1980s the conception acquired a new impetus. The Advisory Council for the Arts in Scotland (AdCAS) held a conference in May 1987 which was probably the most widely representative meeting ever held of the Scottish theatre community. It unanimously resolved that there was a pressing need for a Scottish National Theatre and set up a working party to campaign for it. The Chairman at that time of the Scottish Arts Council (SAC), Sir Allan Peacock, who was present and spoke, wrote to me afterwards as the Convener of AdCAS. "No one", he said, "could fail to be impressed by the strength of the demand fof a National Theatre".

During the next few years the campaign published three reports, including a long list of Scottish plays worthy of revival by a National Theatre. Expectations were high when in 1992 the SAC undertook what they called "the most extensive consultation ever undertaken on the arts in Scotland". At the end of it Joyce McMillan was commissioned to set out the conclusions in *The Charter for the Arts in Scotland*. In it she said:

> The growing confidence in Scotland's indigenous cultural inheritance is also reflected in a strong campaign for a Scottish national theatre. The case for a national theatre rests on the contention that it is absurd for Scotland, which has little indigenous tradition in ballet and opera, to support major national companies in these areas, while having no national theatre to protect and express our much richer inheritance of Scots drama and theatrical tradition. It also pointed out that, although Scotland supports a rich network of theatre companies, none of them has a specific remit to perform and develop Scottish repertoire and languages, and commitment to it therefore varies unpredictably as artistic directors come and go.

She then mentioned some reservations which had been expressed, concern over the possible cost of a building and the idea that the existing diversity of theatre companies made a National Theatre unnecesary. (That is like arguing that we do need a National Library because we have public libraries all over the country). But she concludes:

> It is generally agreed, however — even by those who have some reservations about the idea of a national theatre — that there is a need for an institution whose remit it is to preserve, develop and promote the Scottish dramatic repertoire, to encourage Scottish writing for the stage, and to help actors and directors acquire and maintain the language and performance skills necessary for the most effective performance of drama in all forms of Scots and in Gaelic. Such an institution would provide a valuable resource, not only for the theatre itself, but for all forms of dramatic and literary culture in Scotland, including film and television.

This was a very fair summary of the main points which we had been making in the campaign. In response to it the SAC appointed consultants to make a feasability study, which was completed in December 1994. The SAC then issued a statement that "they would undertake further work to establish the practicability of a Scottish

National Theatre initiative". When I wrote my previous essay, therefore, there was every reason to expect that the SAC had a serious intention to meet the need for a National Theatre which their own *Charter for the Arts* had identified. Unfortunately it has now become clear beyond doubt that their intention has been first to delay and then to prevent any move in this direction. In many respects the SAC has done valuable work, but towards the National Theatre they have been hostile, deceitful and manipulative.

Their response to the first consultant's report was to set up a working party which apparently decided that there was a demand for a national theatre fund but not for a company or a new building, or even, in some versions, any building at all. This theory was perhaps not surprising because consultations had been mainly with theatre managements who were given a broad hint that a National Theatre would probably mean a reduction in their own funding, but that without one more money would probably be found for them. The theory ignored the accumulated evidence for years of the strong demand for a National Theatre and it was, in any case, a nonsense. A National Theatre without a company or a building is no National Theatre at all. It needs a company to build up the skills that follow from a group of actors and directors working together. It needs a building to give it visible reality and establish audience loyalty. Both the Scottish National Players and the Scottish Theatre Company were seriously handicapped because they did not have a base. There is no need for a new building because suitable theatres already exist.

On the basis of the working party's theory, the SAC then commissioned yet another consultant's report. They issued a statement in July 1997, that this had shown "no clear consensus", but that they would review the situation in two years time. They announced in May 1999 a fund of £400,000 to support particular productions, but not a word about the National Theatre. They evidently hope that we have all forgotten about it.

Why have the SAC been so hostile in the last few years to the idea of a National Theatre? At one time it was among their objectives and in the 1980s they funded, though inadequately, the Scottish Theatre Company, evidently as a move in this direction. I recently asked the present Chairman, Magnus Linklater, about this. His answer was very frank: "We have enough trouble already with the national companies without having another one around our neck".

This is far more important than the administrative convenience of the SAC. In any case, should they be concerned with the national companies at all? The National Galleries, Museums and Library are the direct responsiblity of the Scottish Executive. It would be consistent and sensible for the national performing companies to be treated in the same way. Certainly, there are good reasons for a buffer between the Government and the claimants in the allocation of funds to avoid any suspicion of political bias; but that does not apply to the national companies.

The SAC has at present far more power than is healthy for an unelected quango. It disposes of lottery funds as well as Government grants for the arts. Many cultural endeavours survive or perish by their decision. They can determine whether, for example, traditional music and dance remain poor relations or, on the Irish model, achieve the status which they deserve. Parliamentary scrutiny can, and should, introduce an element of democratic responsibility. In addition, the removal of the national companies from their remit would curb their monopoly. It would also avoid competition between the national companies and all the others in the division of funds from the same source.

Now that we have a Parliament again, it is obviously the proper forum for major decisions on cultural matters, including the establishment of the National Theatre. This is not a new question for the political parties. For some years I was the Arts spokesman for the SNP and quite often took part in joint public meetings with my equivalents in the other three main parties. One point on which they usually agreed was the need for a National Theatre. Donald Dewar said in a letter in 1991 to one of my predecessors as President of the Saltire Society. Sir Robert Grieve: "there could be no opposition to the concept of a National Theatre". In a recent debate in the Scottish Parliament on a strategy for the arts Brian Monteith for the Conservatives devoted most of his speech to an eloquent plea for a national theatre. It has been part of SNP policy for years. The way seems open to cross-party agreement, which would be very appropriate in such a matter.

One of the functions of a National Theatre would be to tour widely in Scotland and abroad, but where would it have its permanent base? It should obviously be in a major city with a strong theatrical tradition and a large local audience. Tempting as it may be to think of Aberdeen, Dundee, Kirkaldy, Perth or Stirling (all places to which the National Theatre would tour) in practical terms the answer narrows down to Edinburgh or Glasgow and therefore to the Lyceum or the Citizens. In 1990 Joy Hendry and Hector MacMillan on behalf of the National Theatre Campaign visited theatre companies to ask for their views. The Citizens were alone in saying that while they were happy with the idea of a National Theatre, they did not want to be part of it because they had their own agenda. Of course, directors and opinions may change.

In the past, theatre directors have been reduced to an untypical, embarrassed silence when they have been asked where the National Theatre should have its base. It seems that they do not want to offend the other directors or the SAC. Parliament will have to take the decision for them. In the *Sunday Times* of 22nd August Allan Massie had an article, "Time is right to raise the curtain on a Scottish National Theatre", which was a powerful statement of the case. He proposed that the base should be in Edinburgh, not just because it is the capital, but also because the other national companies are based in Glasgow. The Lyceum had been modernised and was well equpped for the purpose. I think he is right. The Lyceum is a handsome theatre, perfect for drama, and on an ideal site.

Donald Dewar in his letter in 1991 mentioned the problem of resources; but the Lyceum solution would not involve vast cost. The building is already publicly owned, by the City of Edinburgh. Running costs on a scale adequate to a National Theatre would be about £1.5 million to £2 million per year. It is essential that this should be new money and that it does not reduce the funds available for other theatre companies.

Virtually every other country in Europe has a National Theatre as one of its most prized institutions. They aim at establishing a repertoire of the best plays of the country to the best possible standard, to stimulate literature and the arts generally, and to contribute to self-awareness and self-understanding. These functions were well expressed at the AdCAS conference in 1987 by the great literary critic and historian, David Daiches:

> To focus Scottish literary culture, to redefine it, to develop its relations with other cultures, and to enable its language and the literary imagination to be nourished with a new kind of richness, we need a Scottish National Theatre.

When the Bill to establish the National Theatre in London was introduced to the House of Commons in 1949 the Government spokesman, Glanville Hall, said that he hoped that Scotland would follow that example. Now, fiftty years later, the Scottish Parliament has an opportunity to crown its first period of office by the achievement at last of this vital aspiration.

4.10

A National Theatre for Scotland

Statement by Paul H. Scott, President of the Saltire Society, in evidence to the Education, Culture and Sport Committee of the Scottish Parliament, 1st December 1999

I am grateful to the Committee for giving me an opportunity to express the views of the Saltire Society on this important question. The Society, along with many other organisations and individuals, has campaigned for a Scottish Parliament and for a National Theatre for more than 60 years. Now that we have the Parliament, the National Theatre is the only vital institution which Scotland still needs.

It is an historical accident that Scotland has national companies for opera and ballet, where we have little claim to distinctive traditions of our own, but not for drama where we have both a substantial body of plays and our own style of performance. Without a national company committed to Scottish drama, new Scottish plays tend to disappear after only a few performances. We need a National Theatre to give the Scottish tradition an impulse and a focus.

Experience in other countries has shown that their national theatres stimulate not only drama, but literature generally and the whole cultural life of the community. They enhance cultural confidence and are an important means of self expression and self understanding.

A Scottish National Theatre company should be based in one of our existing theatre buildings. It would tour in Scotland and abroad and provide an educational resource for our schools and colleges. By training actors and directors, especially in Scottish texts and Scottish speech, it would support the work of other theatres, broadcasting and film. With adequate rehearsal time and a cast large enough for the needs of the play, it would enhance the reputation and attractiveness of drama in Scotland and of Scotland itself internationally.

Scotland has waited a long time for such a theatre. Its achievement now would be a major accomplishment for the new Parliament and an exciting and encouraging start for the new millennium.

4. 11

The Scottish National Theatre: 'an effective starting point'

Letter to 'The Herald', 26th July 2001

Dear Sir,

To all of those who have been campaigning for a Scottish National Theatre for decades it is very good news that the Scottish Arts Council have largely endorsed the plan drawn up by the working group chaired by Donald Smith. All that is needed now is approval of the funding by the Scottish Executive and the way will be open to what James Boyle, the Chairman of the Scottish Arts Council, has called "a brilliant and dynamic" National Theatre.

James Boyle's enthusiasm is particularly welcome because the SAC before he joined it were, paradoxically, determined opponents of the idea. They fought an ingenious and unscrupulous rearguard action ever since the modern phase of the campaign effectively began with the AdCAS conference of 1987. Boyle is also right to stress that the present proposal is only a first step. The Scottish National Theatre, for the time being at least, will have no building and no permanent ensemble of actors. Both are necessary in the longer term. Its two predecessors, the Scottish National Players and the Scottish Theatre Company, were undermined by the lack of their own theatre. A building is necessary for administration and rehearsal, but also for a stage under their own control. In addition it gives a sense of identity, solidity and continuity. There are a number of theatres in Scotland which would be perfectly suitable for the purpose. A nucleus of an ensemble of actors is necessary to produce the benefits which flow from the experience of working together.

I made these points when I gave evidence to the Education, Culture and Sport Committee of the Scottish Parliament. In their Report they said that proposals of the kind which are now going ahead were "an effective starting point". The essential thing is to make a start. After that I think that we can be confident that the Scottish National Theatre will evolve under its own momentum to make a real difference to the cultural life of Scotland.

Yours sincerely,

Paul Henderson Scott

4. 12

The Tragedie O Macbeth

A Foreword to David Purves's rendering into Scots of Shakespeare's play. (Edinburgh, 1992)

Why, it might be asked, translate *Macbeth* into Scots? Surely everyone who understands Scots also understands English. And so why do they need a translation? There are several answers to these questions. Sometimes translations, as of notices in airports and railway stations, are purely to help people unfamiliar with the local language. David Purves, I am sure, had quite different intentions in mind.

In the first place, I think that he was drawn to the idea because *Macbeth* is set mainly in Scotland, the names of the characters and places are Scottish, and the action is related, with much distortion admittedly, to events in Scottish history. It is therefore tempting to fit the language to the place. To use Scots for this purpose is no more historical than the freedom which Shakespeare takes with his sources, because the language of the courts of Duncan and Macbeth was certainly not Scots but Gaelic. Even so, the use of Scots settles the play more comfortably into its setting than the English of Shakespeare, especially when that is spoken in the manner usually adopted by modern Shakespearian actors.

Secondly, like all good translations of poetry, Purves is not aiming at merely reproducing the sense of the original. Poetry, as someone once said, is the element which is left out in such a process. He is creating a new work of art, based on the original, but which has to stand or fall on its own merits. As a man who has used Scots to good effect in his own poetry and plays, he has the skill to face this challenge. The result, I think, is a play, derived from Shakepeare, but fit to be judged as a work on its own terms.

Like any language, Scots has its own character, its own strengths and limitations. It can be powerful, passionate, humorous , tender, earthy, direct, contemptuous, warm, affectionate, fantastic, outrageous, but it does not lend itself to pomposity or affectation. The result is that a familiar text in another language seems to acquire a new directness and reality when rendered into Scots. You have the feeling that you are dealing with real people who may before have been abstractions. William Lorimer's translation of the New Testament hits you precisely with this shock of recognition. This happens to people who have lost, or never had, the ability to speak Scots, but who still react to it on another level of the mind. This translation by David Purves has the same effect.

T. S. Elliot said that translation should be "done in the idiom of our own language and our own time". This is what Purves has done. Shakespeare, of course, writes poetry of incomparable power and beauty, but the passage of time has made some of his text seem diffuse, obscure and verbose. Purves is always, like the Scots tongue itself, direct and to the point. He cuts away the undergrowth to get at the root of the matter and the play gains in pace accordingly. Scots is a language which works well on the stage and I am sure that this version, in the right hands, would have great force and vitality.

Perhaps there is another purpose. At the end of the fifteenth century, Gavin Douglas wrote his translation of the Aeneid, as he said, "in the language of our Scottish nation". It is plain from his first Prologue that one of his purposes was to extend Scots by measuring it against the "copioss fouth or plenitude" of Vergil's Latin. The flood of translations in our own century which followed the example of MacDiarmid had a similar intention. (A selection can be found in the excellent anthology edited by Peter France and Duncan Glen, *European Poetry in Scotland*, EUP, 1989). They are part of a deliberate and necessary effort to restore Scots and Scottish poetry to the mainstream of European thought and literature and enhance its range and status. This version of *Macbeth* is a notable contribution to this endeavour even if we have to wait until we have a national theatre before we see it on a stage.

Note: *On this last point I was wrong. Theatre Alba (Director: Charles Nowosielski), presented the play at Duddingston Kirk as part of the Festival Fringe in 2002.*

4.13

Language and Literature

Paper for Round Table discussion at 60th International PEN Congress, Santiago de Campostela 6th-12th September, 1993

We are all accustomed to classifying literature in national categories. We speak of French or Italian literature or of English, Scottish, Irish or Welsh. Of course, this involves difficulties of definition. What are the defining characteristics, language, place of birth or education, or the conscious or unconscious following of a national tradition? When you begin to think of these things, you may begin to wonder whether classification by nations serves a useful or meaningful purpose, or whether it might be better to think of writers as part of the literature of the world and of nothing else.

The matter is less complicated in countries which have their own language which is not used to any significant extent anywhere else. All languages have their particular strengths and weaknesses and their own accumulation of associations. Each of them embodies the experience of the people who have spoken them over centuries and who have had many things in common in their history, social relationships, beliefs and attitudes, climate, geography, and economy, but which are different from those of other people. Their language has layers of association which reflect these particular circumstances. Partly for this reason, and partly because of its own nature, a language can carry meanings which cannot be expressed in any other language with precisely the same effect and the same resonances in the mind.

Since language is the raw material of literature, it follows, I think, that a literature in any particular language is likely to have characteristics that are special to it. This is most obvious in poetry where the relationship between the words and the meaning and effect is at its most subtle. As is often said, poetry is the element which is lost in translation. A good translation can still be poetry, but it is poetry which has a different impact from the original. Might I draw an example from Scotland, which is the country which I know best? Here the English language has largely, but not entirely, displaced the indigenous languages, Gaelic and Scots, for most purposes in written prose. The two native languages continue to flourish in poetry where they express aspects of feeling and experience which cannot be so well expressed in any other way. As Edwin Muir said of the Border ballads, "they enshrine the very essence of the Scottish spirit, and they could have been written only in the Scottish tongue." [1]

I think therefore that it is clear that the national classification of literatures has an an obvious meaning and usefulness at least when it is applied to countries which have their own language which they do not share with others.

But there are comparatively few countries in that position. Most of us use languages which are shared with other countries which are quite often in distant parts of the world with conditions which are very different. The obvious examples are the English and Spanish languages and both in consequence of the imperial expansion of the people who first used them. The English language is now used all over the world in countries which have been touched at various times by the expansionist habit of the English people. It began in the Middle Ages in Wales, Scotland and Ireland and then spread to every continent in the world. It included the American colonies in what is now the United States, which as the sole remaining superpower has exercised its own powerful influence in the same language. Similarly the once great Empire of Spain has spread the Spanish language over a vast part of the world.

This presents us with a problem. Are we to describe as English or Spanish literature everything written in one of these languages or does that merely confuse the issue? I do not think that there is much doubt about the answer. The literatures of, for example, the

United States, Ireland and Scotland are all obviously so different from that of England that it would be unhelpful to apply the same label to them.

This is not surprising. The language may be more or less the same in London, New York, Dublin or Edinburgh, but many other things are very different. They include historical development, social conditions, climate and geography and all the attitudes, habits and responses which derive from them. It is the shared experience of all these things which make a people conscious of a national identity, and literature both reflects this shared experience and is a constituent part of it. Lines of continuity run through any national literature which are recognisable, even if they are difficult to define. R. L. Stevenson said that even if a Scot speaks English, "he will still have a strong Scots accent of the mind." [2] I am sure that the same is true of the Americans or the Irish or of all the numerous peoples who make use of the English language in diverse parts of the world.

The effect of all the shared circumstances is so strong that it gives a distinctive character to a national literature even in the works of writers who have not made a particular study of the works of their predecessors. In the experience of many submerged nations, national traditions can survive decades or centuries of suppression. The Scottish example shows, and this may be more surprising, that they can even survive when the schools and universities concentrate on a different literary tradition. We are therefore talking about something which is not frail and artificial, but resilient and natural.

The literature of any country has a special appeal and significance for the people of that country. It refers to familiar places and institutions and habits of behaviour and thought. Understanding and the recognition of shared experience are therefore more direct and immediate that they would be to a reader from another background. For this reason, the literature of one's own country in education is the best introduction to the pleasures and significance of literature as a whole.

This does not mean, of course, that we should shut ourselves up, either as writers or readers, in a water-tight box of our own national tradition. We can all benefit from the stimulation, the shock or the example to emulation of other countries, other languages and other literatures. That is, as long as it is left to our own free choice and is not imposed upon us by a large and expansionist neighbour, or by commercial interests with the financial power to dominate the means of communication. These are roads to cultural imperialism, manipulation by the advertisers and ultimately to sterile uniformity.

We need open minds and open borders and the free movement of literatures and ideas, but we also need the diversity of literatures and cultures to give us the widest possible range of interest and interpretation. More than 50 years ago, the poet, T. S. Eliot, wrote:

> It is to the advantage of England that the Welsh should continue to be Welsh, the Scots Scots and the Irish Irish . . . If the other cultures of the British Isles were wholly superseded by English culture, English culture would disappear too. [3]

Eliot was writing only of the British Isles, but what he said of them is true of the whole world. The vitality of culture, which includes literature, in any country is dependent on international diversity. We should all cherish our distinctiveness, both for its own sake and as a contribution to the cultural vitality of the rest of the world.

References

1. Edwin Muir, *Latitudes* (1924)
2. R. L. Stevenson, 'The Foreigner at Home' in *Memories and Portraits* (1887)
3. T. S. Eliot, *Notes Towards the Definition of Culture* (1947)

4.14

International PEN and the language question

'The Herald' Essay, 26th July 1997

My role in International PEN, the organisation of writers, has involved me recently in meetings in Spain and Slovenia. These discussions have revealed the extent to which many other countries share the concerns which have been troubling us in Scotland for most of this century and even longer. Countries confronted with powerful neighbours have always had to struggle to hold on to their identity and languages. In the contemporary world there are new pressures for conformity exercised by the global market and mass media. The diversity of cultures and languages is a condition of civilisation, but the forces opposed to it have never been stronger. In Scotland we have been working out our own solution to these problems. So have many other countries. It is encouraging to find how similar is their response and how many natural friends and allies we have.

The first of the meetings was in Pamplona in Navarre in north west Spain. It was concerned with linguistic rights, the belief that languages, like individuals, have rights which governments and the international community have an obligation to respect. In Scotland we have tended to suppose that we were exceptional in having two languages, Gaelic and Scots, which governments, especially in the past, have systematically ignored and tried to suppress. On the contrary, there is hardly a country in the world where a similar problem does not exist. All of these languages are part of the diversity of human experience. Each of them has distinct qualities and embodies a particular attitude to the human situation. We are all diminished by the loss of an animal or plant species; we lose even more if a language is lost. This threat is now widely understood and organisations all over the world are responding to it.

The involvement of International PEN in this movement goes back to a Congress in Lugano in 1987. For years PEN has been defending writers persecuted by governments because of their opinions. I went to Lugano as one of the Scottish delegates with a resolution which proposed that we should also defend the rights of languages. The Catalan delegation had a similar proposal and we combined them. This combined resolution was passed virtually unanimously with, as far as I can remember, only the English delegation speaking against it and abstaining.

Since then a committee of PEN, largely organised and financed by the Catalans, has kept up the pressure. They have acted together with a research agency, CIEMEN, sponsored by the Catalan Government, and another, Mercator, which works for the European Commission. In June last year they called a conference in Barcelona which was attended by 250 representatives from about 90 countries. With great ceremony and an air of solid achievement the conference approved a Universal Declaration of Linguistic Rights, the culmination of the work of the previous nine years. The representative of UNESCO accepted the document and undertook to begin the process of submitting it to the United Nations as the basis for an inter-governmental agreement similar to the Universal Declaration of Human Rights.

This Barcelona Declaration is a very comprehensive document which provides for the rights of languages in government, the law, education and the media. The fullest panoply of rights apply to what it calls historical language communities which have their own territorial space. I argued at Barcelona, and again at the recent meeting in Pamplona, that this definition was suitable for Catalonia, but not for countries like Scotland where the same territorial space was shared by more than one language with long historical roots. The majority view seems to be that the language of the Declaration is sufficiently flexible to meet difficulties of this kind.

It is not only PEN and its supporting organisations which have been active. The European Commission has established a European Bureau for Lesser Used Languages. In November 1992 the Council of Europe drew up a European Charter for Regional or Minority

Languages. This was much less binding in its terms than the Barcelona Declaration because, it is full of escape clauses such as "as far as this is reasonably possible". Even so, it does recognise that minority languages are "an expression of cultural wealth" and need to be safeguarded by "resolute action". Like the Barcelona Declaration its tendency is to enhance the status and treatment of Gaelic and Scots, which are minority languages within the UK, whatever they might be in Scotland or parts of it.

So far, the UK Government, to its shame, has failed to sign or ratify the European Charter. Even worse, when the Governments were asked to supply information about regional or minority languages in their territory, the UK supplied a rather grudging statement about Gaelic, but made no reference at all to Scots. Perhaps this was only to be expected of a Tory Government, but it is now the responsibility of the Labour Government to make good the deficiency.

The organisations responsible for the Barcelona meeting, with the support of the European Commission and the Government of Navarre, invited 36 people to Pamplona in early May to consider the next step. Apart from some representatives of PEN, like myself, they were either academics who specialise in the subject or officials of UNESCO and the Council of Europe. There was no disagreement about the objective, but a more realistic recognition of the complexities than had been apparent at Barcelona. Xavier Iriondo of the Basque University said that there were more than 6,000 languages in the world, but only 200 of them had official status. States tended to regard the non-official languages as a threat to their unity or even to their ability to survive. For such reasons as these, Andri Isaksson of UNESCO said that they would have to feel the way forward very carefully. It was accepted that some of the more widely spoken languages (and the predominant one is English) have to be used to facilitate international communication; but this was not inconsistent with the defence of lingistic diversity. It was agreed that an explanatory manual should be drawn up to amplify the Declaration.

I always thought that this would be a slow and laborious process and that many governments would resist very stubbornly. Even so,

I do not think that there can be much doubt that there has been a distinct shift of international opinion on this whole subject. There is an increasing demand in very many countries for more equitable treatment of "unofficial" languages such as Gaelic and Scots. We are not alone in recognising their importance.

The meeting in Slovenia was of a different kind, although the underlying theme was similar. For 30 years Slovenian PEN has invited members of other PEN Centres to an annual conference. The purpose is to discuss the international situation, especially in Eastern Europe, as it affects, or is affected by, writers. I had not taken part before, but I should certainly be happy to go again. The discussions were stimulating, the company and hospitality excellent and the place, Bled, one of astounding beauty. Slovenia has been independent only since 1991 and it has a population of 2 million, less than half of ours in Scotland. The pride of the people in their independence, the air of contentment and optimism, the signs of achievement and progress were very obvious. I had the same feeling of admiration and envy that I have felt in Iceland, Ireland and Norway. All small nations which have recently achieved independence are models of what Scotland might be.

In this part of the world, one might expect that the discussions would have been dominated by the troubles of the Balkans. They were not avoided. The Croatian, Mirko Mirkovic, for example, spoke passionately of the "senseless bloodshed", caused by the "scourge of nationalist hatred". Others deplored Serbian writers whom they accused of violating the PEN Charter by publishing direct incitements to violence and killing. The meeting agreed with me that nationalism was a word of many, and even contradictory, meanings and that in such countries as Slovenia and Scotland it was a constructive and liberating force. Mirkovic said that he had not meant to suggest that any country was ever justified in dominating another.

A paper by Boris Novak of Slovenian PEN was a good summary of the central preoccupation of the meeting. The east of Europe had escaped from the domination of communism, but was now subject to a more subtle and less violent threat. This he called "western fundamentalism", pressures exercised by commercialism and "the omnipresent media, banal brainwashing which wipes out cultural differences". The Charter of PEN, he said, was based on a balance between two seemingly conflicting values, respect for the language and cultural identity of any national literature and faith in the universal spirit which unites all literature as a civilising force.

The PEN Charter is the basic statement of the aims of the organisation. It asserts "the principle of unhampered transmission of thought, within each nation and between all nations" and also that "literature, national though it be in origin, knows no frontiers". This combination of national individuality and wide internationalism accords both with our attitude for centuries and with our current aspirations. I suppose that this is the reason why Scottish writers feel so much at home in PEN and why it provides us with international support and good friends and allies.

The ideas expressed by Novak are very close to those in the statement of the major theme, "Identity and Diversity", of this year's PEN Congress. This is being held in Edinburgh and Glasgow from 5th to 11th August in the 70th anniversary year of the foundation of Scottish PEN on the initiative of Hugh MacDiarmid. It will be the largest meeting of its kind ever held in Scotland with some 400 writers from more than 100 countries. A seminar, held in conjuction with UNESCO, will consider the cultural identity of women. There will be literary exhibitions in the City Art Centre in Edinburgh and in the Mitchell Library in Glasgow. Some of the literary sessions will form part of the programme of the Edinburgh Book Festival.

A PEN Congress of this kind is unlikely to happen again in Scotland for at least 50 years. It is an excellent opportunity for us to make Scotland and Scottish literature better known internationally and to extend our acquaintances with writers from other countries. Above all, it is a chance to exchange ideas on the place of Scotland and other nations in the modern world with many thinkers who share many of our problems and aspirations. This 64th PEN Congress will be a further step in the evolution of the cultural alliance which is embodied in the PEN Charter.

4.15

The Future of the Scottish Language

'Scottish Affairs', No 24, Summer 1998

We are very fortunate in Scotland to have no fewer than three languages (or four if you include Latin), all with distinguished literatures, which are part of our national identity. The memorial window to George Buchanan in Greyfriars' Kirk in Edinburgh claims, not unjustly, that Scotland was the final barrier against the Roman Empire, but was also the last refuge of Latin eloquence. Both Gaelic and Scots are rich in song. John Galt said that the Scots had great resources of expression because of the fortunate circumstance of possessing the whole range of the English language as well as their own'[1]. Lord Cockburn was "really sorry for the poor one-tongued Englishman" [2]. That is the right attitude. We should take pleasure and benefit from our linguistic richness and neither apologise for it nor think of it as a problem.

But, particularly with Scots, there are still people who are reduced to embarrassment or inarticulacy because of a complex about language. You can blame the schools, but they have only reflected the attitudes of society. In the past, they have made great efforts to suppress both Gaelic and Scots and implant a uniform English. Their method (apart from, in its time, the tawse) has been to make the bairns ashamed of the language of their parents. The psychological damage which this must have done is horrifying. I say particularly Scots because, unlike Gaelic, it is so close to English, with which it shares a common origin and much common vocabulary, that its opponents believe that they can treat it as simply incorrect English. This is an attitude which betrays an ignorance of linguistic history, but that does not stop them.

Of course, attitudes are changing. Scots has been retreating in daily use under the pressure of radio and television; but it has also been making notable advances both in literature and scholarship. When R. L. Stevenson published *Underwoods* in 1887, he said in the Introduction to his admirable poems in Scots: "The day draws near when this illustrious and malleable tongue shall be quite forgotten". Its no deid yet for a that. As George Bruce says in his poem about the attempted burial of Scots:

> She's jinkit again, the bitch.
> said the man with the spade. [3]

Since Stevenson, Scots poetry has not only persisted vigorously, but has extended its range and reached new heights in the work of Hugh MacDiarmid, William Soutar, Sydney Goodsir Smith, Violet Jacob, Robert Garioch, Alexander Scott, Tom Scott and scores of others up to the present day. There have also been such notable works in prose as Lorimer's translation of the New Testament and the short stories and plays of Robert McLellan.

Scholarly resources have been given a solid base in the ten volumes of the *Scottish National Dictionary* and in the continuing work on the *Dictionary of the Older Scottish Tongue*. The data which they have collected has been used in a whole family of dictionaries, of which the latest is the electronic *Scots School Dictionary*, launched in April. Many books about the language have been published and several of them in the last few months. The most substantial (and most expensive; it costs £150) is *The Edinburgh History of the Scots Language*, edited by Charles Jones and published by Edinburgh University Press. This impressive book shows the width and depth of modern scholarship on the language. There are contributions from academics, not only in Scotland, but in Canada, the United States, Hungary, Finland, Germany and Australia. The Saltire Society has recently published two short books: a revised edition of Derick McClure's *Why Scots Matters* and *A Scots Grammar* by David Purves. The first of these is a succinct and classic account of the nature and history of the language which McClure describes as "a unique national possession, a highly distinctive and expressive tongue which is also the vehicle for a literature of great antiquity, merit and durability". David Purves's Grammar is full of examples of Scots usage which are so well chosen that anyone who lives in Scotland and keeps his or her ears open will recognise with a shock of delight. It is perhaps the first grammar of any language which is a sheer pleasure to read. Purves says that his book is only a modest first step, offered in the spirit that "bannocks is better nor nae breid"; but it is a good start. He has also written a paper for the Scottish Centre for Economic and Social Research, *The Way Forward for the Scots Language*, which proposes a realistic policy to accord Scots the status which it deserves. This will make an excellent brief for the members of the Scottish Parliament.

The most recent of such books is *The Scots Language: its Place in Education*, edited by Liz Niven and Robin Jackson and published by Northern College, Dundee. This brings together 16 papers which look at the language from a variety of points of view. Two of its most eloquent advocates state the reasons for its value and importance, Derick McClure and Billy Kay (whose book, *Scots: The Mither Tongue*, published by Mainstream in 1986, is also indispensable). There are papers by people responsible for relevant institutions: the Scots Language Resource Centre, the Scots Dictionary Association, the Consultative Council on the Curriculum, the Examination Board and the Education Department of the Scottish Office. A number of teachers with experience of teaching Scots give their views. There is a great deal of interest in all of this, but perhaps the most significant sentence in the whole book is in the Foreword by Sam Galbraith M.P., Minister for the Arts in the Scottish Office. He says of Scots: "It is part of our cultural heritage and, if we value that heritage, we need to cherish the language and aim to see it used with respect and sensitivity". This is the most forthcoming statement on the matter which I have seen from a Government minister. Others, such as Donald Dewar and Calum MacDonald, have brushed it aside as no language at all and as a matter of no importance.

An important advance for Scots in the schools, and the point of departure of this book, was the publication by the Scottish

Education Department in 1991 of the *Guidelines on English Language* for the ages 5-14. This emphasised the value of "the language that children bring to school". The papers in the book by teachers suggest that a literal interpretation of this well-intentioned phrase may defeat the object. In the first place, the language which children bring to school may not be Scots at all, but a mixture of scraps of Australian, Brooklyn and Cockney, acquired from television. It is one thing to avoid deriding the mother tongue of the children and so destroying their self-esteem; it is another to go to the opposite extreme and accept that anything goes. Some of our novelists already seem to act on this principle. The end result is likely to do more to destroy Scots than to preserve it.

In his paper, John Hodgart argues that teachers should "jist accept that the 'best' Scots is whit the local weans bring to their ain schuil". Otherwise, "they will come tae feel that 'Scots' is as alien tae them as posh English". Matthew Fitt is against the idea that "the obvious way into Scots is through a few Scots poems and stories . . . Nobody would dream of starting a class off learning German with an anthology of Rilke's poems".

These papers make it very obvious that there are two distinct approaches to Scots in the school. Is the avoidance of damage to self-esteem and self-expression the only objective? Or, in the words of Sam Galbraith, do we want "to cherish the language and see it used with respect and sensitivity"? Part of the difficulty lies in the belief that Scots has so far degenerated into a number of dialects that teaching must be based on one of them. In fact, this is not the case. Scots is no more divided into dialects than most other languages. The language as it is used in most literature and in poetry and song, in particular, has been essentially consistent for centuries. Of course, some words become obsolete and others are created, as in any other living language.

Scots is worth studying because it expresses certain aspects of the Scottish situation and the Scottish character better than any other and because it gives access to a literature of particular value to us for the same reason. It is a precious asset for its own sake because of its qualities. Few other languages, if any, are so rich in words where the very sound conveys the meaning, which is why it is so powerful a medium for poetry and drama. I mean such words as snell, dreich, slaister, splairge, forfochen, sonsy, braw, fushionless. As in learning any language, including English of course, the study requires effort and the conscious expansion of vocabulary. This need not be inconsistent with a sympathetic response to the "language which children bring to school" and to dialectical variations; but the aim should be the expansion, not the restriction, of linguistic resources. We should also cultivate the sheer pleasure of the expressive sound and infinite associations of the language. I think that the aim should be ability to handle at least two of our languages along with some acquaintance, if no more, with the third. Bi- or tri-lingualism is a positive asset in widening the mind and improving the ability to communicate. It is easily acquired by children from the languages spoken around them and it makes it easier to acquire other languages later on. Scots is a useful bridge to several other European languages.

I speak of bilingualism because our schools will, of course, continue to teach English. In consequence of the extent of the British Empire in the past and (as David Hume forecast) of American power in the present, English has become an almost universal means of international communication. The very success of English in this respect also has disadvantages. Since it is the language of mass commercialism, tourism and entertainment, it tends to be reduced to the basic level of the lowest common denominator. The vitality and richness of the vocabulary of Scots can restore some character and colour, some birr and smeddum. Here the affinity of Scots and English is an advantage because they can readily intermingle in varying degrees. Discrimination against unofficial languages to the point where their survival is threatened is very widespread. Scotland is by no means unique in this regard. With some honourable exceptions such as Switzerland, governments tend to be monolingual and opposed to linguistic diversity because that makes life easier for them. All over the world languages are dying. It is now widely recognised that the loss of a language, as with the loss of an animal or plant species, is an impoverishment of all of us. Every language embodies a particular response to human experience which has its own interest and value.

In recent years there has been a strong international response to this problem. The most ambitious is the Universal Declaration of Linguistic Rights which was approved in Barcelona on 6th June 1996 at a meeting of 220 representatives from 90 countries and all five continents. This was the culmination of nine years of preparation in which the Scottish Centre of International PEN was closely involved. It began at a PEN Congress in Lugano in 1987. On behalf of Scottish PEN, I tabled a resolution which proposed that International PEN (which is a world-wide organisation of writers) should extend its activities beyond the defence of the right of free speech to the rights of languages. Although we had not been in consultation in advance, the Catalans had a similar resolution. We combined them and the joint resolution was adopted without opposition and only one or two abstentions which included English PEN.

The Catalans, with the enthusiastic support of their Government, led subsequent developments. They organised a series of international meetings in which not only PEN centres, but organisations and university departments in many countries, were involved and which drafted the Universal Declaration. One of the organisations was UNESCO (the United Nations organisation concerned with education, science and culture), and their representatives at the signature in Barcelona undertook to work for an intergovernmental agreement on similar lines for presentation to the General Assembly of the UN. Since the Declaration calls for a full panoply of rights in administration, justice, education and the media for language communities and lesser but substantial rights for 'language groups', this is likely to be a slow process. Many governments will certainly resist and argue for a text, if there has to be a text at all, which is less precise and demanding.

There is, however, already another intergovernmental Treaty on the subject which applies in Europe and which is much more flexible. This is the European Charter for Regional or Minority Languages approved by the Council of Europe in November 1992. It is a flexible agreement in two senses. First of all, it allows governments on ratification to declare to which languages it applies in their territory. Secondly, they are also free to choose under each heading (administration, justice, education, media and so on) the degree of support along a wide sliding scale. To the shame both of the previous Conservative, and the present Labour, Government, Britain has not yet ratified. According to press reports, this is now contemplated, but only for Scottish and Irish Gaelic (in Northern Ireland) and Welsh. Even this is said to have been delayed in case the Unionists are upset by a reference to Irish Gaelic in Northern Ireland. If Ulster Scots were also included, as it should be, the Government could appear more even handed.

Why has there been no mention of Scots or of its offspring in Ulster? It was the same in 1995 when the Conservative government replied to a request from the Council of Europe for a report about the situation of "regional or minority languages" in each country. Again no mention of Scots. No doubt, British Governments have been relying on a clause in the Charter which says that it does not apply to "dialects of the official language(s)". Scots shares a common origin with English; but it cannot be dismissed as a dialect because of its centuries of separate development, its use for most of that period as the official language of Scotland, its extensive literature and the fact that it is understood or used by a large part of the Scottish people.

This is where Sam Galbraith has an opportunity to prove that he means what he says in the Foreword which I quoted above. The ratification of the Charter and the specification of both Gaelic and Scots need not commit the Government to doing much more for each language than it already does (although I hope that might follow); but mere specification would give both languages the encouragement of the international recognition which they deserve.

Incidentally, many Gaels, as can be seen from quite frequent letters to the press, object to the term, Scots, because they think that it implies that this is the only language of Scotland. I think that we should call it Lallans. That was good enough for Burns and Stevenson and it should be good enough for the rest of us.

The Scottish Parliament will have to evolve a language policy and do far more for Gaelic and Lallans than British Governments have ever done in the past. It would be a helpful, a gracious and a long overdue gesture, if the British Government would now prepare the way by the ratification of the European Charter in respect of both languages.

Postscript

On 4th June, in a written parliamentary answer, the Government announced that they proposed to sign the European Charter and to specify Gaelic under Part III. Scots, they said, would be "covered by Part II". The significance of this is that Part III deals with measures which it is proposed to adopt. Part II is a statement of objectives and principles. There is nothing in the Charter which suggests that it is possible to specify a language under Part II only.

This is certainly progress, especially as far as Gaelic is concerned. For Scots, the Government seems to be trying to avoid commitment, but they are apparently reluctant to say so clearly. How can they justify such radically different treatment of the two languages? Scots, after all, has an even more substantial literature than Gaelic and is understood and spoken by more people.

References

1. Galt, John, Introduction to the short story, *The Seamstress* in, among other editions, *Selected Short Stories of John Galt*, edited by Ian Gordon, (Edinburgh, 1978), p.21.
2. Cockburn, Henry *Memorials of his Time* (Edinburgh, 1872), p274.
3. Bruce, George *Perspectives, Poems 1970-1986* (Aberdeen, 1987), p77.

4.16

Charter for the Scots Language

Drafted for the Scots Language Cross-Party Group of the Scottish Parliament, February 2001

This Charter has been drawn up by the Cross-Party Group of the Scottish Parliament for the Scots Language in co-operation with the Association for Scottish Literary Studies, the Saltire Society, the Scots Language Society, and the Scottish Centre of International PEN. Its purpose is to explain briefly the nature and importance of the Scots language, or Lallans, and to suggest measures which should be taken to enhance its status and extend its use.

1. Scots is a language which shares a common ancestry with English and a good deal of common vocabulary. During centuries of separate development it evolved its own distinctive character, syntax and vocabulary. It became the State language of Scotland, used for all purposes and by the whole population outwith the Gaidhealtachd. Already by the 14th century it had become the vehicle of some of the finest poetry that was being written in Europe at the time and it has continued to be an important literary language ever since. Because of its deep roots in Scottish experience it has a rich vocabulary which relates to Scottish conditions and is the best expression of many aspects of the Scottish character. It is not a debased form of English, but, on the contrary, it is often closer than English to the common origin of the two languages. Nor has it declined into a clanjamfry of mutually unintelligible dialects. Like most languages, including English, there are local variations; but the essential core of the language extends aver the whole country. The Scottish National Dictionary and the Dictionary of the Older Scottish Tongue have established a solid body of scholarship on the vocabulary of Scots and this has been made readily available in

the Concise Scots Dictionary, the Scots Theasaurus and the Scots Schools Dictionary.

2. Because of the removal of the royal court to London in 1603, the use by the kirk of the Authorised Version of the Bible, and the parliamentary Union of 1707, Scots lost its official status and much of its prestige. The basic similarity to English, which has the advantage of helping towards mutual intelligibility, has also contributed to the displacement of Scots by English. Despite this, outwith the Gaidhealtachd, Scots remained as the first language of many people throughout the 20th century. In many places it still is the first language, although the majority also speak English. Children at school were taught to read and write almost exclusively in English; but in the last 100 years there has been a strong revival in the use of Scots for literature, a convincing demonstration of the vigour and expressiveness of the language.

3. In the last fifty years or so, the use of Scots in daily speech has diminished, largely because of the influence of the schools and of broadcasting. Until quite recently most schools have actively discouraged the use of Scots and radio and television have been overwhelmingly in English. This denigration of Scots has had adverse psychological effects. When children are taught that the language they bring from home is wrong and unacceptable, their self-confidence and ability to express themselves is liable to be seriously damaged. Also, if we lose Scots, which is likely to be the consequence if this process continues, we shall lose important aspects of our national character and access to much of our finest literature.

4. The threat to both Gaelic and Scots is part of a world-wide problem. Many languages in all parts of the world are under pressure and their disappearance would be a serious cultural loss. In response to this situation the Scottish and Catalan Centres of International PEN at the PEN Congress in Lugano in 1987 proposed, and it was agreed, that the organisation should take measures to

help languages to survive. An extensive international study was undertaken and this resulted in the drawing up of the Universal Declaration of Linguistic Rights. This was approved by representatives from organisations in more than 90 countries (including Scottish PEN) in Barcelona in June 1996. UNESCO has undertaken to work for an inter-governmental Declaration on similar lines.

5. The Universal Declaration recognises linguistic communities "established historically in a particular territorial space". It considers that all such languages have equal rights which include their official use, the provision of education in them and access to the media. Both Gaelic and Scots are historic languages of Scotland; but the treatment of both, and especially of Scots, in all of these respects falls far short of the requirerments of the Universal Declaration. That is the standard to which we should aspire.

6. Of course, we do not advocate the abandonment of the English language. In the contemporary world, English is a major means of international communication and therefore a valuable asset. We should like to see Gaelic, Scots and English all co-existing in Scotland, and all treated fairly and regarded with equal esteem. (The co-existence of Swiss and German in Switzerland is an encouraging example). A multi-lingualism of this kind is an intellectual asset in itself and it is an aid towards the acquisition of other languages, especially because of the close affinity of Scots with German, Dutch and the Scandinavian languages and the elements of vocabulary derived from Latin and French.

7. The first requirement is to work for the restoration of the social status of Scots so that children and adults are no longer made to feel ashamed of it. They should be encouraged to realise that it is (in the words of Derrick McClure) "a highly distinctive and expressive tongue which is also the vehicle for a literature of great antiquity, merit and durability as well as one of the most exuberant branches of the contemporary literary scene". A great deal of

valuable work in this direction has been done in Scottish schools in the last 30 years or so and this should be welcomed and encouraged.

8. The agencies which can do most to effect this change are those which have in the past done most to denigrate and discourage the use of Scots; that means the schools and the broadcasters. The newspapers, and indeed all of us, can help as well by using Scots whenever possible. A great deal can happen spontaneously without intervention by Parliament or Executive. We call on everyone to participate in a determined effort to enhance the status and the use of Scots.

9. Now that we again have a Scottish Parliament, however, we have an instrument which can and should play a leading role in this campaign. We call for the following measures:

a) The specification by the British Goverment of Scots, in the same way as Gaelic, under part III of the European Charter for Regional and Minority Languages.

b) Measures to improve the teaching of Scots language and literature in the schools. This should begin in the primary schools which should draw on the great wealth in Scots of stories, poems and songs. At secondary level, the subject at present called "English" should be renamed "Languages and Literature". Questions on both languages should be included in all examinations. Classes should also be provided for adults, especially school teachers, who wish to improve their knowledge of Scots.

c) Improved financial support of the Scottish National Dictionary Association and the Scots Language Resource Centre.

d) The establishment of a fund to encourage programmes in Scots on radio and television.

e) The linguistic diversity and literary richness of Scotland are great assets also for cultural tourism. This is an additional reason why the Anglicisation of place names and signs should be resisted.

4.17

The Scottish Parliament and Scottish Culture

Paper for the conference 'The Scottish Parliament: The Consequences', in Dundee University, September 1999. Published in the proceedings, 'Scotland: the Challenge of Devolution', edited by Alex Wright, 2000

The present and how we arrived at it

From one point of view, the restoration of the Scottish Parliament is a very small and timid step forward. Its powers are so limited and so restricted by Westminster that it is weaker than the subordinate parliaments of most federal states. For an ancient sovereign nation, which has never completely lost its identity and autonomy, it could be said to be more of an insult than a compliment. Can we not be trusted to run our own broadcasting to say nothing of taxation and foreign affairs?

On the other hand, although timid, it is a step which changes everything. It is the greatest constitutional change in Scotland since the Treaty of Union which was ratified by the Parliaments of Scotland and England in 1707. The treaty had one essential provision: it abolished the Parliament of Scotland and, in theory, that of England as well. In their place, it created the United Kingdom of Great Britain with one Parliament. The Westminster Parliament, so created, has frequently violated the Treaty of Union, but it has never before abrogated the essential provision. Now that it has done so, many possibilities are open. They include the dissolution of the United Kingdom, a constitutional arrangement which depends on the Treaty. As Donald Dewar said at the formal opening of the restored Scottish Parliament on 1st July 1999, it was "a new stage on a journey begun long ago and which has no end".

The expectancy and optimism which attended the opening of the feeling that Scotland now enters a new era, are therefore not altogether misplaced. There is an obvious risk that disillusionment will quickly follow. That would certainly happen if the Scottish administration were to insist on following in the footsteps of Westminster and to refuse to find Scottish solutions to Scottish problems and introduce radical changes. On the whole, I think that this is unlikely. One advantage of having our own Parliament on our own doorstep is that public disapproval can easily make itself felt. As Mrs Howden in Scott's *The Heart of Midlothian* memorably remarked: "when we had parliament-men o our ain, we could aye peeble them wi stanes when they werena gude bairns". The Parliament is a public forum, for the discussion and resolution of Scottish issues. That is bound to strengthen Scottish democracy and reinforce our sense of identity.

It may not be the dominant idea in the minds of the politicians or of the drafters of their manifestos, but the movement towards Scottish self-government, which has carried us forward to this point, is closely involved in more ways. than one with our national culture. In the first place, the fundamental reason why we want to run our own affairs is because we are conscious of a national character which should be free to develop in accordance with its own nature. We believe that we have our own particular set of attitudes, ideas and values, expressed in our literature, music and art. If that were not so, if we were identical to our neighbours, then there would be no case for a Scottish Parliament.

Secondly, there is a close inter-relationship between cultural and political self-confidence and without that self-confidence, demonstrated convincingly in the Referendum of September 1997, constitutional advance would not have been possible. The poet, Robert Crawford, is quoted in *The Herald* of 4th June 1999: "There is a confidence abroad among Scottish poets. Imaginatively, devolution happened 10 or 20 years ago". I should say that the imaginative change began much longer ago than that. In 1895 Patrick Geddes wrote about a Scottish renaissance, long before Hugh MacDiarmid gave a new impetus to it in the 1920s and 30s. How it is that ideas and passions, generated by poets, painters and composers, are conveyed to people who know nothing of their work is mysterious. Perhaps it is a two-way process. At all events, it is clear from the record that public opinion tends to follow, sooner or later, the lead of the writers and poets.

Thirdly, we need self-government to remedy the cultural, social and psychological damage inflicted on us by the Union. This an aspect which requires some explanation because we have all been brought up to believe that the Union was a wise and benevolent act of statesmanship which brought nothing but advantage to Scotland. Robert Silver, who was a distinguished scientist as well as the author of a fine play about Robert Bruce, said once that the Scots were "the victims of the strongest attempt to brainwash a whole nation ever mounted in history". It has succeeded in obscuring for generations the reality of our situation.

Usually the brainwashing concentrates on the economic case. In the days of the British Empire, with captive markets and imperial preference, there was no doubt benefit for some branches of the economy. There were also careers in the army and colonial service which compensated for the neglect of Scotland itself. All this has long gone and we now live in a global economy with the free movement of goods and people, not just in the small area of Britain, but in the much larger one of the European Union. A comparison of the present condition of Scotland with small independent countries in north west Europe does not suggest that we have benefited from the imperial or British connection. We have lost millions of our people through emigration. We have also lost most of our industry and ownership and control over most of what is left. We have deplorably low standards of public health and housing and high levels of poverty and long-term unemployment.

In cultural terms, with all that they imply for personal contentment and psychological well-being, the damage has been much more insidious. *A Claim of Right for Scotland* of July 1988, the report of the Constitutional Steering Committee which led to the Constitutional Convention and therefore to the Scottish Parliament, begins with a section on "the essential facts of Scottish history". One of the conclusions is: "the Union has always been, and remains, a threat to the survival of a distinctive culture in Scotland". Recently, a well-informed English observer, John Tusa, in his book, *Art Matters*, made very much the same point:

> For 250 years after the Union, and culminating in the Thatcher years, Scotland was not only subordinated to England politically but culturally as well . . . Scottish culture had been virtually Leninised — that is to say reduced to a few token, vestigial symbols such as bagpipes, tartan, shortbread, haggis, whisky, a folksy accent and the baccanalian celebration of Hogmanay. It is undoubtedly the case that many Scots were happy to collaborate in the process

But there was a rebellious strain of an authentic Scottish identity which was alienated from Thatcherite London and later contributed to the sudden sweep towards the idea of self-government, and possibly even independence. Of course, both the rebellion and the movement towards self-government had very much deeper roots than Tusa supposes. Even so, the close political association with a larger, and a powerful and self confident, country might have led to cultural assimilation. As Colin Bell said at the end of his series of BBC programmes, *Scotland's Century*, Scotland is a nation which could have disappeared, but which refused to die.

The cultural subordination of Scotland is most obvious in language. We have two indigenous languages, Gaelic and Scots. Both have rich literatures. Both, like all languages, embody the shared experiences of the communities which have used them for centuries, and therefore are the best means of expressing aspects of the national character. These languages still exist and are still vehicles of fine literature, but they have been almost entirely displaced by English in education, the law, government and the media. Tacitus said of the acquisition of Latin by the ancient Britons that they thought that it was part of civilisation, but in fact it was a proof of their enslavement. The same might be said of the English language in Scotland.

Certainly, there are many advantages in the modern world in a knowledge of English. It has become so useful a means of international communication that many countries use it as a second language for this purpose. We should want to do the same; but this could have been acquired without generations of Scottish children being reduced to inarticulacy and a sense of inferiority by the denigration of the mother tongue which they brought to school. In other ways as well our educational system has tended to undermine our self-confidence. It has been Anglo-centric, saying little about the extraordinary range of Scottish achievement, but focusing on English conditions, history and literature, and giving the impression that nothing of consequence ever happens in Scotland. The London domination of broadcasting has tended in the same direction. So has the need to look to London for all important decisions in government and business.

The consequence of all this is the so-called Scottish cringe, a massive inferiority complex. Cairns Craig says in his book, *Out of History*: "Scottish culture has cowered in the consciousness of its own inadequacy, recognising the achievements of individual Scots simply as proof of the failure of the culture as a whole. And the consequence of accepting ourselves as parochial has been a profound self-hatred". Iain Macwhirter in the *Sunday Herald* of 27th June 1999 says that: "Lack of self-respect and self-government have left us prone to a kind of national infantilism". Of course by no means all Scots have succumbed to such feelings, but there are signs which suggest that they are sufficiently prevalent to amount to a serious weakness. The restoration of national self-confidence must be one of the first objectives of the Scottish Parliament.

What can the Parliament do about it?

The American sociologist, Michael Hechter in his book, *Internal Colonialism* argued that England, as the core of the British state, denigrated the cultures of Scotland, Wales and Ireland to justify its political domination and that it used the "voluntary assimilation of peripheral elites" for the purpose. This is the process which I have been describing. I do not think that it has happened as a result of a deliberate policy, but as the automatic result of the overwhelming size and wealth of England. As Tusa says, many Scots were happy to collaborate and that has included the school teachers. They have done this with the best of motives because they thought it was the best way to prepare their pupils for careers in the British Empire and state. The teaching profession now recognises the consequences of inadequate attention to Scottish history and culture. The Scottish Consultative Council on the Curriculum has drawn up reports to make recommendations on both of these. The first of them has been published, but the second is so far in suspense, apparently because of a sudden loss of courage. Blue prints therefore already exist for the remedy of the Scottish deficit in Scottish education.

It is not only Scottish history, but all history, which has been given too little attention by the schools. This is unfortunate for two reasons. First of all because we cannot understand the present without some understanding of how we arrived here. Secondly because history, properly taught, is an excellent training in the critical examination of the evidence. In this age of sound-bites and high pressure advertising there is more need than ever for the cultivation of the habits of logical, objective and sceptical thought. George Davie in his important book, *The Democratic Intellect*, stressed the importance of the study of philosophy in the Scottish universities in the past. An intelligent approach to history can serve very much the same purpose. With history, as with literature, music and art, we should begin in Scotland because that has most immediate relevance and then radiate outwards to the international connections.

All political parties and people generally agree that the improvement of education is an urgent necessity. In Scotland this is particularly so because, as I have been arguing, it relates so intimately to self-confidence, and therefore to happiness and social usefulness, as well as to the technological skills which the modern world demands. Where once we led, we have fallen behind international standards, and that gives an additional need for urgency. In addressing these problems, the members of Parliament and the civil servants should not yield to the temptation to suppose that they have a monopoly of wisdom. I hope that they will use the committees to seek advice from both the teachers and the taught and from people with ideas.

The Scottish Parliament is responsible for cultural policy; but broadcasting, the most potent means of cultural expression, is reserved to Westminster. This is absurd. In an essay, *The Backwardness of Scottish Television*, Stuart Hood, the novelist and former Controller of Programmes for BBC Television, said that there were societies "which have not achieved self-awareness because the dominant instruments of mass culture do not provide a mirror in which their citizens can see themselves truthfully". This is precisely our situation in Scotland. Not only is the BBC controlled from London, but the structure of commercial television ensures that most of the programmes, even of the Scottish companies, are produced in England. For most of the time, we are made to look at ourselves and the rest of the world through London eyes. This was confusing and demoralising enough when our Government and Parliament were also there. It is now intolerable and must be changed.

Many of the most important cultural institutions, such as the National Library, Galleries and Museums, the Scottish Museums Council and Scottish Screen, are state funded but controlled by their own boards. The Scottish Arts Council is such a body. It is responsible for the distribution of Government funds for the support of the arts in Scotland, a hands-off device which avoids suspicion of political favouritism and also shelters the Government from the criticism of unpopular decisions. It is through these organisations that the State has its most significant, if indirect, influence on the cultural life of the country. It can stimulate artistic and intellectual achievement by adequate funding or curtail it by a reduction.

The Scottish Arts Council is a major factor in the cultural life of Scotland, but it has also been fiercely criticised. In its origin it was a subcommittee of the Arts Council of Great Britain and therefore followed their policies. For years it more or less ignored Scottish indigenous music and dance, but this has changed for the better since the Scottish Council became autonomous and since an extensive consultation in 1992 revealed that Scottish traditional music was very much alive and deserved much more recognition and support. A stand-still on funding in the last years of the Conservative govermnent, which was in effect an annual reduction, put great strain on the Council. That was not their fault, but they have also been criticised for too much secrecy, too much bureaucracy and too much arbitrary power. Most of these points can probably be remedied if the Council becomes answerable to a committee of the Scottish Parliament.

On the other hand, it may well be true that the Arts Council has exercised more power than is appropriate for a single body since it became responsible for the distribution of lottery funding for the arts as well as the direct Government grant. I think that there is a good case for the national companies (Scottish Opera, Scottish Ballet, the RSNO and the Scottish Chamber Orchestra) becoming directly funded by the Cultural Department of the Scottish Executive in the same way as the National Library, Galleries and Museums. At present the national companies require such a large proportion of the Arts Council budget that they distract attention from the multiplicity of other companies which are an essential part of the cultural life of the country. The same risk of suspicion of party political favouritism does not apply to the national companies which clearly have to be funded.

Another advantage would follow from this change. It would make it easier to achieve the National Theatre which has been an aspiration for about a century. The case for it was stated very fairly in *The Charter for the Arts* in Scotland, drafted by Joyce Macmillan and published by the Scottish Arts Council as a statement of 'a shared vision' for the future development of the arts into the next century:

> The case for a national theatre rests on the contention that it is absurd for Scotland, which has little indigenous tradition in ballet and opera, to support major national companies in these areas, while having no

> national theatre to protect and express our much richer inheritance of Scots drama and theatrical tradition. It is also pointed out that, although Scotland supports a rich network of theatre companies, none of them has a specific remit to perform and develop Scottish repertoire and languages, and commitment to it therefore varies unpredictably as artistic directors come and go . . .

There is a need for an institution whose remit it is to preserve, develop and promote the Scottish dramatic repertoire, to encourage Scottish writing for the stage, and to help actors and directors acquire and maintain the language and performance skills necessary for the most effective performance of drama in all forms of Scots and in Gaelic. Such an institution would provide a valuable resource not only for the theatre itself, but for all forms of dramatic and literary culture in Scotland, including film and television.

Why then, when the need is so obvious, has the Scottish Arts Council always resisted it and fobbed off demands with yet another feasibility study? I think it is because they have been reluctant to accept responsibility for an additional national company and because of opposition from the existing theatre companies who were afraid of a competitor for Scottish Arts Council funds. Neither of these would arise if all national companies were funded directly by the Scottish Office. In the experience of most other European countries a national theatre has a vital role as a stimulus of the national literature and of national self-awareness and self-understanding.

There seems already to be a real prospect of the expansion of the resources for film making. If that happens, I think that we need only one other new institution, in addition to the National Theatre. That is a body to encourage cultural exchange with other countries in both directions. Until Scotland acquires its own diplomatic representation abroad, this could be combined with offices to promote trade and tourism and there is in fact a relationship between all of these.

No government or parliament, as far as I am aware, has ever written a play, a symphony or a novel, although they have provided material for them. Their main cultural function is to provide the financial support which in the past was provided by royal or aristocratic patrons. The Scottish Government is going to be under very severe financial restraint. It has denied itself the use of even its very limited power to vary income tax and the grant under the Barnett formula is designed to squeeze more tightly year by year. The poor standards of housing and public health will make strong and legitimate demands. On the other hand, the share which the arts need is only a very small proportion of total Government expenditure. Last year (1998) the Scottish Office spent about 0.5% of the total on museums and galleries and about 0.2% on the performing and visual arts through the Arts Council. There is room for improvement without any substantial change in the overall pattern of expenditure.

In any case, the benefit from expenditure on the arts is out of all proportion to the cost. Nothing does more to enhance the international reputation of the country with direct benefit to the tourist trade, inward investment and even to our exports. We have the advantages of having in Edinburgh the greatest international festival of arts in the world and of having our own traditions in literature, music, painting and architecture which are a valuable and distinctive part of European diversity. We should encourage both the international and the national. We need to experience the best that can be produced in the rest of the world, but we have a special responsibility for our own arts because they speak to us directly and because they cannot be found anywhere else. Above all, we should encourage the arts because they enrich the lives of our people, broaden their understanding and contribute to civilisation.

We should study the practice of other comparable countries in encouraging their cultural and intellectual life. Many of them do far more than we have been able to do so far. There is, for example, in the Irish Republic a tax regime which encourages works of art. Norway has a scheme for the purchase of new Norwegian books for distribution to libraries throughout the country.

Financial restraints are not the only problem. There is another which is much more insidious and damaging. Cultural standards everywhere are under the very real threat of the trans-Atlantic fashion of 'dumbing-down'. There are insistent calls for the rejection of cultural values and the acceptance of any music, writing or entertainment as though it were as good as any other. Anything which is difficult and which requires application and effort is condemned. This approach can be represented as a crusade for equality and the rights of the common people, although it is in fact condescending and insulting to them. The use of the word, elitist, as a term of abuse is a warning that this spirit is abroad. Even the Scottish Arts Council is not free from it A recent paper, *Scottish Arts in the 21st Century* contains this ominous sentence: "Why are young people more interested in screen-based arts, rock music, and fashion than in the areas which SAC has traditionally supported?"

At the Congress of International PEN in Warsaw in June 1999 the dramatist, Ronald Harwood, spoke passionately about what he called the virus which was attacking the standards of cultural achievement:

> The virus feeds most voraciously on the demands of the market place, to some extent on lower and lower educational standards, and most unfortunately on those who believe that popularity is preferable to anything else . . . Anyone who seeks to defend high standards is immediately branded old-fashioned, reactionary, living in the past, out of touch, boring or even fascist . . . In all of the media, as a matter of survival, standards are constantly being lowered in order to attract the greatest numbers. Junk food and junk culture are soul mates.

This is a world-wide challenge, but in Scotland we are well placed to resist. We have a long tradition of respect for education and for the broad philosophical approach of the democratic intellect. Our contribution to the arts and sciences is very remarkable for so small a country. As a result of several centuries of these traditions, and of close interchange with intellectual movements in continental Europe, we led many aspects of enlightened thought in the 18th century. There is no reason why we should not be bold enough to aim at a similar role again. We should be open to beneficial influences from other countries; but we should resist the damaging and destructive. Our habits of logical and sceptical thought should be a barrier against mere fashion. I am not alone in this optimism. Peter Jones, Professor of Philosophy in Edinburgh, in 1989 called on Scotland, "To proclaim itself as unashamedly intellectual, the thinking nation". He suggested that we should once again not hesitate to give a lead to the rest of the world in critical intelligence and innovative thought, a new Enlightenment in fact. This idea is now widespread. For example, the City of Edinburgh has drawn up a cultural policy which it calls "Towards the New Enlightenment".

Public reaction to the official opening of the Scottish Parliament on 1st July 1999 made it very obvious that expectations are high that it will lead to a radical transformation of Scotland. There is no point in having a Parliament unless it makes real improvements. Education and culture are within its responsibilities. Of course, it is not possible to create a new Enlightenment by passing a few laws. That requires a sustained endeavour by our schools, universities, writers, artists, thinkers and people at large; but Parliament can give a lead and help to create favourable conditions. Scotland for too long has suffered from the absence of a body with the power to mobilise and inspire the popular will. In an article in *The Scotsman* on 30th June 1999 Ian Bell said that the Parliament had no hiding place. Among other things it would have to show that Scotland was "a country that takes education and intellectual ambition as seriously as it likes to claim". That is the challenge and the opportunity.

Parliament
and
Independence

5.1

Scotland and England

'Glasgow Herald', 8th December 1990

In a recent article in this newspaper (10th September) Allan Massie said that he thought that I underestimated the English influence on Scottish Culture. This surprised me because my view of English influence on Scotland is that it has long been excessive, is increasing and ought to be diminished. This is not because English influence is always bad. On the contrary there are many admirable things about the English, although usually not the things on which they generally pride themselves. They have a great literature, for example, but their vaunted form of parliamentary democracy is a sham and an absurdity. The most objectionable thing about English influence is quite simply that it is forced on us whether we like it or not. External influence on any country can be very beneficial and stimulating, but generally the essential condition for that to happen is that it is voluntary. Something which we chose because we like the look of it is quite another matter from something imposed, regardless of our own wishes, tastes or interests. In his famous book, *Small is Beautiful*, E. F. Schumacher remarked that it is not necessary to be annexed by a country before you can trade with it. The same is true of cultural influence. We could take what we may happen to like from the English example without being subject to their political control.

Of course, the reason why England is in a position to impose itself on us is partly because we share an island in which they are ten times more numerous; but it is mainly because of the strange arrangements which were made in the Treaty of Union of 1707. The Treaty purported to abolish the Parliaments of both Scotland and England and create a new entity, the Parliament of Great Britain. This is a fact which the English prefer to forget as they have always behaved as though the English Parliament simply carried on without change other than the absorption of a few Scottish members and the extension of its authority over Scotland. They were encouraged in this view by two factors: the absence of any machinery to safeguard Scottish interests and the fact that Scottish membership of the two Houses of Parliament was so small that it could be ignored. Scotland had 45 members in the Commons, which was about the same as Cornwall. The 15 representative Scottish Peers in the House of Lords were outnumbered by English bishops alone.

Historians have long had great difficulty in explaining how it was that Scotland came to accept such a poor bargain. This was especially remarkable of a country which was probably the first to evolve the idea of national self-determination and which had defended its national independence against heavy odds for more than 300 years. Historians in the 19th Century thought that they had found an explanation in trade. They suggested that the Scottish ruling class, against the wishes of the great majority of the people, had deliberately exchanged Scottish independence for access for Scottish trade to England and the colonies. This theory, which is highly implausible when you think about it, still lingers on as the established wisdom on the matter. In fact, a study of the contemporary evidence shows that considerations of trade played a very small part. The Scottish trading interests were opposed to the Union because they saw that they would suffer great damage from the imposition of duties and regulations designed for English conditions and the unrestrained flood of English goods into the Scottish market. They were right. The Scottish economy was devastated and only recovered, through Scottish efforts alone, towards the end of the 18th Century.

For a long time, historians clung to their trade theory, with a sort of historical prudery, because it was more palatable than the sordid facts of bribery and military intimidation which did no credit to either side. Now that the Union is no longer a sacred cow and it is probable that it soon either be abolished or radically changed, there is no need for this polite evasion. The distinguished English historian, Christopher Hill, admitted recently that "Scotland was bribed and swindled into Union with England". It is now widely accepted that, apart from the bribery and the swindling, the Scottish ruling class surrendered independence largely because the alternative was invasion by Marlborough's army and the imposition of worse terms. In fact, the Union settlement could have been much worse. Scotland lost her Parliament, and therefore any capacity to legislate for her own needs and in accordance with her own wishes; but virtually everything else was left intact and even guaranteed under the Treaty or in an entrenched Act associated with it. This applied to the Church, the Universities, the Legal system and local government. All of these affected the daily lives of the people far more than Parliament and Government did at that time. Schools and welfare provisions, for instance, were mainly in the hands of the church. The Government only started to intervene, slowly at first and then with increasing momentum from early in the 19th Century. Scotland after centuries of independence, followed by this semi-independence, has developed strong and distinctive traditions. They are not dead yet in spite of all the anglo-centralising efforts of the Thatcher administration.

In the early part of this century two distinguished constitutional historians, one English and one Scottish, A. V. Dicey and R. S. Rait, jointly wrote one of the most substantial books ever written on this subject, *Thoughts on the Union between England and Scotland*. They both took the then conventional, and now widely discredited, view that the Union was an act of wise and enlightened statesmanship. Even so, their final conclusion was that the "supreme glory" of the Union was that "while creating political unity, it kept alive the nationalism both of England and of Scotland". It is simply untrue, as unionist politicians argue when it suits them, that Britain is a unitary state. It is, and has been since 1707, a clumsy and unsatisfactory association between two nations, in which one of them, Scotland, is in a particularly vulnerable position. The English doctrine of Parliamentary Sovereignty, according to which

Parliament can do whatever it pleases, allows Westminster to disregard both the safeguards of the Treaty and the evident wishes of the Scottish people. Our history since 1707 is full of examples.

Of course, much has changed since Dicey and Rait wrote their book. The factors which made the Union more or less tolerable in the 19th Century have all evaporated. Britain is no longer a model, as people used to believe, of freedom and parliamentary democracy. It is an increasingly intolerant state, riddled with secrecy, patronage and pompous absurdity, with a parliamentary system that allows a Prime Minister, usually elected on a minority vote, to assume virtually absolute power. It is no longer a Great Power with a vast Empire which provided jobs for the boys on a massive scale. It has an economy with endemic problems of inflation and balance of trade which steadily declines in prosperity in comparison to the other countries of Western Europe.

At the same time, the European Community, to which so many of the English react with distrust and hostility, has many solid attractions for Scotland. The E.C. makes Scottish independence more necessary, because otherwise we are pushed further to the periphery. It also makes independence easier to achieve since it removes any worry about a small market and customs posts on the Tweed. All international organisations have special advantages for small nations. They curb the excesses and the bullying of larger countries and have a tendency to regard all member states as equal. Even the weighted voting system, which the E.C. uses for certain decisions, is so arranged that the larger countries cannot take a decision without the support of some of the smaller ones. In 1704 Andrew Fletcher of Saltoun, one of the leading opponents of the Union, looked forward to a Europe of small autonomous states co-operating to preserve peace and promote trade. Nearly 300 years later such a European settlement is now emerging. Scottish membership of the European community, 'Independence in Europe', would be a valuable contribution to this process. John Robertson, in a recent article in *Chapman* about Fletcher, reached the same conclusion: "A separate Scottish presence within the E.C., aligning itself with the smaller nations of the community, is thus desirable in its own right, representing a more constructive response to Franco-German predominance than Mrs Thatcher's little England obstructiveness". One of the worst effects of the Union was that it cut Scotland off from direct contact with the rest of the world. Before that Scotland had for centuries been very closely involved in Europe. To this day, our law and our educational system are closer to the European norm than the insular self-sufficiency of England. In a very real sense, Scotland as a full and independent member of the E.C. would be returning to the associations which served us well in the past.

The pooling of aspects of sovereignty in Europe does not frighten us in Scoland because we should have infinitely more control over our own affairs than we have at present and a say in the evolution of common European policies. At present, we have internally a Government imposed on us, which we have repeatedly rejected at the polls, and no right to participate in European decision making. Luxembourg, with a population of about the same size as Edinburgh and no coastline, has more say in European fishing policy than Scotland which has most of the fish.

In the matter of cultural identity, Europe is much more likely to be supportive than threatening because this is something which all European countries value. European agencies, for example, are already taking a more constructive interest in lesser-used languages, such as Gaelic and Scots, than British Governments are ever likely to do. European influence is beneficial, partly because it is diverse. The same is true of the freedom of movement which allow nationals of any member state to take employment in any other.

On the other hand, the strongest threat to our cultural identity at present is the extraordinary extent to which the top posts in many areas of our national life have been virtually monopolised by immigrants from one country, England. This applies especially to posts which are particularly crucial for the way in which we see ourselves and are seen by others, the arts, the universities, local government, public bodies even those who are responsible for presenting us to the tourist industry. Many of the people appointed to these jobs are new to Scotland and know very little about our history, literature, attitudes and traditions. They are likely to weaken and confuse our identity. What can be done about this, without curbing that freedom of movement which is desirable in itself and part of the ethos of Europeanism?

In 1988 the Advisory Council for the Arts in Scotland, (AdCAS) suggested that the obvious course was to include among the essential qualifications, whenever such posts are advertised, a knowledge of the appropriate segment of Scottish life. You would expect, for example, the director of a major art gallery in Scotland to be familiar with Scottish painting, the director of a theatre to know about the Scottish acting tradition, and the corpus of Scottish plays and have an appreciation of spoken Scots. You would expect a director of tourism to have a deep knowledge and experience of the part of the country that he represents. Curiously enough, there is usually no such requirement. Often it seems that ignorance is preferred.

I think that the explanation lies in a deep-seated sense of inferiority which is a consequence of our historical position and is one of our major problems. In a recent interview, the playwright, Chris Hannan, said: "the Scots still believe in imported culture. They call their own culture parochial and that of others, the true culture". I think that this is true of some people in Scotland and perhaps that includes many of those responsible for these curious appointments. It is an attitude fostered by our system of education and by most of the media which concentrate on the English experience, as though everything important always happens there and nothing Scottish is of any consequence. This may not be designed to breed an inferiority complex, but that is certainly the effect. The less people know about our own history and literature the more likely they are to succumb. In the final analysis, it is a result of the fact that we have been deprived of the dignity of responsibility for our own government. A critic writing recently about Neil Gunn noted that he was conscious in Scotland of "the absence of hope, and of the lacerating self-contempt which is a marked component in the psyche of colonised peoples."

There is a risk that this is one of these chicken and egg questions. Perhaps we can only free ourselves from this debilitating sense of inferiority when we have the responsibility of independence. But can we have the spirit to achieve independence as long as we are plagued by ideas of inferiority, even if they are false and ill-founded? Fortunately, there are many signs that we are recovering the spirit. We have been remarkable for resilience in the past and we may be again.

5.2

What do the Unionists want to save?

Letter to 'The Herald' of 27th March 1992

Dear Sir,

Lord Weir and other distinguished and venerable gentlemen have written to the newspapers (27th March) to "save the Union"; but what is it that they are trying to save?

The Union, foisted on us in its origin by bribery and intimidation, has had both good and bad effects in the course of its history. As a political or constitutional arrangement it has long outlived any usefulness that it may have had. It means at best that Scottish affairs are neglected in the absence of a democratic forum to discuss our problems and seek remedies. We have to tolerate legislation designed to suit English conditions and ideas and not our own. At its worst (and we have had many examples of that in the last thirteen years), it means that we have a Government and policies forced on us which we have rejected at the polls. It is a denial of democracy which no people with an instinct for freedom can tolerate.

As what has been called a social union, as distinct from the constitutional or political, it has great advantages as an area of peaceful co-operation and the free movement of people, ideas and trade. No one wants to interfere with this, and it has now become part of the much wider area of the European single market. If this is what Lord Weir wishes to preserve, then there is no dispute.

The present constitutional arrangement provokes precisely the "rivalry and conflict", "bitterness and instability" and "dangerous uncertainty" which Lord Weir deplores. This is because any self-respecting nation must resent, and struggle against, their powerlessness in the face of a larger and insensitive neighbour which inflicts on us measures like the Poll Tax and the distortion of our educational system. It would not be much better under the devolution proposals of the Labour and the Liberal Democrats because they would still leave control of most of the purse strings and most of the important decisions to Whitehall.

The only way to remove the causes of resentment, and therefore of bitterness and uncertainty and all the rest of it, is the independence in Europe for which the SNP stands. We should then have no one to blame but ourselves and we should have a normal, friendly and co-operative relationship with England. Look at the example of all the scores of previously dependent territories which have achieved independence.

Paradoxically therefore, if Lord Weir and his friends want to preserve the social union (which is the only part worth preserving), they should give their support to the SNP.

Yours faithfully,

Paul H. Scott

5. 3

The European Summit: Edinburgh, December 1992

Dialogue with an enquiring visitor

'The Herald', 5th December, 1992

Paul H. Scott's latest book, 'Scotland in Europe: A Dialogue with a Sceptical Friend', considers the arguments for and against Scottish independence and membership of the European Community. For 'The Herald' he has written an additional dialogue about a conversation with E.V., an enquiring visitor from Italy who has come to Edinburgh for the European Summit.

E.V. I hear that your latest book is called *Scotland in Europe.* It is presumably not a coincidence that it is published just before the European Summit in Edinburgh. There was, as far as I know, no particular political significance in the fact that the previous one was held in Birmingham. Does the choice of Edinburgh for this one have any more point than that?

P. H. S. Certainly. Even John Major has said that "Edinburgh is a capital city and a capital city should be the scene of great events". His chief representative in Scotland, the Secretary of State, Ian Lang, for his part has added: "We must draw more on Scotland's status as a nation and on Edinburgh's status as a capital city". So far they have refused to draw what I should regard as the obvious conclusions from these facts, but they acknowledge the essential point. It is because Edinburgh is not a provincial city, but the capital of an ancient European nation with close connexions with the rest of Europe, that the Summit there has special implications.

E. V. Forgive me, but this is where I begin to have difficulties. In my language, Italian, we use the same word, Inghilterra, for the whole of this island. We do not distinguish between what you call Britain or the United Kingdom and England. We have some vague ideas about Scotland in the past; but as our language reveals, we have assumed that it has long ago been absorbed in England. Is that not the position?

P. H. S. I am sorry that there is no simple answer to that question. It confuses people not only in the rest of the world, but even some in Scotland itself and nearly everybody in England. To cut a long story short, the facts briefly are these. In 1707 the Scottish Parliament was induced by various means, including bribery and military threat, and against the wishes of the great majority of the Scottish people, to ratify a Treaty of Union with England.

The Treaty abolished the Parliament of both Scotland and England and replaced them with a new entity, the Parliament of Great Britain. At least that is what the Treaty said. In practice both houses of the English Parliament carried on as before, except that some Scottish members were added. The Scottish Parliament ceased to exist. England was hardly changed by the Union. Scotland lost the ability to legislate for itself and it disappeared from view internationally. Because of this, you could say that Scotland was absorbed in fact, if not in law.

On the other hand, many other institutions in Scotland, such as the legal system, the Church, the local administration and the Universities, not only continued in being but their separate existence was guaranteed by the Treaty. Until quite recent times, these institutions had far more effect on the lives of the people than the remote Parliament and Government. In a very real sense, therefore, Scotland was not absorbed but continued to exercise its own distinctive national existence.

E.V. But Scotland, if I understand correctly, has been subject to the London Parliament since 1707?

P. H.S. That is true and it is a Parliament which has in the meantime evolved the peculiarly English doctrine of parliamentary sovereignity. That means that it claims the right to pass any law it chooses without the restraint of a written constitution or constitutional court. It has never hesitated to violate the Treaty of Union, although that is the instrument to which it owes its own existence.

E.V. So Scotland has a legal system, a Church and an administration, as well as its long history as an independent country, but has no legislative body to exercise democratic control over its own affairs. It claims to be a nation and has many of the attributes of one, but it has no Parliament or legislative assembly of any kind. That presumably means that it has less power than a region in Italy or a land in Germany.

P.H.S. Yes, that is the position.

E.V. From the Scottish point of view, that seems to me unsatisfactory, unstable and humiliating.

P.H.S. I must agree again.

E.V. Why then have the Scots tolerated this state of affairs for so long?

P.H.S. I find that difficult to understand myself. Part of the explanation is historical. Until about the middle of the 19th century Scotland did very well under its own institutions with very little interference from London. By the time the London Government began to intervene, the situation was complicated by the existence of the Empire and involvement in European wars. The population as a whole did not have the right to vote until this century, but there has been increasing agitation for Scottish self-government for more than 100 years.

E.V. Well, you deserve credit for patience if nothing else, but was there not a referendum on the matter some time ago?

P.H.S Yes, there was a referendum in 1979 on a proposal for an Assembly with limited powers over internal Scottish affairs. The Conservatives campaigned for a 'No' vote with the promise that, if they suceeded, they would immediately call a constitutional conference to improve the government of Scotland. This confused the whole issue. In spite of it, the 'Yes' side had a majority of over 77,000 votes which was 51.6% of the votes cast. Normally this would have settled the matter because every other decision in our political history has been taken in the belief that a majority of one is sufficient. In this case alone, however, the British Parliament had introduced the requirement that the result would be regarded as positive only if at least 40% of the total electorate voted 'Yes', an impossibly difficult condition since the electoral rolls contains many people who have died, moved away, gone on holiday or to hospital and so on. The Conservatives, who came to power shortly afterwards, repealed the legislation for an Assembly and have never honoured this committment to call a constitutional conference. Under Edward Heath they had been in favour of a Scottish Parliament, but Margaret Thatcher reversed the policy and John Major has followed her example.

E.V. What is the evidence about the present state of Scottish opinion on this issue?

P.H.S. Every opinion poll on the subject since polls began has shown between 75% and 80% in favour of a measure of self-government and therefore only 20% to 25%, or even less, in favour of the constitutional status quo. The division of opinion between independence and a Parliament with more limited powers has fluctuated. The latter has usually been in the lead, but independence has been gaining ground. The results of the last four elections have been consistent with these polls. The parties in favour of a Scottish Parliament have always had about 75% of the vote and the Conservatives, the only party in favour of the *status quo*, 25% or less. They have formed the Government at Westminster for the last 13 years on the strength of votes in England and have used this position to impose policies on Scotland which the Scottish electorate have repeatedly rejected.

E.V. But I have the impression from what I have read in the press that the Conservatives did rather better in Scotland in the last Elections in April.

P.H.S They have worked hard to give that impression but the fact is that their vote in Scotland increased by only 1.7%. This is a very small amount when you consider that John Major, who was at that time still quite popular, had replaced Margaret Thatcher who was generally detested in Scotland. Also many voters opposed to the Conservatives had removed themselves from the electoral roll because they wanted to avoid the poll tax. On the other hand, the Conservatives spent millions of pounds on an organisation which mobilised their vote very effectively. Any one of these factors could account for the small increase.

John Major had made the constitutional *status quo* a major issue which, he said, transcended the whole campaign. That point of view can take little comfort from the fact that it was, once again, rejected by 75% of the Scottish votes. The votes of the Scottish National Party, the party of independence, increased by 7.5%

E.V. From what you tell me there seems to be no doubt that the Scots have consistently demonstrated over many years that they want their own Parliament, but that the Conservatives since Margaret Thatcher became their leader have steadily refused to listen, and that John Major seems to be even more opposed to any constitutional change.

P.H.S. Yes. In a speech in Glasgow on 10th September John Major said that he would defend with equal vigour "the remarkable, magical Union" and the value of sterling within the ERM. Admittedly his strong commitment on the second of these lasted only about another week.

E.V. The point about this which interests me most is that this is the same John Major who is always lecturing his EC colleagues about the importance of national identity and national decision making and subsidiarity. He accepts the Scotland is a nation, but refuses to allow Scotland to make her own decisions about her own affairs. How can he simultaneously hold such different views towards the EC and towards Scotland? That looks to me like a high degree of hypocrisy and inconsistency.

P.H.S. Exactly. That is what makes the Summit in Edinburgh so significant.

5. 4

Lang in Wonderland

'Scotland on Sunday', 21st March 1993

"When I use a word", Humpty Dumpty said in a rather scornful tone, "it means just what I choose it to mean, — neither more nor less".

Lewis Carroll, *Through the Looking Glass*

Ian Lang is the new Humpty Dumpty and just as scornful, although rather less amiable. His White Paper, with its embarassing pun as a title, "A Partnership for Good" is a sustained exercise in Humpty Dumpty speak.

It begins with his Introduction. He tells us that the proposals which follow "effectively address such shortcomings as may be perceived" in present constitutional arrangements. You might suppose that he is about to face the clear demand by a substantial majority of Scots for an end to the scandalous denial of our elementary democratic rights. We are in fact treated to an elaborate pretence that such a problem does not exist.

We are told that the Scottish Parliament in 1707 "having decided that Union was the best way forward for the future relationship with England, passed the Act of Union by a substantial majority". Only in Humpty Dumpty speak could that sordid story of bribery and intimidation be so described.

Then we are asked to believe that the Government has a "drive to devolve more decision-making power to Scotland and within Scotland" and "to shift decision-making, where practicable, to Scotland's local communities". This comes from a Government that has not only ignored the clear desire of the Scottish people for a Parliament, but has systematically curbed, undermined and "capped" the power and functions of local government. This is Humpty-Dumptyism at its most extreme.

Another Lewis Carroll principle comes into play in the frequent repetition that it is good for Scotland, in spite of all the talk about devolving decision-making, that all the important decisions should nevertheless be taken by the Westminster Parliament with its overwhelming English majority. If you can believe that, you can believe anything. So how is it explained? By the other principle, "What I tell you three times is true".

Does this extraordinary document amount to anything more than an insult to the intelligence of the Scottish people? Is there anything of any substance in it at all? Most of the concrete proposals (which in any case he has threatened to withdraw if the opposition parties do not play according to his rules) amount to very little. There is not much merit in extra opportunities for MPs to question Ministers since the procedure always leaves them with the last word. It is probably significant that the one real advance is the transfer of responsibility of the Scottish Arts Council to the Scottish Office. This is something which AdCAS, the Saltire Society and other bodies have been advocating for years because it should mean less interference from London.

This is the one sign in the whole document that the Government may mean something when it talks about "the recognition of Scotland's status as a nation, . . . the development of a stronger Scottish identity" and a desire to "respect and cherish the difference between each of the constituent parts of the United Kingdom". It also mentions the possibility of the creation of "new bodies to take account of the distinctive Scottish identity". Do they have one of the most obvious needs, a Scottish National Theatre, in mind? An early test of the sincerity of these points will be the reaction of the Government to the outrageous proposal to abolish one of the finest of Scottish institutions, the Scottish National Portrait Gallery.

All of these points about the cherishing of the Scottish identity come in the last chapter of the White Paper, which has the strange and incongruous title, 'Bring the Union Alive'. The language which it uses is in sharp contrast to the tired old platitudes and double-speak of the rest of the paper and it strikes a new tone for a Tory statement. Has something of the reality of the Scottish situation penetrated to the mandarins who drafted it? The truth is, in the words of *A Claim of Right for Scotland* of 1988, that "The Union has always been, and remains, a threat to the survival of a distinctive culture in Scotland". It is proof of its inherent vitality that, in spite of the discouraging circumstances of external control, so much has survived, and is now growing in strength and confidence.

Is there a hint here that Lang hopes that he might be able to appease the Scottish hunger for normality and self-respect by recognising cultural, if not political, freedom? A vain hope, no doubt, but autonomy for the Scottish Arts Council is a step in that direction. The next, and a vital one, will be autonomy for public service broadcasting in Scotland. The revision of the BBC Charter will provide an opportunity for this necessary and long overdue reform.

5.5

The End of Britishness

'Cencrastus', Autumn 1993

In Scotland there has long been profound discontent with the British constitution or system of government. Every opinion poll on the subject since polls began has shown a large majority in favour of constitutional change. What is new is the sudden collapse of faith in the system also in England. It is the culmination of a long process. Robert Worcester, the chairman of MORI, whose polls have recorded the process, says that there is no doubt that for some decades there has been a decline of confidence in British institutions, "in monarchy, in Westminster and Whitehall, in the judiciary and the system of government as a whole". [1]

This steady decline has now reached the point of crisis with a collapse of morale and a wide-spread feeling of despair. Since 1962 Anthony Sampson in the successive editions of *The Anatomy of Britain* has given a detailed account of the state of British institutions. His latest book, published at the end of last year, *The Essential Anatomy of Britain*, reflects the new pessimism. It has the subtitle, *Democracy in Crisis*, and Tom Nairn has described it as "a cry of mingled horror and alarm". [2] As Henry Porter has said in *The Guardian*, "Suddenly what seems to be at stake is not economic and material well-being, but the Britishness of being British".[3] According to a recent poll, about half of the British public would emigrate if they could. A headline in *The Scotsman* concluded that the mood and morale of the nation (meaning Britain) has never been at such a low ebb.[4]

Of course, there have been many recent events which are likely to contribute to disillusionment and despair. Major's government has shown nothing but indecision, incompetence and confusion, with no apparent purpose beyond clinging to power. Even the Tory press finds it derisory. There is an unmistakeable air of deceit and corruption. Ministers refuse to resign in circumstances where common decency, to put it no higher, would have demanded it in the past. Unemployment exceeds three million. Since the humiliation of Black Wednesday the Government has staggered from one muddle to another. The British economy has been in steady decline for decades. In 1960 the UK was 9th in terms of GDP per head out of the 24 members of the OECD; by 1991 it was 18th. The courts have had to release people who have been wrongly imprisoned for years. The despair of the young erupts in violence in the streets. The myth of the monarchy turns into a bedroom farce. The "stock-taking" White Paper has shown again that the Government cannot, or will not, respond to the need for democratic normality in Scotland. The shambles of the Grand National was an apt symbol of the state of Britishness.

Some of these tendencies, although bad enough, may be checked or reversed and their effects may be only temporary. After all, the Government will change eventually; there will be some recovery in the economy, even if there is little sign of any escape from its fundamental weakness; the failings of the law courts and of the royal family may be forgotten and forgiven. These changes by themselves are, however, unlikely to halt the steady decline of confidence in the British system because its troubles are far more deep-seated than any temporary difficulty.

The British system has been in existence for nearly 300 years and has had far-reaching consequences. It is therefore surprising how little investigation has been made of its origins and nature. Historians have tended to regard it as the mere continuation of England under another name or have taken its existence for granted. In fact, one of the few serious attempts to explain what it is and how it came about appears in a book published only last year. This is *Britain: Forging the Nation, 1707-1837*, by the distinguished historian, Linda Colley. She has blind spots, particularly towards Scotland, but her book is the most thorough and penetrating account so far of the nature of Britishness.

Colley begins at the Union of 1707 when "as a would-be nation rather than a name, Great Britain was invented". The Union was "profoundly unpopular" in Scotland and there were "profound cultural and historical divisions between the English, the Scottish and the Welsh". This new nation was an artificial invention, "forged above all by war", especially the long war with France from 1689 to 1815. Partly because France was the leading Catholic power, "an uncompromising Protestantism was the foundation on which the state was explicitly and unapologetically based". [5]

In spite of these unpromising origins, the idea of Britain became widely accepted in the course of the 19th century, even in Scotland. (In fact, one might say particularly in Scotland, because the English always seem to have had difficulty in understanding the distinction between England and Britain.) As Colley continues, "an extraordinarily large number of Britons seem to have believed that, under God, they were particularly free and particularly prosperous". This is curious because, until recent times, both the freedom and the prosperity applied to only a very small part of the population. The idea of Britishness rested on a mass illusion which Colley calls an "enormous conceit". She identifies a number of factors behind it, apart from Protestantism. "Aggression channelled into war and imperial expansion" led to the Empire which was a British, as opposed to an English, institution. "A reverence for Parliament became an increasingly important part of élite attitudes, and a vital part of élite patriotism", The myth of monarchy was part of it as well, although in the period of Colley's book it had not yet reached the height of apotheosis which it later achieved. [6]

It is not part of Colley's purpose to describe the consolidation of this system in the latter half of the 19th century or to speculate about how long it might last. She does allow herself to "express the hope that if Britishness survives (and it may not) it will in the future find a more pragmatic and more generous form". Britishness, as it emerges from her frank account, is not something which any fair-minded person would want to perpetuate. Its essential characteristics have been as "an artificial nation, governed at the highest level by a predominantly landed — and in the early decades especially — an aggressively Anglocentric oligarchy", depending for its identity on war and on an irrational conviction of superiority.[7]

One of the virtues of this important book is that, although its period ends in 1837, it helps us to understand the nature of Britishness in its heyday and to see why it now inevitably faces collapse. No one would now dare to claim that Britain was vastly superior to her European neighbours in either freedom or prosperity, but the decline has been still more radical. The fact is that the four props, on which Britishness rested, have now all either disappeared or changed and weakened beyond recognition.

Protestantism may once have been a unifying force, although there have always been substantial differences between the Churches of England and Scotland. It no longer has any political weight in a society of diverse religions which is predominantly secular. The exception, of course, is Northern Ireland where 17th century attitudes have survived and Protestantism is still equated with Britishness and the Crown. More profoudly than they probably realise, the loyalists of Ulster reflect the origins of the Britlsh idea. The great majority of people in mainland Britain regard their attitudes as no more than eccentric and distasteful sectarianism.

The Empire has disappeared into history. In its day, it was the major factor which made the British idea acceptable in Scotland, even if it benefitted individual Scots, rather than Scotland as a nation. As Michael Lynch said in his recent *Scotland: A New History*, the Scots embraced, not Britain, but the British Empire.[8] For this reason, Scotland should logically have terminated the Union as soon as the Empire dissolved after the last War. Almost all of the component parts of the Empire have achieved independence. Scotland, which contributed greatly to their development, has still not recovered what Hamish Henderson calls "the elementary civilised right, of a nation to control over its own affairs".[9]

The institution of Monarchy, although part of the British idea, does not affect the question of the Union very much one way or the other. It has been no obstacle to the independence of the other countries which used to be parts of the Empire. In any case, Monarchy itself now faces a very dubious future. Within a few months it has declined from something apparently unassailable and sacrosanct to a questionable anachronism. It is not its cost nor the indiscretions of the younger members of the family which are the real objections to it, but again much more fundamental defects.

At the end of the 17th century Andrew Fletcher of Saltoun said that a hereditary prince is as absurd as a hereditory professor would be. [10] Certainly, nothing could be more illogical than choosing a head of state, or the holder of any other important office, not by personal qualities, but by parentage alone. This involves the high risk that the accident of birth can land you with someone who is quite incapable of the job. This happens all the time with family businesses, which is why very few of them survive for more than two or three generations. It might be argued that this does not matter in the case of the monarchy which has no power, but then why preserve an expensive institution which does so little? The fact is that the role of the monarch in the British state, although residual in a constitutional sense, still has a pervasive influence on social and political attitudes, and this influence is wholly undesirable. It is probably one of the main reasons for the failures and decline of the British state.

In the first place, the monarchy by its nature endorses the medieval idea of inherited privilege which is repugnant to social justice and common sense. You cannot logically object to inherited privilege in the House of Lords, or any other British Institution, if you accept it at the top. Consequently, a largely unconscious acceptance of this antiquated and pernicious principle runs through the whole of British life.

Apologists for the monarchy often tell us that it is an institution which is greatly admired abroad. We are told how lucky we are to have it and how good it is for the tourist trade. I have some experience in other countries and have had opportunities to witness reactions in this matter. My impression is that some people in other countries are titillated by the soap opera, but that most intelligent people regard it as a ludicrous survival which no modern society should tolerate. We are regarded with more pity than admiration.

But the worse thing of all about monarchy, and especially the British version of it, is that it cultivates an attitude of reverence and humility towards people of very ordinary capacity, which is an insult to intelligence and fills heads with nonsense. This has been wearing a bit thin recently in some quarters, but the British press still expects its readers to respond to royal photographs as to a mystical icon. This whole attitude of unreality introduces a large element of myth and make-believe into the process of government which conceals and confuses the reality of power.

This myth and make-believe badly corrupts the last of the four pillars of Britishness, the Westminster Parliament. Unionist politicians in the British parties speak much about the sovereignty of Parliament. According to this theory, Parliament is supposed to be the supreme authority which controls the Executive. The truth is the opposite. It is the Executive which controls Parliament. As long as the Prime Minister has the support of his own party and they have an overall majority, the Prime Minister has more individual and arbitrary power than any monarch in history. Parliament fought long to curb royal power, but the result has been the transfer of the royal prerogative to the Prime Minister. This is true even of an inadequate Prime Minister like John Major. His power is secure until his own party turns against him.

Lord Hailsham has described this system as "elective dictatorship" and Lord Home said in his autobiography: "But now a party can be elected on a minority vote, and in spite of that gain a Parliamentary majority, and use it to force down the throats of the electorate policies which the majority do not approve. This is a caricature of democracy. It was never meant to be like that." [11] These two prominent Conservatives expressed their anxieties at a time of Labour rule, but the erosion of the checks and balances which once curbed Prime Ministerial power has proceeded at a much fiercer pace under Thatcher and Major. Anthony Sampson points out in his latest book that centralising power has been diminished all over Europe, but that Britain has done the opposite. "The British in the last decade have seen concentrations of power which the Victorians never dreamt of." [12] Every rival to the central power of the Prime Minister, particularly the local authorities and the trade unions, has been curbed and emasculated. All contrary opinion has been derided or ignored. Ruthless use of Prime Ministerial patronage has packed public bodies with yes men.

The British parliamentary system has always been liable to abuse. There is no written constitution to curb the misuse of power, no guarantee of human rights and no freedom of information. The first past the post electoral system works with the reliability and fairness of a roulette wheel. In the absence of fixed terms, the Government can fix the date of elections to suit itself and manipulate fiscal policy to influence the result. In addition to the Honours system, the Government has at its disposal a large number of influential and lucrative appointments. There is no limit on the amount of money which political parties can spend centrally on propaganda and election campaigns. Parties are under no legal obligation to publish their accounts nor information about donations from firms or individuals, domestic or foreign. The procedures of the House of Commons (as the Maastricht debate amply demonstrated) are arcane and absurd.

In the past, this ramshackle and easily abused system survived because of a tacit agreement between Government and Opposition to operate it with restraint and resist the temptation to exploit its weaknesses. Alternative centres of power and influence, such as the local authorities, the trade unions, the universities and the broadcasters were tolerated with very little interference by the Government. Patronage was shared between the parties and the quangos were not packed with Government nominees. Sophisticated and expensive publicity techniques had not yet been introduced into British elections and money therefore played a lesser role. The first past the post electoral system worked fairly well as long as there were only two major parties.

The remnants of this old system of fair play, mutual restraint and consensus (which is all that substituted for a written constitution to shield the British system from the risks of tyranny and corruption) was shattered by Margaret Thatcher. She despised consensus and was determined not only to impose her dogma but to curb all alternative centres of power. When it suited her, she had no hesitation in reneging on promises, such as the commitment to give a measure of autonomy to Scotland. She used the power of patronage to extend the influence of the governing party and to attract donations to party funds. Honours were given to compliant newspaper editors and to directors of firms who used their company funds to make large donations to the Tory Party. By these means and by the creation of artificial booms before she called elections, she seemed to be set on creating a permanent one-party state, at least in England. She was eventually sacked by her own party, not for any of these reasons, but because they thought she had become an electoral liability

The semi-secret conspiracy between certain businessmen and the Tory Party has become even more flagrant, or at least more exposed, under John Major. It has long been evident that this Government tends to award knighthoods and peerages to directors of companies which have made substantial donations to the Tory Party. This is a misuse of money which properly belongs to the shareholders or customers, who are not consulted, for the purposes of private vanity. It is much more sinister when the awards are appointments to senior, and often well-paid, posts in the new quangos set up by the Government to take over powers previously exercised by elected councillors. The most recent examples are the police authorities proposed for England and Wales and the water boards proposed for Scotland. It is still more sinister if the donations (which, as we have seen recently, can be from foreign businesmen of doubtful integrity) are intended to influence Government policy. This is difficult to prove, but is it a coincidence that the tobacco companies are large donors and the Government stubbornly refuses to ban tobacco advertising? Is the illogical and anti-social preference for road over rail unconnected with the donations from the car manufacturers and road builders?

The over-all impression is of a thoroughly corrupt system under which businessmen finance the expensive election campaigns which keep the Tories in power and they repay the favour with policies designed to favour the private interests of the donors. Margaret Thatcher used to be fond of invoking the authority of Adam Smith, at least during her visits to Scotland. Her Party have conspicuously ignored his advice on this matter. He said in *The Wealth of Nations* that Governments should regard the advice of "merchants and master manufacturers" with the most scrupulous and suspicious attention. "It comes from an order of men whose interest is never exactly the same with that of the public, who have generally an interest to deceive and even to oppress the public". In another passage he said that "people of the same trade seldom meet together, even for merriment and diversion, but the conversation ends in a conspiracy against the public" [13] Under the British system, Government has been reduced to exactly such a conspiracy.

This system has worked to the particular disadvantage of Scotland. Our evident desire for self-government has been disregarded. For more than a decade Scotland has been governed by a party which it rejects at the polls and which has imposed policies opposed by the great majority of the people. The Government makes promises to serve its immediate purposes, such as Lord Home's before the Referendum, and the "guarantees" to Britoil, Ravenscraig and Rosyth; it then ignores them when they become inconvenient. Scotland has been treated with contempt like a helpless and despised colony. James VI boasted that he was able, with the backing of English power, to rule Scotland from London by the stroke of a pen. Ian Lang is under the same illusion. So far, he has got away with it, partly because the official Opposition has been feeble. He may now have gone too far. The Scottish people are long-suffering to a fault, but even they cannot stomach the blatant breach of trust over Rosyth, followed so quickly by the gerrymandering (or langrigging) of the local government proposals, with their implied threat of the eventual privatisation of water. The Government, by its own actions, has now destroyed all credibility in itself because its guarantees and promises have been exposed as worthless. A Government and a system in which hardly anyone now has any faith does not deserve to survive, and it is unlikely that it will.

5.6

The European Union: a New Chance for Scotland

'Scotland on Sunday', 27th May 1994

Scotland, at present, can only look on enviously as Austria, Finland, Norway and Sweden, countries comparable to us in size and in other ways, are about to become member states of the European Union. There are advantages in separate membership which are denied to us as long as we are treated as a region of Britain. With about the same population as Scotland, Denmark has sixteen seats in the European Parliament. Scotland as a 'region' has only eight. That is a fact of increasing practical importance as the Parliament gains in power; but it is only a symbol of a much greater distinction.

The fact is that independent governments, in spite of the limitations of independence which now apply to all of them, have powers and rights utterly different in kind from those of regions, provinces and other subordinated territories. International relations are conducted between independent governments. They are the members of the international organisations which are like clubs where the members have privileges denied to everyone else. The views and interests of even the smallest and poorest of them have to be taken into account by the other members in a way which simply does not apply to the regions.

This is one of the basic rules of international life. I am very conscious of it because I was involved in it for years as a diplomat. I have been the assistant head of the United Nations Department of the Foreign Office and I have conducted negotiations with eastern European countries on behalf of the European Community during a period when the UK held the Presidency. Always in such matters you have to have regard for the views of other member states and they are the only players on the board.

The consequence is that the international organisations have limited the power of the larger countries but have actually enhanced the influence of the smaller ones. In the bad old days large countries could achieve their purposes by sending a gun boat. Now they normally have to play by the rules and work towards a consensus with their fellow member states. Even Michael Heseltine has recognised this. He said in a television discussion in November 1991: "if you are relatively small and relatively without power, it's obvious that as a state in such a circumstance, if you can become part of a club and can be heard at the centre of that club, you can actually enhance your sovereignty, because you're influencing a wider power grouping".

The European Union is a case in point. The advantages which it gives to the smaller countries have been analysed in a paper just published by the Scottish Centre for Economic and Social Research, *The Power of Small Nations in the New Europe*. It quotes former Danish and Irish Prime Ministers explaining how much more influence membership of the European Union has given to their countries. Garret Fitzgerald, for instance has said that this is the clearest justification of Irish independence. It is also a strong additional reason why Scotland needs independence and why the half-way house of Labour or Liberal Democrat devolution would be inadequate.

The British Government in the current election campaign is laying emphasis on what they curiously call the "British veto". In fact, such veto rights as there are, and this is something which can only be used very rarely if at all, apply equally to every member state. They do not apply to the great majority of decisions which are taken by qualified majority voting. Here the rules are designed to prevent the larger states imposing their will on the smaller ones. No decision can be taken without the agreement of several of the smaller countries. They will have even more influence when the new applicants join next January. This is why the British Government recently tried with humiliating bluster and ineffectiveness to change the rules. The new members along with

Denmark and Ireland, and I trust eventually Scotland, will have together 23 votes compared to the 10 of the UK and the small northern countries are likely to agree on most issues.

What then do the unionist parties mean when they tell us that Scotland is well served within the 10 votes of the UK? This is simply fantasy or the delusion of former grandeur. Whenever the interests of Scotland and England differ, the views of England must prevail for good democratic reasons because they have ten times our population. Our interests therefore tend to go by default. A good example is the case of steel. The European Union has agreed to preserve the steel production of countries with a single plant. If Scotland was independent, Ravenscraig would still be alive and thriving. Scottish fishing would be in a happier position as well. You have only to visit Dublin or Copenhagen to see the evident economic and cultural stimulus of independent membership. Neither the Danes nor the Irish would thank you for the suggestion that they should be represented by a neighbouring country with 10 votes.

It is not surprising that the Conservatives should want to deny Scotland independence because they see little chance of power in Scotland except on the back of English votes. Labour and the Liberal Democrats are UK parties with their eyes on power in Westminster and for that they need the help of Scottish seats. All of these parties are in effect sacrificing Scotland for the sake of their party interest.

The Parliamentary Union of 1707 and the European Union are very different creatures. The first destroyed the international identity of Scotland and subjected Scotland to a Parliament with no defined limit to its powers and in which Scotland had a small minority voice. The European Union respects the identity of its member states and accords to each of them defined powers and rights. At present Scotland is powerless and invisible internationally. Independent membership would give us the same advantages as Denmark or Ireland.

It is one of the paradoxes of the Scottish situation that the segments of the population which would benefit most directly from independence seem to be the slowest in realising it. There are members of the business and financial communities who are apparently blind to the opportunities. There are people living in Edinburgh who fail to see the enormous increase in status, activity, employment and property values that would follow when it becomes a real capital again. But more and more people are beginning to understand the advantage of recovering direct and independent involvement in Europe. We are fortunate that it can be achieved through the ballot box by votes for the SNP.

5.7

Imperial Nostalgia

'The Herald', 6th October 1995

In his column last Saturday, George Birrell revealed a bad case of nostalgia for the supposedly great days of the British Empire. He prefers *Rule Britannia* to *Flower of Scotland*. He laments the loss of the feel good factor "when the Scots and the English . . . felt a Christian mission to scatter the spores of our civilisation". Presumably he has noticed that Britannia no longer rules the waves and that those on whom the spores were scattered were only too anxious to dispense with the privilege. All of these countries are now independent (with the odd exception such as Scotland) and none of them regret the change.

Birrell also seems to admire the Parliament at Westminster. He thinks that it would be a shame and a waste if George Robertson gave up his seat there in exchange for one in a Scottish Parliament. Has he failed to notice that Westminster has long lost any reputation it once had as a model of democracy? It has an electoral system which gives absolute power to the leader of a party supported by only a minority of the electorate. It is antiquated, corrupt, absurd and largely impotent . As long as a Prime Minister can control his or her own party, he or she controls the House of Commons. A restored Scottish Parliament will be able to make a fresh start and avoid the bad example of Westminster.

Birrell regrets a growing hostility to England, but he fails to see the cause. Of course, there are many historical roots, but the real reason is much more recent. For 16 years we have had policies, which we detest, imposed on us by a party, which we have soundly rejected at the polls, but which a sufficiently large minority of English voters have chosen. To be ruled from the outside by people with different interests and standards of value is the essence of colonialism which is universally regarded as intolerable. In these circumstances is it any wonder that people resent and blame the English?

Certainly it is desirable to have good relations with our English neighbours but this is only likely when we are no longer subject to remote control from London. When we stand on our own feet as a free and equal partner in the European Union, we can treat one another as close allies and friends, not as master and dependent. The English in the great majority are a fair-minded people and have understood this point in scores of formerly dependent territories. Recent opinion polls have suggested that they understand it in our case as well.

In an earlier piece Birrell described the SNP policy of independence in Europe as spurious. The aim of the policy is the same degree of independence as any other member of the European Union. Birrell seems to be entirely unaware of the advantages of this for the smaller countries, such as Denmark or potentially Scotland. All countries in the modern world accept limitations on their independence through their membership of international organisations such as the United Nations or the European Union. These organisations impose restraints on the larger powers, but they enhance the influence of the smaller countries. This is especially true of the European Union where the voting system is designed to give a disproportionate weight to them, and it is why John Major tried and failed to change the rules at the last expansion of membership. Ministers of the smaller countries frequently comment on the way in which membership has increased and not diminished their influence. The sooner Scotland becomes a member in our own right the better.

George Birrell's wallowing in nostalgia would be picturesque and funny if it were not so pernicious. This old fogey tendency is an obstacle to the emancipation and progress of Scotland. Usually the victims of the tendency are sensible enough to keep their prejudices to themselves. Perhaps Birrell is performing a public service by speaking out and revealing the real absurdity of Unionist reaction.

5.8

Culture is Fundamental

Remarks by Paul H. Scott to inaugural conference of the Elphinstone Institute, 9th September 1996.

I greatly welcome the establishment of the Elphinstone Institute. The north of Scotland is the source of vital elements of our traditional culture and the Institute is well placed to preserve, enhance and increase awareness of them. It is highly appropriate that it should take the name of Bishop Elphinstone, one of the great men of one of the greatest periods in our history. If his advice had been taken, the disaster of Flodden might have been avoided and the subsequent history of Scotland would have been very different. As it is, one of the great achievements of the brilliant renaissance in the reign of James IV is still visible in this University which he founded. I am confident that the Institute will make a significant contribution to the University and to the modern renaissance of our culture which has been growing in strength since Patrick Geddes first used the phrase just over a hundred years ago. I congratulate Professor Porter and everyone else involved in this important and inspiring venture.

I have been asked to speak to you today on behalf of the Scottish National Party. There is a very close relationship between the evolution of this political party and the recovery of our national cultural awareness and self confidence. The Scottish Home Rule Association was founded in 1886 at the same time as Geddes was proclaiming a new cultural, revival. After the first World War Hugh MacDiarmid gave a fresh impulse to both the political and the cultural movements. This sort of relationship between the poets, thinkers and artists and the politicians is common to independence movements everywhere and there is a good reason for it. Scotland needs independence for self-respect, for democratic principle, for economic prosperity, to make our own contribution to international affairs; but the fundamental reason is cultural. It is because we have a distinctive, diverse and valuable national culture that we need independence to fulfill our potential and give expression to our identity.

Struan Stevenson has spoken at some length about the Darien scheme. Since this is a period which I have studied for years and on which I have written two books, I am tempted to follow him. I shall refrain because I do not think it would be very relevant; but I shall mention a document of that time, the Claim of Right of 1689. It was because I was writing a book which referred to it while I was also a member of the Constitutional Steering Committee that I suggested that we should use the same name for our report. This was *A Claim of Right for Scotland*, published in July 1988 and which led to the formation of the Constitutional Convention.

Confusingly enough, this Convention at its inaugural meeting in March 1989 signed another document which they also called a Claim of Right. In this all but one of the Scottish Labour, and all the Scottish Liberal Democrat, Members of Parliament acknowledged the sovereign right of the Scottish people. This is, of course, entirely contrary to the doctrine recently asserted by Tony Blair that his devolution scheme would leave sovereignty at Westminster. When he was questioned about this in an interview with *The Scotsman*, he gave the impression that he did not understand the point at all.

But this is a digression. I mention all this because I want to quote a passage in the report of 1988, which was brilliantly drafted by Jim Ross and approved by the Constitutional Steering Committee, of which the late Sir Robert Grieve was the chairman. There is an introductory section, "The Past: essential facts of Scottish history", in which it says:

> Scottish nationhood does not rest on constitutional history alone. It is supported by a culture reaching back over centuries and bearing

> European comparison in depth and quality, nourished from a relatively early stage by an education system once remarkable by European standards. Since the Union, the strength of that culture has fluctuated but there is no ground for any claim that, overall or even at any particular time, it has benefitted from the Union. On the contrary the Union has always been, and remains a threat to the survival of a distinctive culture in Scotland.

This report has been described as one of the best analyses of the situation in which Scotland finds itself. It seems to me that the passage which I have just quoted goes to the roots of the cultural issues which we are discussing today.

The fact that this culture has so long survived the threat imposed by the Union is due to two factors: its inherent strength and the large measure of *de facto* autonomy which continued after the Union and partly even to the present. That autonomy is now being steadily eroded with such developments as the impairment of local government, pressure to make Scottish education conform to English ideas, a mass of legislation based on an English conception of society, the domination of broadcasting by London, political parties which pretend to be Scottish, but are in fact controlled by London. All of these parties, for their own reasons, want to preserve the Union; but it is the Union which is the problem. It is frustrating, distorting and intolerable. It is time that we put an end to it.

The achievement of independence will by itself be a powerful stimulus to cultural, as well as economic, creativity and self-confidence. This has been the experience of other countries and there is no reason why this should not happen in Scotland as well. In addition an SNP Government of an independent Scotland would take positive measures to stimulate and invigorate the cultural environment. We should have a Scottish Broadcasting Corporation, a National Theatre, an organisation to encourage cultural exchange with other countries, better facilities for training in traditional music and dance, more attention in the schools to our history, languages, literature, geography and environment, favourable tax arrangements to encourage the arts, including the film industry.

I was particularly encouraged today by the very interesting contribution by Matthew Rooke and by his assurance that the Scottish Arts Council was determined to make "the support of Scotland's indigenous culture central to all its activities". As he made clear himself, this is a radical change of policy. It began only in 1990 when the SAC undertook a survey of the arts in Scotland and discovered that Scottish music and dance were flourishing all around us and that there was a great public demand for their recognition and encouragement. Why was this only discovered in 1990 when the Council had been in existence, originally as a sub-committee of the Arts Council of Great Britain, since 1947? The answer, of course, lies in that origin. It was assumed by those who founded that sub-committee that London was the source of all wisdom and that what Scotland needed was the closest possible replica of the institutions and practices to be found in England. It has taken more than 40 years for a more responsive attitude to the needs and wishes of Scotland to prevail.

5.9

The Union is the Problem

'The Herald', 5th May 1997

The unionist parties in Scotland (and that means the leadership of Labour and the Liberal Democrats as well as what remains of the Tories) all talk as though it was self-evident that the Union of 1707 should be preserved at all costs. This betrays an ignorance of both history and of our future potential. The Union was imposed on a reluctant Scotland to meet the strategic needs of England at the time. It took about 60 years for our economy to recover through our own efforts. It may have been of some benefit to Scotland, or to some Scots at least, in the days of the Empire. By now it has long outlasted its usefulness and it is a serious obstacle to Scotland emulating the prosperity, well-being and contentment of other small and comparable European countries where the quality of life is so much higher than our own.

The Unionists have failed to make a serious case for the Union. They tend to argue that Scotland is too small or too poor, when it is about the ideal size and has the capacity to be the eighth richest country per head in the industrialised world. They suggest that we should lose financially, when in fact Scotland pays more to the UK Treasury than it receives back. They hint darkly that independence would interfere with the free movement of goods and people across the Border, although we are part of the much larger area of free movement and trade of the European Union. They ridicule any idea of Scotland having its own defence forces and diplomatic service; but forces on the scale of Denmark and without outrageous expenditure on the dangerous nonsense of nuclear weapons would be rational and our representation abroad would do wonders for our trade, reputation and self-respect.

There is one respectable argument for unionism. None of the unionist parties rely on it, but it was stated in a consultative paper on Scottish culture in education recently issued by the Consultative Council on the Curriculum. In Scotland, it said, there were some people for whom "the Union is political and cultural" and who had "a strong sense of common UK purposes". In other words, there are people in Scotland who feel either more British than Scottish or entirely British and not Scottish at all. There is nothing surprising about this when you consider the deluge of British propaganda to which we have all been subjected, particularly since the introduction of broadcasting and especially television.

The unionist parties do not rely on an appeal to Britishness because they know that it would not work. All the opinion polls and academic studies on the subject have shown that only about 10% of the population regard themselves as only British or more British than Scottish. Consequently all of these parties in Scotland, even the Tories, emphasise their Scottishness and cultivate Scottish symbols. Labour has adopted the English rose and the English bulldog and it covers its platforms in England with the Union Jack; but in Scotland the Saltire is prominent as well.

It is inevitable that British parties, controlled from London and aiming at power in the Westminster Parliament, should follow a predominantly British agenda. Even if they are willing to concede a Scottish Parliament, and all of them have a various times professed this, they always add in the next breath, within the United Kingdom, and they propose to leave real power at Westminster. There are obvious reasons why Westminster wants to hold on to Scotland. They want the oil revenues and the taxation raised in Scotland. If we were really the financial liabilty which they pretend, the situation would be different. Also Scotland is useful as a conveniently remote base for the submarines with nuclear weapons. Vast sums have been spent on building it and you can imagine the outcry if it was proposed to remove the whole thing to an English back-yard. Since it has no real military purpose, they might be glad of an excuse to abolish it, except that it is the last remaining pretext to justify Britain's declining claim to be regarded as a major power.

Until the Election on 1st May radically changed the situation, there were also particular reasons why the Tories and Labour wanted to keep the Union. It meant that the Tories could enjoy the fruits of office in Scotland without having to win our votes. Labour used to think that it needed the Scottish seats to have any chance of achieving power at Westminster. Now both of these motives have disappeared. The Tories have been wiped out, partly because of the accumulated disgust of the electorate, partly because of the crazy effects of first past the post, but also at least partly because of their stubborn hostility to constitutional change. As many Tories have already realised, their best hope now lies in a Scottish Parliament with proportional representation. Labour is now so strong in England that they now longer depend on Scottish seats.

We should therefore now be able to conduct an intelligent and serious debate about our constitutional future without the distortion of these party political factors.

George Robertson and other Labour leaders have suggested that the Election settled the issue between independence and devolution, but of course people were voting for a great many different reasons. I do not think that there is much doubt that the main motive was an overwhelming desire to get rid of the Tories. The only constitutional implication of which we can be certain is that few people agreed with John Major's crusade to defend the Union.

Labour leaders have also suggested that they want "entrenchment" of a devolved Parliament, not to protect it against abolition by Westminster, but to attempt to deny it the right even to hold a referendum on independence. Perhaps what happened to the Tories in the Election may have persuaded them of the dangers of opposing the popular will. It showed that there is more reality in the Scottish belief that sovereignty lies with the people than in the English notion, shared evidently by Tony Blair, that it belongs to the Westminster Parliament.

5.10

The Age of the Small Nation: a reply to John Reid

'The Scotsman', 29th May 1998

The lecture by John Reid MP, Minister for the Armed Forces, on 25th May was widely trailed as the launch of a Labour campaign to deploy an intellectual case against the SNP. In fact, it was stronger on rhetoric than on any solid or original argument.

Reid's first point was that the constitutional issue was settled by the Referendum last September which, he insisted, showed that "the expressed will of the Scottish people" was for devolution, not independence. This was a shaky start. We all know that the strong 'Yes' vote was partly due to the support of Alex Salmond and the SNP. There was a decisive majority for a Scottish Parliament; but we do not know how many were for devolution and how many for independence because the Labour Government refused to put that question to the vote. If they are so sure that the majority of the Scottish people do not want independence, why do they refuse to ask them?

Next, John Reid advanced a somewhat tortuous argument which seemed to be designed to imply, although it is not true, that Scotland had never been independent of England. Scottish nationhood, he said, had always been "established and maintained through the relationships with the world beyond its boundaries". That, I suppose, is true of every country in the world. Even the Declaration of Arbroath, said Reid, warming to his theme, asserted Scottish nationhood "in relation to our larger English neighbour". That is true as well, but only in the sense that the Scots said very firmly that they would resist all English attempts to conquer them.

In defiance of the poll evidence (which shows the opposite) Reid maintained that most Scots felt as much British as Scottish. The Scots, he believed, had not rejected Britain, but Conservative policies. This is a dangerous line when you consider how little Blair has departed from these policies. And can we be sure that Scotland will never again have to suffer a real Tory Government, elected by mainly English votes? That is one of the hazards of Unionism. Reid was honest enough to concede that Britain has lost the Empire and has declined economically and in general prestige. He asked us to believe that Labour would change all that.

Reid's conclusion was that Labour was modern, but the SNP was old-fashioned. The SNP would "wrench Scotland out of the United Kingdom and the British single market". It would therefore, he thought, create economic and political instability. He seems to have forgotten that Scotland is now in a European market of 270 million (which will rise to about 400 million after enlargement), not a British one of 40 million. The existence of the European Union, and the increasing part which it plays in our affairs, is the reason which makes it necessary for Scotland to become a member in its own right. This will be much more stable than the contradictions of devolution, which pretends to give Scotland freedom, but simultaneously maintains London control. It is this, and not the clearly established status of membership of the European Union, which is a recipe for instablity.

The most prosperous, socially just and contented parts of the European Union are the small nation states, many of them much smaller than Scotland. It is widely recognised that this is the age of the small nation. That is the modern course, not the maintenance of the United Kingdom, one of the few surviving multi-national states, the dinosaurs of the past. In raising the question of modernity, John Reid has revealed the extent to which Labour Unionists are living in the past, still relying on arguments used in the days of the British Empire. They have failed to notice how much the world has changed.

5.11

The Recovery of Self-Respect

Letter to 'The Scotsman' of 25th July 1998

Dear Sir,

As one would expect, Andrew Marr's qualified defence of the Union (25th July) is more sensible than such things usually are. He does, however, still rely on two old, tired and unconvincing arguments.

The first is that "it seems handy to pool expensive functions like defence". That means that we have to pay a share of the heavy cost of nuclear weapons which we neither need or want. A defence force suitable to our needs would be a more rational and cheaper option than helping to sustain the pretensions of a former great power.

Secondly, he says that says that "small nations won't count" in the re-organisation of the EU. In fact, the system of weighted voting is such that no decision is possible under it without the vote of a number of the smaller member countries. The admission of new members will increase the number of the smaller countries and put them into an even stronger position, especially when they act together, as is likely over most aspects of re-organisation.

Marr suggests that the existence of a devolved Parliament will end the need for Scotland to complain about Westminster, but is that likely when Westminster still retains 17 pages of reserved powers and financial control?

George Kerevan makes some good points, but Scotland has had a distinct culture for centuries, not just for 30 years. He suggests that "the real reason for independence is jobs and international relations"; but there is also the recovery of self-respect, the confidence that goes with it, and the ability to form a society that meets our needs and aspirations.

Paul Henderson Scott

5.12

Does Scotland need Embassies?

'The Scotsman', 13th October 1998

A Scottish newspaper has described the office which the Scottish Office are opening in Brussels as the first Scottish Embassy. This is wrong on two counts. First of all, the independent Scotland before the king flitted to London in 1603 had active diplomatic relations with the rest of Europe. At that time countries did not normally maintain permanent establishments in other countries, but sent embassies for particular negotiations. So the office in Brussels is by no means the first. Neither is it an embassy in the real sense of the term. Only independent countries responsible for their own foreign relations can aspire to them, just as they alone have votes in international organisations. The office in Brussels is a step in the right direction. It is an embryonic embassy, just as a devolved parliament is a step towards a real parliament, free from London control.

This first step raises many questions. Do we need embassies at all in the modern world of instant communications? Do they have to be in grandiose buildings and run in a lavish and expensive style? Would an independent Scotland have to have them all over the world?

I think that the answer to the first question has to be yes. The interdependence of the modern world creates more and not fewer points of contact between governments. There are many questions which arise between them, on such matters as trade, economic and military assistance, cultural exchange, regional co-operation and so forth, down to personal problems of individuals. Embassies provide a channel of communication between officials who can establish a working relationship. Between member states of international organisations and with the staff of the organisations there is a need for a permanent dialogue of this kind so that each government can try to ensure that its views and interests are taken into account in the drafting of agreements and in the final vote. Embassies can also help our exporters and tourist industry. They have a responsibility to keep their government informed about political and economic developments which may affect them.

This is all routine civil service work, which you might suppose could be conducted in similar buildings and with a similar life style to government departments at home. But what is the reality? The recent programme on BBC 2. "The Secret Art of Government", gave a glimpse inside the British Embassy in Paris. It showed a building like a royal palace with furniture, works of art, cuisine, cellar, and an army of servants to match. Admittedly, this is the grandest of British Embassies, although others in large and important countries are in a similar league. I suspect that Paris is the most magnificent of British Embassies, not so much because of an English desire to impress their traditional enemy (although our ally), as because French confidence in their cultural superiority is an irresistible challenge.

The word, embassy, officially applies not to the offices where the bulk of the work is done, but to the residence of the ambassador. I say the bulk of the work because, of course, the entertainment in the residence of members of the government of the host country, and of opinion formers generally, are part of the process of building up good relations. The quality of the surroundings and of the food and wine do doubt helps, but it does not really need the splendour of a palace. Perhaps this habit is a relic of the time when diplomacy was the business of Kings.

The building itself is meant to convey to the public at large an image of the wealth and power of the country. There is a parallel with the banks and head offices of major companies. Until quite recently, banks evidently felt the need to display their solidity and reliability by putting even quite small branches into buildings of classical style with marble floors and mahogany counters. In Scotland at least this policy has been abandoned. They have kept the least impressive of their buildings and sold the grandest to become night clubs, pubs or humble shops. Is there a lesson here for the embassies?

I remark in passing that banks and large companies are as lavish as embassies in their entertainment of those they wish to influence. Perhaps they have found that this is cost effective; but they have evidently decided that they no longer have to rely on their architecture to create the right impression on the public. Governments may not always have the same degree of self-confidence. It is a matter of keeping up with the Joneses. Many countries seem to believe that people will judge their standing in the world by the splendour of their embassies. I not suppose that many people in fact care about such things. It is probably only great powers who worry about them, particularly great powers in decline.

British Embassies are a case in point. The Government is about to spend £80 million on a new building in Moscow. One of the failings of the British system (and one of the reasons why we should escape from it) is that it involves a desperate, and expensive, clinging to the trappings of past greatness. Accordingly, Britain still has embassies of the size and grandeur appropriate to a great power, and in almost every country in the world. Scotland as a small nation would be well served with something much more modest, comparable to Norway, Denmark or Ireland, and we need them only in countries where we have important interests. At present the Scottish tax payer helps to finance the British diplomatic service. Our own service would not only look after our interests more effectively and suitably but would cost less. The same is true of defence expenditure. Palatial embassies and nuclear weapons are expensive status symbols which we can do without.

5.13

The Third Claim of Right: a Decisive Document

'The Herald', 16th November 1998

Andrew Marr said recently in the *Observer* that the Campaign for a Scottish Assembly "was built up by amateurs from scratch, until it changed the whole game of British politics". This is true, if by amateurs you mean people who are not professional politicians. It is strange how little comment there has been about this remarkable event. Even the tenth anniverary of the publication in July 1988 of *A Claim of Right for Scotland* passed without remark, although it is probably the most influential political document published in Scotland in this century.

I can speak about this from the inside because I was involved in the events which led to it. When I came back to live in Scotland in November 1980, after working abroad, it was to a subdued and pessimistic country. The 'Yes' majority in the 1979 Referendum had been by so small a margin that it could safely be disregarded. This was precisely what the new Government under Mrs Thatcher proceeded to do, despite all their previous promises of a stronger and better Act. The Labour Party was preoccupied with its heavy defeat and its own internal problems. Blame for the failure of the Labour measure was unfairly attached to the SNP and their support drained away for some years. Scottish Home Rule disappeared as an issue from the press. It seemed that Scotland had had its chance and had blown it.

But there were people who refused to accept defeat. Shortly after my return I went to a meeting of the Campaign for a Scottish Assembly with Jack Brand as Convener and was enlisted in its executive committee. This was a very small organisation at first, but we gradually involved like-minded people all over Scotland. Brand was succeeded as Convener by Jim Boyack and then Alan Armstrong. Such people as Hugh Millar, Alan Lawson, Greg McCara and Peter Finlay worked long and hard. We did the usual things, leaflets and public meetings which filled places like the Assembly Rooms in Edinburgh; but we aimed at more constructive measures.

Other countries in a similar situation had used the device of a Constitutional Convention. Gordon Wilson, then leader of the SNP, had once proposed it for Scotland in the House of Commons. It offered a sensible, co-operative and democratic way forward. Hugh Millar has reminded me that the decision to work for it was taken at a meeting in my flat, but the real problem was how was it to be achieved. Here Alan Lawson was a key figure. He had given the Campaign a public voice in his admirable magazine, *Radical Scotland*, and he was ingenious in devising the machinery and establishing contacts with the political parties. It was, I think, his idea that we should establish a Constitutional Steering Committee of "prominent Scots" to make practical recommendations.

This committee, after some months of steady work, issued its report in July 1988 as *A Claim of Right for Scotland*. It should not be confused with a much shorter document, confusingly with the same title, which the Constitutional Convention signed at their first meeting on 30th March in the following year. This second document pledged the members to "acknowledge the sovereign right of the Scottish people to determine the form of government best suited to their needs". It was signed by, among others, all but one of the Scottish Labour MPs, in blatant contradiction to Tony Blair's subsequent claim that "sovereignty rests with me as a Westminster MP" and to a similar assertion in the White Paper and the Bill for the Scottish Parliament. The term, 'Claim of Right', has, of course, historical resonance in Scotland. It was used in 1689, when the Scottish Parliament deposed James VII, and again in 1842 during the Disruption crisis. I suggested that we should use it again in 1988 because I had been writing about the 1689 events for my book on Andrew Fletcher and the parallels were obvious.

In this Steering Committee we were very fortunate in both our chairman, Sir Robert Grieve, and our secretary, Jim Ross. The late Sir Robert Grieve, the distinguished town and country planner, was, as always, patient, amiable and open-minded. He kept the business moving forward, but never stifled debate. Jim Ross is a former senior official of the Scottish Office who had been concerned with the Scotland Act of the 1970s and is a long-standing member of the Labour Party. He was the real author of the Report. He tabled drafts of each section in turn, listened to the discussion and for the next meeting produced a revision which miraculously incorporated a mass of ideas into a text which was lucid, coherent and even eloquent with which we were all not only satisfied, but delighted. (Jim was also, by the way, a leader of the attempt to keep the TSB in the ownership of its depositors. He succeeded in the Court of Session, but their judgement was overturned by the House of Lords.)

There were 14 other members of the committee with a wide range of experience such as Maxwell Craig, Nigel Grant, Joy Hendry, Isobel Lindsay, Neil MacCormick, Una Macintosh and Judy Steel. We all participated as individuals and not as party members. Indeed, this has always been the practice of the Campaign for a Scottish Assembly. We never enquired about party affiliations. It was a cross-party, or rather non-party, organisation.

As it happens, because it was not deliberate, our report was closer to the views of the SNP than of Labour. In reading it again, I recognise many points which I suggested: "the union has always been, and remains, a threat to the survival of a distinctive culture in Scotland"; "the British Prime Minister has in practice a degree of arbitrary power which few, if any, English and no Scottish Monarchs have rivalled"; "the UK has been an anomaly from its inception and is a glaring anomaly now"; "we believe there are good arguments for returning to the traditional usage of Parliament rather than Assembly". I am sure that my colleagues would say the same because the Report was an amalgam of the views of all of us. It did several things; it made detailed proposals for ways in which a Constitutional Convention could be set up; but it was also a clear statement of the inadequacies of both the Scottish and British systems of government. Neal Ascherson said that it was "the most penetrating constitutional critique of the United Kingdom which I have read in this decade". We were building on a century of debate, but after *A Claim of Right* I think that the constitutional status quo became simply untenable.

Discussions between the CSA and the political parties began immediately after the publication of the Report to see if they were willing to create a Convention either by direct elections,or by involving existing elected Members of Parliament and Councillors or in some other way. At first, the CSA was fairly confident of the SNP and of the Liberal Democrats. We were less sure of the Labour Party and they were crucial because their dominant position in Scottish politics at that time. Labour hesitations disappeared when Jim Sillars won the Govan by-election in October 1988; they have always been more pro-Scottish when they perceive a threat from the SNP. They opted for a Constitutional Convention formed mainly from existing MPs and Councillors which gave them a strong majority in it. Partly for this reason, and partly because Labour insisted that the objective was to strengthen the Union by devolution within the UK, the SNP felt obliged to withdraw. The Liberal Democrats stayed on board.

Many people felt that the SNP withdrawal was a mistake and I argued against it myself. But the SNP had bitter memories of 1979 when they worked harder for a Labour measure than Labour itself, only to suffer the blame when it failed. We could hardly be expected again to participate with Labour in an attempt, according to them, to strengthen the Union from which we wanted to escape.

By the usual time-scale of such events, subsequent events have been very fast. *A Claim of Right*, July 1988; Constitutional Convention established, March 1989; its agreed recommendations, 30th November 1995; Government White Paper, July 1997; Referendum, 11th September, 1997; Bill , 17th December, 1997 and now completing its parliamentary process. All within 10 years and all derived from *A Claim of Right*, which is why it is such an important document.

The clear verdict of the Scottish people was achieved with the strong support of the SNP. The Government had refused to include a question on independence as an option, but the SNP made it clear that they advocated a double 'Yes' vote as a step towards independence. The Referendum therefore demonstrated an overwhelming majority for a Scottish Parliament, but left open the decision whether it should remain devolutionary or move on to independence. Whatever the outcome, I have little doubt that future historians will regard *A Claim of Right* of 1988 as a constitutional statement of comparable importance to the Declaration of Arbroath, Buchanan's *De Jure Regni Apud Scotos*, the National Covenant of 1638, the speeches of Andrew Fletcher or Walter Scott's *Letters of Malachi Malagrowther*.

5.14

A Stranger at Loss in a Strange Land

'The Times', 28th August 1998

The Prime Minister is in Scotland this week, no doubt hoping to do something to reverse the decline there in the fortunes of the Labour Party. His previous visits have had the opposite effect. Like Margaret Thatcher he has a tendency to make remarks which set Scottish teeth on edge. Notorious examples are his insistence that sovereignty rested with him as an English MP, although all but one of his Scottish MPs had signed a solemnn declaration that it belonged to the Scottish people; or his comparison of the future Scottish Parliament to an English village council, although his Scottish ministers had repeatedly assured the Scots that it would be a real Parliament with real powers.

The experience of these British Prime Ministers, who are as unpopular in Scotland as they are popular in England, suggests that the great Victorian English historian, H. T. Buckle, was right. He spent many years studying the intellectual development of both Scotland and England in preparation for his *History of Civilisation.* His conclusion was that in spite of all the influences which they shared, the "essential antagonism" between them was as great "as if there had never been any means of their influencing each other and as if they had never had anything in common". It is a point which English politicians should bear in mind.

But, of course, Blair is only English by choice. He was born and educated in Scotland, but not in an ordinary Scottish school but at Fettes, an imitation English public school planted in Scotland. His lack of feel for Scottish opinion suggests that Fettes is firmly insulated from the Scottish life which surrounds it.

At the same time, it has to be said that Blair's unquestionably Scottish lieutenants have not fared much better. Donald Dewar is an intelligent, cultivated man who is steeped in Scottish life, law, literature and politics; but since he became Secretary of State for Scotland he has staggered from one disaster to another. Again some examples: the denial of a knighthood to Sean Connery which the Tories had recommended (trivial perhaps, but he is very popular in Scotland and is a prominent supporter of the SNP); the decision to put the Scottish Parliament at Holyrood, although public opinion was clearly in favour of the more conspicuous and accessible site on the Calton Hill; the suppression of a Scottish Office funded report on the place of Scottish history, literature and languages in the schools.

The reason in each case was the same, a fear that an appeal to Scottish sentiment would help the SNP. When Michael Forsyth was the last Tory Scottish Secretary he followed the opposite policy of trying to outflank the the SNP by showing that he was as Scottish as anybody else. He appeared in a kilt at the premiere of *Braveheart*. He returned the Stone of Destiny from Westminster Abbey to Edinburgh Castle. None of this did him much good because he and all the other Tories in Scotland lost their seats at the next election; but long before that the Tories had become a hopeless case in Scotland whatever thy did.

The Labour Party in Scotland has a particular weakness in the face of the SNP advance. It is split not only between old and new Labour, but between nationalist and centralist wings. In its origins the Labour Party in Scotland was strongly in favour of Home Rule. When the first batch of Labour MPs left Glasgow station for London, they assured their supporters that they would soon be back to establish a Scottish Parliament. Like the Liberals before them, however, they soon discovered that British parties had a different sense of priorities and that life at Westminster had its own attractions. After the Labour victory in 1945, central planning became the enthusiasm of the day and Scottish Home Rule was gradually forgotten. The 1950 Election was the first in which it had no place in Labour's manifesto. When the SNP in the 1970s began to snap at the heels of Labour in Scottish seats, it was the London headquarers which insisted on the adoption of Devolution (the new word for Home Rule) as a defensive tactic. In the 1979 Referendum many Labour activists in Scotland took no part and several of their leaders, such as Robin Cook and Brian Wilson, campaigned for a 'No' vote.

Since then, most of the Labour Party in Scotland have accepted the Devolution policy but for two conflicting reasons. Some, including the nationalist wing, are genuinely in favour of it as something desirable on its own merits. Others, especially the centralists, support it as a means of defusing, or attempting to defuse, the SNP. George Robertson, the Shadow Scottish Secretary before the last Election, frequently asserted that Devolution would "kill the SNP stone dead".

It should have been obvious that the effect would be the opposite. When the Scottish Parliament is restored, there will no longer be a need for a Labour Government to legislate to bring it about or to prevent the return of the Tories. The Scottish electorate will be able to concentrate on Scottish issues. Devolution has failed as a tactic to destroy the SNP.

So what is Labour to do? In the belief that playing to Scottish sentiment helps the SNP, they have purged the list of candidates for the Scottish Parliament both of old Labour and of the nationalist wing. But this is a mistake too because the rebuttal of Scottish sentiment also causes resentment which helps the SNP. Labour is damned if it is pro-Scottish and damned too if it is anti-Scottish. A dilemma.

A solution has been suggested by Tommy Sheppard, a former Assistant General-Secretary of the Labour Party in Scotland. He said that Labour had succeeded in England by occupying the ground of thir chief opponent, the Conservatives. They could only succeed in Scotland by doing the same to their chief opponent there, the SNP. This idea was unwelcome to new labour and Sheppard was duly purged from the candidates list, but perhaps he is right. The Labour Party used to be opposed to independence for Scotland because they needed the Scottish seats to have any chance of power at Westminster. Since they no longer need the seats, is there any good reason why they should still resist Scottish independence?

5.15

Scotland: the Invisible Country

'The Herald', 14th January 1999

In this newspaper on 2nd January there was a report about Thomas Glover, the Scot who in the last century played a major part in introducing industry to Japan. Two Scottish residents had succeeded in having his nationality on a memorial plaque changed from English to Scottish. One of them remarked: "British is not a concept the Japanese understand. Where we would use the word, British, they substitute English".

Of course, it is not only the Japanese who are confused. The confusion began much closer to home and centuries ago. In England itself the terms English and British are habitually treated as synonymous. If the English cannot grasp the distinction, we cannot expect other countries to see the point. In most other languages the word which is the equivalent of England is generally applied to the whole island. Scotland has become so invisible internationally that it is hardly ever mentioned at all. We are all accustomed to this and irritated by it, but how much does it matter?

The first point is that the confusion applies even in contexts where precision is important. Take, for instance, a book which has recently been published in translation, *Europe: A Cultural History* by Peter Rietbergen, who is a professor of cultural history in the Netherlands. He refers to James Macpherson, the translator or author of Ossian, as an "English poet" and to Adam Smith as an "English economic theorist". Both of these men, and Macpherson in particular, are so much the product of their Scottish background than it is highly misleading to look at them as part of an English tradition. The book refers to Hume and Livingstone as Scots, but there is no reference at all to all the other Scots who have made important contributions to civilisation, such as Wallace, Buchanan, Fletcher, Burns, Watt, Scott, Byron, Clerk Maxwell and Patrick Geddes.

These omissions suggest that the invisibility of Scotland encourages a view of history which is false because it ignores the significant part which Scotland has in fact played and which is out of all proportion to its size. As Douglas Dunn has said, the Scottish contribution "is almost disturbing in its scale". Christopher Harvie has remarked that "the peculiar history of the Scots has meant that, man for man, they have probably done more to create the modern world than any other nation".

We may find it difficult to believe that the outside world knows so little about us. Most of us are confident in our identity. We have the impression that there are Scottish symbols which are recognised all over the world (and which incidentally we should value for that reason). This means such things as tartan, the pipes and whisky; but they do not help us much if the world has been taught to regard them as English. There is plenty of evidence of the extent to which Scotland is invisible to many people. Margaret Bennett in her recent book about Scottish Gaelic settlers in Quebec says that many French Canadians "have never even heard of Scotland". In the current issue of *The Times Literary Supplement* Ian Bamford tells us that "Scotland has no recognised identity in Europe". I have been told that post offices in America will not accept mail addressed to Scotland because it does not exist in their reference books.

This state of affairs has, of course, practical economic effects, apart from the damage to our self esteem and to historical understanding. Importers are unlikely to buy goods from a country which is unknown to them. Tourists are unlikely to find us by mere chance. Certainly there are some enlightened people everywhere who are interested in Scotland, but as long as they are a minority, the promoters of "Scotland the brand" and of the Scottish tourist industry will have an uphill struggle.

Robert Burns understood the reason. 'What are all the boasted advantages which my country reaps from a certain union", he asked in a letter, "that can counterbalance the annihilation of her independence and even her very name?" The Union deprived Scotland of an international identity and name. To the outside world we became part of England. Only independent countries can take part in international relationships and attract international recognition. The restoration of the Scottish Parliament is a step in the right direction, but until we are independent, we shall remain largely invisible to the outside world.

5.16

Cultural Identity

Letter to 'The Herald', of 17th July 1999

Dear Sir,

Gerry Hassan (Essay, 17th July) is not the first Scot to want to create a sense of Britishness. Some Scots have been innocent enough to believe that the Treaty of Union meant what it said and that both Scotland and England had been replaced by a new entity called Britain. The trouble is that the English have never believed that. If they use the term 'Britain' at all, it is as a synomym for England. Since they are about ten times more numerous than we are, we have neither the power, nor the right, to make them change their attitude.

As Linda Colley has said, Britain had some meaning while the Empire existed. It was a joint venture which was always called British, although that did not stop the English habitually referring to the Queen of England and to the English Navy and Parliament. Now that the Empire has gone, so has any reality of Britishness.

England is a great country with a remarkable culture of which their people have every reason to feel proud. To their credit, they have never attempted consciously to impose their culture on Scotland, although some Scots have tried to do the job for them. Scotland has retained a distinct and valuable culture which has made an important contribution to world civilisation. Britain is a temporary and artificial political construct, but not a cultural identity.

It is a separate point perhaps, but what are we to make of Hassan's statement that he is "deeply proud to be British" because of Kosovo? The bombing of Serbia was highly questionable legally and morally. In the short term, it greatly increased the suffering of both the Kosovars and the Serbs. In the long term, it has deepened the problems of relationships in the Balkans to an extent that will last for generations, to say nothing of the economic and environmental damage. If this is what Britishness means, the sooner we have no part in it, the better.

Yours faithfully,

Paul Henderson Scott

5.17

Independence is the Key

'The Herald', 18th September 2000

Recently some columnists and other people have been suggesting that independence is an old-fashioned concept and that Scotland should therefore stop worrying about it. Of course it is true that no government, even the most powerful, is as free as in the past to act as it pleases. The member states of the European Union, in particular, have accepted very substantial limitations of their power and these are likely to increase. If independence in these circumstances has become meaningless, then that would apply to France, Denmark, Ireland and the rest as well as to Scotland. It is easy to imagine the answer you would get if you suggested that to them.

Certainly, there is a very clear distinction between Scotland in its present status and, to take only examples of comparable population, Denmark and Ireland. No other single country, as opposed to the European Union, has the right to legislate for them and they are therefore member states of the Union and of other international organisations in their own right. This is the point of fundamental importance. Member states have the right to participate in decision-making and have notice taken of their views and interests. If a country, or part of a country, is not a member state, it may sometimes be treated sympathetically, but it has no such rights at all. In a very real sense, it does not exist internationally. You have to be accepted as independent to be a member state and therefore a participant in international negotiation.

It has also been suggested that the steady transfer of powers from the member states to the EU in some way diminishes the need for Scottish independence. In fact, it has the opposite effect. The powers which are likely to move, those over foreign affairs, defence, taxation and social security, are at present reserved to Westminster.

The more this happens, the less relevance will Westminster have for Scotland. But there will be a corresponding greater need for Scotland to have the right to share in decision making in Brussels. Under the present system, our case is simply not presented there at all whenever our views and interests are different from those of the Westminster Government.

The effect of international organisations, and of the EU in particular, is to curb the influence of the larger countries and increase that of the smaller. Because of this Norman Davies ended his important book, *The Isles* (which has transformed the understanding of 'British' history) on an optimistic note:

> The main source of optimism lies in the existence of the EU . . . It gives a place in the sun to Europe's smaller and middle-sized nations . . . In the old European jungle of sovereign states, an independent Scotland, or an independent Wales, or even an independent England, would have been vulnerable creations living precariously among larger predators. But now the jungle has been banished. Under the umbrella of the European Union, a 'Scotland in Europe', a 'Wales in Europe' and a 'England in Europe' have every chance of doing as well as 'Ireland in Europe'. The richest and most satisfied country in Europe is Luxembourg.

It is independence, the essential condition of membership, which is the key to those advantages.

Gordon Wilson recently suggested that the SNP should now aim for "national status" instead of independence. He did not define the term, but said that it would give representation in the Council of Ministers and the Commission and more members in the European Parliament. But these follow only from independence and acceptance as a member state. The same is true of what Wyn Jones of Plaid Cymru calls "full national status" for Wales. He says that this would mean the same status as Ireland has within the EU; but Ireland is a member state only because it is independent.

In other words all this talk of alternatives to independence is merely playing with words. Scotland needs membership of the EU as a member state and that is not possible without independence.

5.18

Independence: a Practical Guide

Review of 'Scottish Independence: A Practical Guide', Jo Eric Murkens with Peter Jones and Michael Keating (Edinburgh, 2002)

'Scottish Affairs' No. 44, Summer 2003)

This book is the result of research by the Constitution Unit of University College London. It is the most ambitious study so far of the means by which Scotland could achieve independence and of its consequences. According to the Introduction, the book strives to be "strictly neutral on the desirability of independence". With the best will in the world, however, the essays inevitably tend to reflect the prejudices and idiosyncracies of the authors. That is particularly true of the contribution of the leader of the research team, Jo Murkens.

His first point is to assert that Scotland does not have a right in law to self-determination on the grounds that this right applies only in "the colonial context". (p. 10) The wording of the United Nations Covenant on the subject gives no support to this idea, but the point is irrelevant in the Scottish case. As Murkens recognises, the right of Scotland to self-determination has been accepted by a succession of British political leaders. As an example he quotes from Margaret Thatcher's memoirs: "As a nation, they have an undoubted right to national self-determination".

Murkens then argues (p. 11) that the relevant Union is not that of 1707 but of 1801 when Ireland was added. The relevance of this is not clear, especially as the scope of the 1801 Union was radically changed in 1921 when Ireland became independent. Also, the Scotland Act of 1998, on which Murkens relies in other connections, refers specifically to the Union of 1707 between Scotland and England. It even maintains (in Section 37) that the Acts of the

Scottish and English Parliaments which enacted the terms of the Treaty of Union are still in force, subject to the 1998 Act. In other words, the Scotland Act amends the terms of the Union. If the Acts establishing the Union can be amended, they can also be abrogated.

This last point is one which Murkens denies. He quotes (p. 108) from a book by Robert Lane: "there is no possibility of abrogation of the 1707 Treaty of Union because the parties have ceased to exist and could not, in any case, restore the *status quo ante*". This seems to me a very dubious proposition. The Treaty which the Parliaments of both Scotland and England ratified in 1707 replaced both of these Parliaments with a new Parliament of Great Britain. Otherwise the two states continued much as before. Scotland retained, and still has, its own established church, its own laws and legal and educational systems, and its own Parliament has been restored. (Lane was writing in 1991 before the restoration of the Scottish Parliament, which may be the reason for his statement.) At an earlier point in the book, (p. 20) Murkens himself says: "The clarity of Scotland as a territorial and political unit and the national identity of the Scottish people means that no one can seriously dispute that Scotland possesses all the necessary ingredients of statehood". So, of course, does England. Even if England does not at present have a separate Parliament, the British one is overwhelmingly English and it has always regarded itself as the continuation of the historic English Parliament. Neither of the two parties to the Treaty have "ceased to exist".

I can see no reason therefore why the Treaty cannot now be abrogated by agreement between the two parties or (although this would be less desirable) by the withdrawal of one of them. It is a highly questionable instrument in any case. England forced a reluctant Scotland (or at least a majority in an unrepresentative Parliament) to accept it by various forms of pressure, including the threat of military force. Subsequent British governments have often ignored or violated it and the restoration of the Scottish Parliament, even if Westminster still claims ultimate sovereignty, destroyed its fundamental provision.

Murkens accepts that the process of establishing independence would be initiated by the SNP, or a coalition headed by it, achieving power in the Scottish Parliament. The Scottish Parliament would then hold what Murkens calls an "advisory referendum to determine the will of the Scottish people". If the result is positive, Murkens says that negotiations could then begin with the UK Government. He suggests that the outcome of the negotiations would be "embodied in a prospectus and draft constitutional document". Westminster would then hold a second referendum and, if that was positive, it would pass the necessary legislation to give effect to Scottish independence". (pp. 39-40)

These proposals by Murkens are not entirely clear, but it sounds as if he envisages that the negotiations would be concerned not only with the relations between the two countries, but also with the constitution of an independent Scotland. It is clearly inappropriate and unacceptable that the Westminster Parliament, where Scottish members are a small minority, should debate and decide matters which are internal to Scotland, especially something so important as the constitution. The Scottish referendum will be concerned with the draft constitution which the SNP have already published, and (in Murkens's words) that referendum will "determine the will of the Scottish people". The Scottish view is that sovereignty rests with the people. This referendum will therefore decide whether Scotland will be independent on the basis of the proposed constitution. If it is positive, it would be appropriate for both Parliaments to recognise the recovery of Scottish independence in Acts which, in effect, abrogate their ratifications of the Treaty of Union.

Murkens, in suggesting (pp. 39-40) that Westminster should legislate on the new Scottish constitution and hold a second referendum, presumably relies on the Scotland Act, under Section 30.1 of which "the Union of the Kingdoms of Scotland and England" is reserved to Westminster. A positive Scottish referendum would, however, create a new situation and the repeated assurances by British Governments that they would recognise the right of Scotland to self-determination would then be overriding.

Negotiations between the two countries on such matters as the division of assets and liabilities and the future of the nuclear submarine bases at Faslane and Coulport are another matter. They will be complex and will take several months or even years. Except for the nuclear bases there will be nothing unusal about them; the British Government has great experience of such negotiations over the independence of scores of former colonies. One of the advantages of independence is that it will improve relations between Scotland and England by removing the fundamental cause of tension. Both countries will see advantage in reaching an equitable settlement as soon as possible. It will be more of a process than an event, and a second referendum about it would be unsuitable and unnecessary.

The nuclear bases, to which public opinion in Scotland is strongly opposed, are likely to be the most difficult problem. As Murkens says, their removal to a site in England would be very costly. He also remarks (p. 89) there would be public hostility from people who would object to having them in their backyard. (He does not explain why it should be thought acceptable to have them in Scotland, close to our major centre of population) The best possible answer to the problem would be a decision by the British Government to abolish these nuclear weapons altogether. Their maintenance is hideously expensive; they serve no useful purpose; they involve the risk of a catastrophic nuclear accident. We should all be better off without them.

There is then the question of membership of the European Union. In my book, *Scotland in Europe: Dialogue with a Sceptical Friend* of 1992, I quoted statements by well qualified authorities which seemed to dispel any doubt on the matter. For instance, Emile Noel, the former Secretary-General of the European Commission wrote:

> There is no precedent and no provision for the expulsion of a member state, therefore Scottish independence would create two new member states out of one. They would have equal status with each other and the other 11 states. The remainder of the United Kingdom would not be in a more powerful position than Scotland . . . Anyone who is attacking the claim in respect of one country is attacking it in respect of the other. It is not possible to divide the cases.

But attacking it in respect of Scotland is precisely what Murkens does. He refers to Noel's statement, but only in part, and then without citing any other statement of comparable authority he asserts the opposite. He maintains that the remainder of the UK would continue to be the member state, but that an independent Scotland would have to apply for membership. He argues that Scottish independence would come about as a "break-away" from the UK, not as a abrogation of the Treaty of Union, and that it is only in the second of these possibilities that Scotland would inherit membership of the European Union. This is inconsistent with his assumption in the rest of the book that independence would be "granted" (I should prefer to say 'recognised') by Westmister. That would surely amount to the dissolution of a previously agreed union. Certainly, the two new states would have to negotiate with the European Union over such matters as the number of votes in the Council of Ministers and number of seats in the European Parliament, but neither would be expelled.

Murkens has therefore introduced to this debate a number of original propositions: that Scotland has no right to self-determination; that it is the Union of 1801 which is relevant; that the Union of 1707 cannot be abrogated; that Westminster should legislate on the Scottish constitution and hold a second referendum; that an independent Scotland would not inherit membership of the European Union. He fails to make a convincing case for any of them and gives the impression that he is contriving obstacles and difficulties that do not really exist. This might be interesting as an intellectual exercise, but it is certainly not a "practical guide".

The next section of the book, on the economics of independence by Peter Jones, is much more realistic and useful and is clearly based on substantial research. He concludes that "an independent Scotland would have a trade surplus under almost all conceivable conditions" (p. 198) and substantial resources from her share of UK assets. (p. 215) He suggests that the approach to independence might create a climate of uncertainty which would disturb the economy, and refers to the effect of the referendum in Quebec. (It was Jack MacConnell's quotation of this passage which drew a strong denial from the the Agent Général of Quebec). Of course, the effects might be the opposite. Independence has brought economic and other benefits to other small countries in Europe and there is no reason why Scotland would be different.

There is an interesting final chapter by Michael Keating. He makes one very questionable statement: "almost complete absence of a debate in Scotland on defence and foreign policy would seem to suggest that these are not areas where there is a strong demand to diverge from UK policy". (p. 297) On the contrary, the opposition in Scotland to nuclear weapons and to such policies as the bombing of Serbia and the alignment with Bush over Iraq show a vigorous Scottish concern. Keating is right to draw attention to the divergence of views between Scotland and England on the nature of sovereignty He points out that Labour MPs asserted the sovereignty of the Scottish people in signing the 4th Claim of Right and then passed the Scotland Act which insisted on that of Westminster. (p. 296)

Finally, Keating hits the nail on the head by one sentence which states the real issue which faces us: "The question here has always been whether Scotland can gain more influence as a small part of a member state of the EU, or as a small member state itself." (p. 294) I do not think that there is much room for doubt. As a part of a member state our views and interests are simply ignored when the differ from those of England; but they would be expressed and taken into account if we were a member state. Also, in cases where we agree with England, we should together have more votes and more influence as two states than we have as one. And, as Keating concludes (p.295):

> Enlargement of the Union to include the countries of central and eastern Europe along with Cyprus further reinforces the case for independence, since it would become difficult to explain why Slovenia should have a voice in the Council of Ministers and Scotland should not.

Other Saltire Books by Paul H Scott

Walter Scott and Scotland

This stimulating introduction to Sir Walter Scott throws new light on both the great man himself and on the dilemma which faced Scotland at the time and which faces it still. It is a succinct and penetrating account of the influences on Scott of both classical and enlightened Edinburgh, and of border and Jacobite traditions.

ISBN 0 85411 056 9 Price £7.99

Still in Bed with an Elephant

A study of Scotland's relations with England which is, of course, the elephant in question. As well as a cultural history in the period since the Union of 1707, the book offers individual studies of leading observers such as Sir Walter Scott, Robert Burns, Andrew Fletcher of Saltoun and Sir John Clerk of Penicuik. The author identifies the distinctive contribution made by Scottish culture to world civilisation and at the same time helps remove some myths and misunderstandings. He makes a the case for independence as part of a world-wide need to conserve individuality and diversity.

ISBN 0 85411 073 9 Price £7.99

The Boasted Advantages

In this new work Paul Scott attempts to answer Robert Burns' question posed in 1790: 'what are the boasted advantages which my country reaps from a certain union?' Scott examines the often advanced theories that the union was a bargain over trade and that it brought, and indeed continues to bring, great advantages to Scotland. In so doing he helps sweep away the fog of myth and propaganda allowing a rational judgement about the course of Scotland's post union history and the best road to follow in the future.

ISBN 0 85411 072 0 Price £6.99

Andrew Fletcher and the Treaty of Union

Andrew Fletcher has been known since his own lifefime as 'The Patriot' because of his determined resistance to the parliamentary Union of Scotland and England in 1707. This book, the first on Fletcher since 1953, combines a biography with a full account of the events leading to the Union and an up-to-date analysis of Fletcher's essays and speeches.

"impeccably researched and convincing ... will remain the definitive study for many years."
Michael Lynch in *The Scotsman*

ISBN 0 85411 057 7 Price £12.99

The Saltoun Papers: Reflections on Andrew Fletcher

Since the 1960s Andrew Fletcher has been commemorated each September by a short lecture in East Saltoun Parish Church where he is buried. Over the years some of the country's most distinguished historians, politicians and writers have offered their thoughts on Fletcher, and on Scotland past and present. In *The Saltoun Papers* fifteen of these talks selected from the years 1979 to 1999 are reproduced, including those by historians Gordon Donaldson, Geoffrey Barrow, Bruce Lenman, William Ferguson, David Simpson, Edward Cowan and Murray Pittock, politicians Neil MacCormick and John Hume Robertson, philosopher Alexander Broadie, writers Arnold Kemp, Billy Kay and Sheila Douglas, and the businessman, Sir Iain Noble. Paul Scott, the distinguished historian and writer on Fletcher and his period, edited the papers and his own address at East Saltoun in 1984 is included.

A wide range of topics is covered: identity, nationalism, language, patriotism, the Union of 1707 in all its manifestations, and relations with Europe and the world, and controversial and often opposing views are argued with passion and authority.

ISBN 0 85411 081 X Price £9.99

A Scottish Postbag (edited with George Bruce)

This is an updated version of the very successful 1986 edition in which the Scottish poet George Bruce and historian Paul Scott compiled a selection of Scottish letters covering eight centuries and involving many of the great historical, literary and political figures in Scotland's past. Wallace, Mary Queen of Scots, Hume, Knox, Boswell, Burns, Livingstone, Carlyle, Scott, Stevenson, Ramsay MacDonald, and Hugh MacDiarmid are among the 150 famous Scots, nearly 350 letters in all. Together they illuminate Scotland's history in a very direct and entertaining way. The editors have added a number of letters from the last decade.

ISBN 085411 078 X Price £9.99

Some Comments on Paul Scott's Books

Walter Scott and Scotland

"Rewarding and delightful to read . . . Mr Scott's elegant and economical prose brings his great predecessor vividly to life"

(Maurice Lindsay in *The Scottish Field*)

"An important book...which fundamentally challenges Edwin Muir's restrictive and unhistoric view of Scottish literature".

(David Hewitt in *The Scottish Review*)

Andrew Fletcher and the Treaty of Union

"What emerges clearly in this lucid account of his life and thought is Fletcher's comprehensiveness of vision and, passionate Scot though he was, the generous internationalism of his thinking".

(David Daiches in *Books in Scotland*)

"It ought also to be bought by anyone interested in Britain's constitutional history, and in the history of ideas".

(Andrew Marr in *The Economist*)

The Boasted Advantages

"Not too many books have challenged the Union's worth with such anthority. Paul Scott is the pre-eminent nationalist historian in Scotland".

(Murray Ritchie in *The Herald*)

A Twentieth Century Life

"It is one of the most agreeable things in life to be pleasurably surprised by a book. Paul Henderson Scott's autobiography has given me what my mother used to call 'a rare treat' (using rare in the sense of extremely good). Paul Scott is perhaps the leading nationalist intellectual of our time. His autobiography is a delightful read . . . The narrative is fluent and graceful".

(Arnold Kemp in *The Observer*)

"This is a belter of a book". (Alex Salmond in *The Scotsman*)

Note: Paul Scott's autobiography *A Twentieth Century Life* was published in 2002 by Argyll Publishing, price £20 hardback.

Saltire Publications

Alexander Broadie: *Why Scottish Philosophy Matters*	0 85411 075 5
Ian Campbell: *Thomas Carlyle*	0 85411 052 6
Thomas Crawford: *Boswell, Burns and the French Revolution*	0 85411 046 1
William Ferguson: *Scotland's Relations with England*	0 85411 058 5
Johan Findlay: *All Manner of People*	0 85411 076 3
Andrew Fletcher: *United and Separate Parliaments*	0 85411 025 9
Robin Fulton: *The Way the Words are Taken*	0 86334 064 4
John Galt: *Annals of the Parish/ The Ayrshire Legatees / The Provost*	0 85411 074 7
Robert Garioch: *Complete Poetical Works* ed. Fulton	0 90426 593 5
Robert Garioch: *Garioch Miscellany* ed. Fulton	0 86334 057 1
John S. Gibson: *Deacon Brodie: Father to Jekyll & Hyde*	0 85411 050 X
John S. Gibson: *Edinburgh in the '45*	0 85411 067 4
Carol Gow: *Mirror & Marble: Poetry of Iain Crichton Smith*	0 86334 070 9
Ian Grimble: *The Trial of Patrick Sellar*	0 85411 053 4
Ian Grimble: *Chief of Mackay*	0 85411 051 8
Ian Grimble: *The World of Rob Donn*	0 85411 062 3
J. Derrick McClure: *Why Scots Matters*	0 85411 071 2
Pol MacAonghas: *An Guth Aoibhneach*	0 85411 054 2
Rosalind Mitchison: *Why Scottish History Matters*	0 85411 070 4
William Neill: *Tales frae the Odyssey o Homer*	0 85411 049 6
David Purves: *A Scots Grammar: Scots Grammar and Usage*	0 85411 079 8
Murray Ritchie: *Scotland Reclaimed*	0 85411 077 1
Paul H. Scott: *Andrew Fletcher and the Treaty of Union*	0 85411 057 7
Paul H. Scott: *Walter Scott and Scotland*	0 85411 056 9
Paul H. Scott: *Still in Bed with an Elephant*	0 85411 073 9
Paul H Scott: *The Boasted Advantages*	0 85411 072 0
Paul H Scott (ed.): *The Saltoun Papers*	0 85411 081 X
Paul H Scott and George Bruce (eds.): *A Scottish Postbag*	0 85411 078 X
Raymond Vettese: *A Keen New Air*	0 85411 063 1
Eilidh Watt: *Gun Fhois*	0 86334 060 1
Wemyss, Alice: *Elcho of the '45*	0 85411 080 X

Saltire publications are available from Booksource, 32 Finlas Street, Glasgow. G22 5DU Tel: 0870 240 2182. FAX: 0141 557 0189 email: orders@booksource.net

About the Saltire Society

The Saltire Society was founded in 1936 at a time when many of the distinctive features of Scotland and its culture seemed in jeopardy. Over the years its members, who have included many of Scotland's most distinguished scholars and creative artists, have fought to preserve and present the nation's cultural heritage so that Scotland might once again be a creative force in European civilisation. As well as publishing books and producing recordings the Society makes a number of national awards for excellence in fields as diverse as housing design, civil engineering, historical publication and scientific research. There are Saltire Society branches in many towns and cities in Scotland and beyond, and each year members organise dozens of lectures, seminars and conferences on important aspects of Scottish culture.

The Society has no political affiliation and welcomes as members all who share its aims. Further information from The Administrator, The Saltire Society, Fountain Close, 22 High Street, Edinburgh, EH1 1TF Telephone 0131 556 1836.

Alternatively, you can make contact by email at saltire@saltiresociety.org.uk. and visit the Society web site at www.saltire-society.demon.co.uk